CHARLES DICKENS
AS AN AGENT OF CHANGE

IN MEMORIAM

EDGAR ROSENBERG AND HERBERT FOLTINEK

CHARLES DICKENS
AS AN AGENT OF CHANGE

EDITED BY
JOACHIM FRENK AND LENA STEVEKER

CORNELL UNIVERSITY PRESS
ITHACA AND LONDON

Copyright © 2019 by Cornell University

Originally published in 2015 by AMS Press, Inc.
First Cornell University Press paperback printing 2019

All rights reserved. Except for brief quotations in a review, this book, or parts thereof, must not be reproduced in any form without permission in writing from the publisher.

For information, address
Cornell University Press, Sage House, 512 East State Street,
Ithaca, New York 14850.

Visit our website at cornellpress.cornell.edu.

Librarians: a CIP record is available from the Library of Congress.

Acknowledgments

The idea for this book first took form during an international seminar, "Dickens as an Agent of Change," which we hosted in June 2010. We are grateful to our keynote speaker, our revered colleague Michael Slater, whose gracious presence was a paradigm of the great scholarly spirit of this seminar in general, and crucial for its success. We also owe thanks to our seminar attendees and book contributors. The stimulating and instructive discussions with these brilliant Dickens scholars have been a wonderful and enriching experience for us.

Our thanks also go to our team, our efficient agents of positive change. Before and during the seminar, Petra Jakob solved many problems, and Hubertus Weyer took care of all things technological, both analog and digital. Verena Bernardi, Christina Holzer, Sabine Jung, and Esther Lorscheider were all invaluable helpers. We also thank Volker Linneweber, the president of the Universität des Saarlandes, and Erich Steiner, the then dean of our faculty, for their unfailing support in the organizational stages of the seminar. The university's Kontaktstelle für Wissens- und Technologietransfer, Uta Merkle's team, were indispensable specialists in all organizational matters. Moreover, we are grateful to our colleague Manfred Pinkal, who graciously let us convene in his superb conference venue. Charlotte Britz, the Lord Mayor of Saarbrücken, kindly gave us permission to use the splendid town hall for the opening ceremony. In long working hours, Eva Michely helped us generously with the formatting of our typescript. We are also much obliged to David Ramm and Albert Rolls of AMS Press for their editorial help and support.

Contents

Acknowledgments   v

List of Abbreviations   ix

Introduction: Changing Dickens
Joachim Frenk and Lena Steveker   xi

I. <u>Dickens and Social Change</u>

**Repetitions and Reversals: Patterns for Social Change
in *Pickwick Papers***
Jerome Meckier   3
Three Revolutions: Alternate Routes to Social Change in *Bleak House*
Joel J. Brattin   19
**Dickens, Society, and Art: Change in Dickens's View of
Effecting Social Reform**
Robert Heaman   33
The World Changing Dickens, Dickens Changing the World
Bert Hornback   47

II. <u>Dickens and Changes of Power</u>

Parrots, Birds of Prey, and Snorting Cattle: Dickens's Whig Agenda
David Paroissien   61
**"The Tremendous Potency of the Small": Dickens, the Individual,
and Social Change in a Post-America, Post-Catastrophist Age**
Nancy Aycock Metz   75
Money, Power, and Appearance in *Dombey and Son*
Michael Hollington   85

III. <u>Dickens and Literary Change</u>

The Passing of the *Pickwick* Moment
Malcolm Andrews   99
The *Chimes* and the Rhythm of Life
Matthias Bauer   111

Radical Dickens: Dickens and the Tradition of Romantic Radicalism
Norbert Lennartz 129
Modern Characters in the Late Novels of Charles Dickens
Herbert Foltinek 145

IV. Dickens and Changes in Popular Culture and in the Theater

The Cultural Politics of Dickens's *Hard Times*
Doris Feldmann 159
Conjuring Dickens: Magic, Intellectual Property, and *The Old Curiosity Shop*
Christopher Pittard 173
Popular Dickens: Changing *Bleak House* for the East End Stage
Chris Louttit 191
The Frozen Deep: Gad's Hill, June–July 1857
Robert Tracy 205

How to Read Dickens in English: A Last Retrospect
Edgar Rosenberg 219

Index 235

List of Abbreviations

The following abbreviations are used in all parenthetical references to Charles Dickens's novels. For full bibliographical information on the editions used in the individual essays, please consult the respective bibliographies.

Pickwick Papers	*PP*
Oliver Twist	*OT*
Nicholas Nickleby	*NN*
The Old Curiosity Shop	*OCS*
Barnaby Rudge	*BR*
A Christmas Carol	*CC*
The Chimes	*TC*
Martin Chuzzlewit	*MC*
Dombey and Son	*DS*
David Copperfield	*DC*
Bleak House	*BH*
Hard Times	*HT*
Little Dorrit	*LD*
A Tale of Two Cities	*TTC*
Great Expectations	*GE*
Our Mutual Friend	*OMF*
The Mystery of Edwin Drood	*MED*

Introduction: Changing Dickens

Joachim Frenk and Lena Steveker
Universität des Saarlandes

Cloisterham, the non-London setting of *The Mystery of Edwin Drood* that conjures up the Rochester Dickens knew as a child, is initially presented, in a somewhat timeless present tense, as immune to any kind of change: "A drowsy city, Cloisterham, whose inhabitants seem to suppose, with an inconsistency more strange than rare, that all its changes lie behind it, and that there are no more to come" (*MED* 23). Although the mindless bourgeoisie embodied by the new mayor, Mr. Sapsea, celebrate this changelessness, it seems to be one reason for Mr. Jasper's spiritual unrest and his need for an escape, which he satisfies in the Princess Puffer's opium den. Cloisterham's dreary initial changelessness changes completely in chapter 23, which still must serve as the ending of the novel:

> A brilliant morning shines on the old city. Its antiquities and ruins are surpassingly beautiful, with a lusty ivy gleaming in the sun, and the rich trees waving in the balmy air. Changes of glorious light from moving boughs, songs of birds, scents from gardens, woods, and fields—or rather, from the one great garden of the whole cultivated island in its yielding time—penetrate into the Cathedral, subdue its earthy odour, and preach the Resurrection and the Life. (*MED* 270)

At its conclusively provisional ending, Dickens's last novel offers one last change. Cloisterham changes from a city that is spiritually all but dead, its necropolis cathedral haunted by Durdles and Jasper, into a place joyously filled with the light of hope for the (capitalized) Resurrection and the Life. Dickens wrote the passage above in his

Swiss Châlet at Gad's Hill, with a view of the Kentish countryside in the summer, very probably in the knowledge that he would have to die soon. Shortly afterward, John Forster encouraged every reader to see an analogy between Dickens's last finished chapter and his fading life: "the reader will observe with a painful interest, not alone its evidence of minute labour at this fast-closing hour of time with him, but the direction his thoughts had taken" (521). It was the direction of one last change for the better.

On 9 June 1870, having finished this chapter of *Edwin Drood*, Charles Dickens stopped changing, but the many readers of his works have made sure that he keeps being regarded as an agent of change. The images of Dickens himself, Michael Slater notes, only started changing more than sixty years after his death:

> It was not until the mid-1930s, when revelations about his connection with Ellen Ternan began to surface, that [the prevailing] perception of Dickens [. . .] began to change, and a darker, more turbulent, and altogether more complex figure began emerging into the public consciousness. (623)

As this essay collection documents, it is a rewarding undertaking to discuss the numerous ways in which Charles Dickens was (and still is) an agent of change in an age of changes—of the plurality of Weltanschauungen, of the political system and the social cosmos, of technology, of the definitions, of the writing and the distribution of literature. And, we may add, of the changing notions of change itself.

In the twenty-first century, the notion of constant change has become the norm rather than the exception. Both in international companies and in other areas of the globalized, post- (or not-so-post)industrial societies, change has become ubiquitous, and change management is a familiar term in the economic discourse. Changes are sometimes highly welcome: in 2008, for instance, Barack Obama was elected president of the United States largely because he promised change, and most Europeans applauded his message of change, too. Although so many areas of life are restructured and changed for the most diverse reasons— and, occasionally, there seems to be no reason but change for its own sake—it is highly instructive to look at our immediate prehistory, the Victorian Age, to see how change was instigated, described, and managed then.

Charles Dickens's works, as agents and representations of all sorts of changes big and small, are excellent starting points for such an investigation. During his career as a writer and as a figure of public life, Dickens, who was initially irritated by isolated faults of the society surrounding him, became ever more dissatisfied with society as a whole. Consequently, the changes Dickens wanted to see changed; the longer and the more Dickens wrote, the more radical the changes he proposed became. Still, Dickens's ideas of change never condensed into an overarching system based on monumental abstractions.[1] They primarily focused on the change of the individual, the famous change of heart toward kindness and generosity, often brought about by suffering and compassion—in contrast to, say, Karl Marx's ideas of necessary and, in his view, quasi-inevitable changes to come. For a time, Marx worked next to Dickens in the reading room of the British Library, but, as George Bernard Shaw commented in 1947, they were "living in the same city [. . .] yet they seem to us like creatures of a different species living in different worlds" (633). Dickens's idea of change was not Marx's, yet both saw the need to change the signs of their time, to minimize the collateral damages of technological capitalist modernity.

There are for instance the massive changes caused by the new railways, a new technology that physically, perceptually, and otherwise changed British society irreversibly within less than a century. Dickens is of course not the only contemporary to comment on the railway shock, but his prose is among the most powerful, for instance, when it describes a "hellish" railway construction site in *Dombey and Son*:

> There were a hundred thousand shapes and substances of incompleteness, wildly mingled out of their places, upside down, burrowing in the earth, aspiring in the air, mouldering in the water, and unintelligible as any dream. Hot springs and fiery eruptions, the usual attendants upon earthquakes, lent their contributions of confusion to the scene. Boiling water hissed and heaved within dilapidated walls; whence, also, the glare and roar of flames came issuing forth; and mounds of ashes blocked up rights of way, and wholly changed the law and custom of the neighbourhood. (*DS* 79)

This passage spells out that the coming railway is "unintelligible as any dream," but at the same time, it seeks to render the change intelligible through its daring syntax and imagery—and ultimately through acknowledging how radical this change is, particularly in terms of the culture affected by the new technology.

Dombey and Son not only registers the enormous disruption of the cityscape caused by the railway; it also deals with the enormous acceleration of travel, perceived as a condensation of time and space, the changed attitudes toward the railway, the enormous array of railway-related products that commodified the new phenomenon and the terrible power of the new machines that must be controlled and in the end is let loose in the death of the villain Carker. When Mr. Dombey, mourning for his lost son, travels to Leamington by railway, the narrative voice takes over Dombey's analogy between the power of the railway and then turns it into a virtuoso piece of rhythmical and onomatopoetic exuberance that imitates the sound of the train journey itself:

> Away, with a shriek, and a roar, and a rattle, from the town, burrowing among the dwellings of men and making the streets hum, flashing out into the meadows for a moment, mining in through the damp earth, booming on in darkness and heavy air, bursting out again into the sunny day so bright and wide; away, with a shriek, and a roar, and a rattle, through the fields, through the woods, through the corn, through the hay, through the chalk, through the mould, through the clay, through the rock, among objects close at hand and almost in the grasp, ever flying from the traveller, and a deceitful distance ever moving slowly with him: like as in the track of the remorseless monster, Death! (*DS* 311)

The impression given here is that of a perceptive apparatus working at its limit to cope with the change of transport speed. Although the rhythm of the passage drives on mechanically and mercilessly, dissolving after a long syntactical period only to reaffirm itself triumphantly after the semicolon, the staccato impressions fired at the reader, forcing him or her to adapt to changes in a fleeting moment, indicate how much received ideas of time and space are threatened by a glance out of the window. "Away"—the traveler is always already gone, removed from any kind of fixed standpoint, dissolving like the surrounding land- or cityscape. The same goes for the deceptively close objects that keep changing their position from the moment they come into view. The shriek and the roar of the railway serve to animate it—elsewhere, locomotives are compared to "tame dragons" (*DS* 245)—and the verbs of the first syntactical period all signal the sheer physical power of the train to change the space it passes through: burrowing, flashing, booming, bursting. Toward the end of the paragraph, the rhythm starts to slow, similar to a train entering a station, and comes to a standstill in the last, mobility-denying word, an emphatic monosyllable whose final fricative mimics the locomotive's hissing when it has come to a standstill: death.

Dickens's mastery of the English language spells out a perceptual change that, 130 years later, Wolfgang Schivelbusch defined as one of the central characteristics of railway travel in the nineteenth century:

> [. . .] the idea that the railroad annihilated time and space must be seen as the reaction of perceptive powers that, formed by a certain transport technology, find suddenly that technology has been replaced by an entirely new one. [. . .] the railroad did not appear embedded in the space of the landscape the way coach and highway are, but seemed to strike its way through it. (37)[2]

The new train station, "the heart of this great change" (*DS* 245), is a hub of restless Dickensian vitality and profusion, both admirable and uncanny. There is no single, stable view of the railway in Dickens's writing; instead, the new transportation technology and its implications are being constantly revisited and revised (see Philpotts; Mengel).

London, the prime space of Dickens's imagination, also changed at an unprecedented speed and to an unprecedented extent in the nineteenth century. Dickens, the "special correspondent for posterity," from the beginning of his writing career onwards traced London's many changes, as it were, obsessively. Although Dickens's narrators, in keeping with their creator's view of his own time and his regular derision of "the good old times," more often welcome change than they condemn it, there are also moments in which a sense of loss is evident. Here is one early example from *Sketches by Boz*, a description of the change of Scotland Yard first published in the *Morning Chronicle* on 4 October 1836:

> Amidst all this change, and restlessness, and innovation, there remains but one old man, who seems to mourn the downfall of this ancient place. [. . .] A few years hence, and the antiquary of another generation looking into some mouldy record of the strife and passions that agitated the world in these times, may glance his eye over the pages we have just filled: and not all his knowledge of the history of the past, not all his black-letter lore, or his skill in book-collecting, not all the dry studies of a long life, or the dusty volumes that have cost him a fortune, may help him to the whereabouts, either of Scotland-yard, or of any one of the landmarks we have mentioned in describing it. (89–90)

What is lamented here is not the change of Scotland Yard per se, but the fact that it cannot be documented, while, ironically, the sketch sets out to do exactly that. At the same time, the pejorative way in which all kinds of written matter are described here—"mouldy record," "black-letter lore," dry studies of long life," "dusty volumes"—implicitly poses the question why it should be different with the newspaper, certainly even less connoted with a long shelf life than the coming antiquary's dusty volumes, in which this sketch first appeared. Dickens restlessly registers the changes around him, and his works, self-conscious, self-confident, and full of appeals to their readers, strive to be accounts of change as much as agents of it.

In its eagerness to come to terms with the numerous transformations that were going on, the nineteenth century produced an entire discourse of change, which consisted of texts that differed widely in terms of quality and relevance. Dickens was sure enough aware of this discourse, and in his representations of change, he commented on it on a meta-level, as the following example illustrates. Of all Dickens's characters, the insufferable Mrs. Chick is given a little monologue on the topic of change:

> "It's a world of change. Any one would surprise me very much, Lucretia, and would greatly alter my opinion of their understanding, if they attempted to contradict or evade what is so perfectly evident. Change!" exclaimed Mrs Chick, with severe philosophy. "Why, my gracious me, what is there that does *not* change! even the silkworm, who I am sure might be supposed not to trouble itself about such subjects, changes into all sorts of unexpected things continually." (*DS* 448–49)

In this passage, the rhetoric of change is a target of Dickens's satire. Mrs. Chick, perfectly incapable of anything approaching "severe philosophy," drones on in the most conventional platitudes about change to prepare Miss Tox for news of great changes in the small world of the two scheming ladies, of Mr. Dombey's second marriage, and of Miss Tox being disconnected from the House of Dombey altogether. The monumentally insignificant silkworm seems to have no direct connection to the relevant changes going on in the novel; it will never appear again. However, with a potentially telling analogy to the condition of the English working class, the silkworm produces a luxury material the Dombeys need for their conspicuous consumption. Yet it is, for Mrs. Chick, as unimportant as all non-Dombeys, such as, for instance, the unfortunate Miss Tox. Over and above Mrs. Chick's fishing for a convenient illustrative image of uncontrolled change, then, the silkworm serves as an ironic reminder that change is indeed ubiquitous and unstoppable, a process of life quite unimpressed by Mrs. Chick's opinions or by nineteenth-century change debates. Those who do not actively participate in the changes of their own time, like the ideologically petrified Mrs. Chick, will be forced to change. Dickens chose to participate in the changes of his time, to be an agent of change, and his ways of representing, advocating, criticizing, and instigating change are fascinating subjects of study. The essays assembled in this book address the multitudinous ways in which the notion of change has found entry into and is negotiated in Dickens's works.

The first section of this volume focuses on Dickens's strategies of promoting social change in and through his novels. Jerome Meckier argues that *Pickwick Papers* relies on a structural pattern of repetitions and reversals that at the same time represents the novel's privileged concept of effecting social change. Whereas Meckier's discussion of this early text shows Dickens as preferring *reversal*, the so-called change of heart, to *revolution* as the basic recipe for improving the *condition humaine*, Joel J. Brattin's essay focuses on Dickens's return to the idea of revolution in *Bleak House*. Brattin identifies and discusses three different kinds of revolution in this novel: violent struggle, the Industrial Revolution, and the gentle revolution of love, embodied by Esther Summerson in her social commitment and social responsibility. Bob Heaman adds one more dimension to our understanding of Dickens as an agent of social change. In his reading of *Great Expectations*, Heaman analyses Dickens's fundamentally artistic conception of social reform. In the essay that concludes this section, Bert Hornback also focuses on Dickens's concern with fiction as a means of reforming society. Touching on thirteen novels, Hornback explores the "power of doing good," which can be traced in both Dickens's novels and in his career as a writer.

The essays in the second section broaden the volume's critical perspective on Dickens's commitment to the public, taking into view what we would argue are changes of power—political and ideological—featuring in his writing. David Paroissien is concerned with analyzing the ambivalent and complex attitudes toward politics and progress expressed in Dickens's journalistic and fictional texts. In her reading of *Martin Chuzzlewit*, Nancy Metz explores how the novel's intersecting discourses of politics, history, and science reveal an interesting change in Dickens's beliefs about agency, authorship, and society following his American journey. Michael Hollington discusses Dickens's representation of capitalism in *Dombey and Son*. Analyzing this novel through the lens provided by Georg Simmel's *Die Philosophie des Geldes* (*The Philosophy of Money*), Hollington argues that Dickens criticizes nineteenth-century monetary culture for effecting a catastrophic change: estranging human beings from themselves.

Moving from Dickens as social critic to Dickens as writer of fiction, the third section of this volume looks at literary changes in Dickens's works. Malcolm Andrews's reading of *The Pickwick Papers* examines the comic techniques Dickens develops at the early stages of his career, adapting the original Pickwick remit to suit his own particular strengths as a humorist and adjusting inherited Regency styles of comedy to meet changing tastes on the eve of Victoria's succession. The following essay links satirical comedy to literary aesthetics as Matthias Bauer looks at acoustic changes in *The Chimes* (1844). His analysis of the text's dynamic sound patterns demonstrates how the story's eponymous chimes, and their reinterpreted rhythm, serve to represent the movements of life and human relationships. Turning from changes in Dickens's literature to Dickens as an agent of literary change, the essays by Norbert Lennartz and Herbert Foltinek focus on Dickens's relation to both his literary predecessors and successors. Whereas Lennartz detects elements of anti-Victorianism in *Oliver Twist* and *David Copperfield* that align Dickens with Romantic radicalism, Foltinek's discussion of *Little Dorrit* and *Our Mutual Friend* identifies these novels' characters as complex figures whose self-doubt, listlessness, and uncertainty anticipate the characters of modern literature.

The fourth section focuses on the changes that Dickens and his works evoked in popular culture and the theater. Dickens was both involved in and fascinated with nineteenth-century popular culture. Not only did he write for a large and diverse readership, producing literary commodities for mass consumption; popular culture also features strongly in his novels, as Doris Feldmann and Chris Pittard argue in their essays. Focusing on popular entertainments in *Hard Times*, Feldmann investigates Dickens's conception of popular culture as a vehicle for a "kinder understanding" across different social strata that forms part of a radical agenda subverting Victorian cultural hierarchies. Pittard traces the resonances of conjuring as a form of nineteenth-century popular entertainment in *The Old Curiosity Shop*. Reading the novel as a narrative of secular magic, he situates it within the mid-nineteenth-century debate about property and copyright. In his essay on Victorian dramatic adaptations of *Bleak House*, Chris Louttit focuses on yet another form of popular culture, the mid-Victorian East End theater scene. Louttit's reading of hitherto marginalized plays not only offers insight into the tastes and interests of Dickens's mass audience, but also presents Dickens as an agent of radical change in this arena as well as a great popular entertainer. The essay by Robert Tracy, which concludes this section, takes us to twenty-first-century drama. Focusing on Sebastian Barry's play *Andersen's English* (2010), Tracy sheds light on the theater's continuing engagement with Dickens. Thus Barry's play, which Tracy reads as a commentary on Dickens's self-image as a man in charge of his fictional plots and of his life, indicates the ongoing changes in perception to which Dickens is still subjected today. Just as Andersen failed to read the dynamics of the Dickens household properly in 1857, we are always in danger of constructing a Dickens that suits our twenty-first-century tastes.

In his afterword, Edgar Rosenberg provides a Dickens retrospect of a more personal kind. Recalling his own first encounter with Dickens's texts as a teenage boy, Rosenberg's autobiographical essay portrays Dickens as a writer who not only fuelled his love for literature, but also taught a young Jewish refugee from Nazi Germany a new language to live in, and thus a new way of life. More than seventy years after his death, Dickens thus acted as the agent of a momentous change he cannot even have remotely foreseen.

NOTES

1 In his (unsigned) *Household Words* article "On Strike" (February 11, 1854), Dickens, who is close to the narrator persona in this short piece, is confronted with the question, "'Pray, what would you have, sir, [. . .] in the relations between Capital and Labor, *but* Political Economy?'" The narrator's comment is telling: "I always avoid the stereotyped terms in these discussions as much as I can, for I have observed, in my little way, that they often supply the place of sense and moderation" (qtd. in Flint 61).

2 On the same page, Schivelbusch gives a quotation from Heinrich Heine's *Lutezia*, (1843) which, although rhythmically less complex than Dickens's passage quoted here, gives vent to the same impression from an observing point of view.

BIBLIOGRAPHY

Dickens, Charles. *Dombey and Son*. Ed. Andrew Sanders. London, 2002.
———. *Great Expectations*. Ed. Edgar Rosenberg. New York, 1999.
———. *Sketches by Boz*. Ed. Dennis Walder. Harmondsworth, 1995.
———. *The Mystery of Edwin Drood*. Ed. David Paroissien. London, 2002.
Flint, Kate, ed. *The Victorian Novelist: Social Problems and Social Change*. London, 1987.
Forster, John. *The Life of Charles Dickens*. New York, 1908.
Mengel, Ewald, ed. *The Railway Through Dickens's World: Texts from* Household Words *and* All the Year Round. Frankfurt a. M., 1989.
Philpotts, Trey. "Dickens and Technology." *A Companion to Charles Dickens*. Ed. David Paroissien. London, 2011. 199–215.
Schivelbusch, Wolfgang. *The Railway Journey: The Industrialization of Time and Space in the 19th Century*. 1986. Berkeley, 1977.
Shaw, George Bernard. "Introduction to *Great Expectations*." *Great Expectations*. By Charles Dickens. London, 1947. v–xx. Rpt. in Dickens, *Great Expectations*. Ed. Edgar Rosenberg. New York, 1999. 631–41.
Slater, Michael. *Charles Dickens*. New Haven, 2009.

I. Dickens and Social Change

Repetitions and Reversals: Patterns for Social Change in *Pickwick Papers*

Jerome Meckier
University of Kentucky

Contrary to Steven Marcus's arguments, sheer brilliance of language does not provide the structural foundation of *Pickwick Papers*. Patterns architectural rather than linguistic become increasingly discernible as Dickens ponders which method of reversing repeated wrongdoing constitutes the surest way to achieve social change. Pickwick is hoodwinked repeatedly until he stops trying to outwit his adversaries and begins to return good for evil, charity, and compassion for cruelty and injustice. In two stunning reversals, he first succors Jingle and Job Trotter, then goes back on his word in order to release Mrs. Bardell from the Fleet. Instead of turning the tables in order to get even, Pickwick learns to strike back through merciful acts of kindness and forgiveness. Repetitions corrected by reversals emerge as both plot and theme; the pattern for structuring the novel and the means of effecting social change turn out to be the same.

Despite the consternation of admirers such as George Orwell, Dickens remained committed to *reversal*, the so-called change of heart, which he preferred to *revolution* as the basic recipe for improving human nature. However, the latter half of *Pickwick Papers* is actually constructed around a skillful counterpoint: at the same time that Pickwick absolves his tormentors, Sam and Tony Weller retaliate physically against Stiggins. In the discombobulation of the red-nosed reverend, another pattern begins to appear. One has an early indication of the sensational realist who warned wrong reverends, Chancery courts, and circumlocutionary government offices that catastrophic reversals are built into the life process.

Throughout *Pickwick Papers*, Steven Marcus claimed, Dickens "let the writing write the book" (225). The novel is generated by its own "linguistic energy," as if an author's "writing" were capable of "writing itself" (228). "Somehow," Marcus asserted, "language is spontaneously creating this novel" (228); it "provides the dramatic substructure" (228). Supposedly, *Pickwick Papers* was able "to make itself" with Dickens functioning primarily as "stenographer" (229).[1] Preposterous if taken literally, Marcus's remarks do a disservice to Dickens and the craft of novel writing.

Even if one dismisses the nine interpolated tales as fillers,[2] the remaining forty-seven chapters exhibit architectural skill as well as linguistic inventiveness. One observes a growing correlation between theme and plot, on the one hand, and the novel's shape and structure, on the other.[3] Dickens's awareness of this correlation increased the more he insisted upon the nonviolent reversing of repeated wrongdoing as the surest method of achieving positive social change.[4] *Pickwick Papers* is held together by multiple repetitions of socially despicable behavior and by fruitless attempts to prevent or punish it; two dramatic reversals of the novel's comic but toxic pattern set things to rights. The first occurs in chapter 42, installment 15, when Pickwick relieves Jingle and Job Trotter. The other happens five chapters later, in installment 17, when Pickwick reverses himself in order to free Mrs. Bardwell from the Fleet. His change of heart affords Dickens's first novel a second climax ethically more intricate than the first one.

Detestable behavior in *Pickwick Papers* always takes some form of humbuggery, whether it be hypocrisy, fraud, or deception, all of which generate a humorous though seemingly irredeemable world full of hustlers, cheats, and phonies. Ineffectual antidotes are revenge or exposure (or exposure as revenge) at first, but these have to be resorted to repeatedly. True redress for social disorder enters the novel only when Pickwick, having been several times embarrassed, stops trying to outsmart his adversaries and begins to return good for evil. Instead of trying to gull those who gulled him—it would mean a never-ending crusade—Pickwick retaliates decisively through Christ-like acts of mercy and benevolence.

Each new manifestation of humbuggery, every additional appearance (or reappearance) of someone not qualified to be what he or she claims or who willfully deceives or deliberately fosters misunderstanding, is a repetition that contributes to the reader's growing sense of pandemic.[5] There are as many humbugs in *Pickwick Papers* as one finds snobs in Thackeray's *Book of Snobs*. The cavalcade begins with the cab driver who claims his horse is "Forty-two" years old, while Jingle boasts that his dog, Ponto, could read signs (*PP* 27, 35). The list swells quickly to include Pott of the *Eatanswill Gazette*, Slumkey of the Blues, Fizkin of the Buffs, Mrs. Leo Hunter, Count Smorltork, and Stiggins, the red-nosed reverend—all within the first half of the novel—not to mention shortly thereafter, Serjeant Buzfuz, Mr. Justice Starleigh, and the concerted humbuggery of Bardell against Pickwick (ch. 34). Each of the Pickwickians fails to demonstrate the prowess supposedly associated with his specialty: Tupman as a ladies' man, for example, and Winkle as a crack shot. What chance, Dickens asks, do honesty, sincerity, and straightforwardness stand when repetitions of their opposites create a society on the verge of becoming a comic version of Dante's underworld.

Efforts to expose a conniving fraud or to exact punishment for having been bamboozled prove disappointing. Dickens feared that life itself obeys a picaresque pattern in which one problem follows another or endlessly repeats itself through unpleasant variations. In other words, the basic rhythm of life may be picaresque, a situation not as funny overall as the separate mishaps of which it consists. Not even utopic Dingley Dell is exempt. From there, Jingle, having duped Tupman, runs off with Rachel Wardle, a repetition of his misconduct at the charity ball when he cut out Dr. Slammer with Mrs. Badger (ch. 2). Pickwick, who introduced Jingle to Dingley Dell, swears revenge: "If ever I meet that man again, I'll—" he blusters, little realizing that their paths will cross repeatedly (*PP* 146).

Pickwick helps Wardle recover his sister, the spinster aunt; they give Jingle £120 for her (ch. 10). However, he resurfaces five chapters later at Ms. Leo Hunter's breakfast disguised as Charles Fitz-Marshall, a naval officer. Pickwick resolves to track the rascal to Bury Saint Edmonds in order to "expose" him once for all (*PP* 239). Instead, Pickwick falls into a well-laid trap. Job Trotter, Jingle's man, reveals that his master intends "to run away with an immense rich heiress from boarding-school" (*PP* 246), a repetition of his running off with Rachel Wardle. There is, of course, no such plan. Pickwick breaks into Westgate House to prevent it, only to be caught by Miss Tomkins and her thirty boarders. This time, Wardle comes to Pickwick's rescue, Jingle having outfoxed him "for the second time" (*PP* 251). Undaunted, Pickwick renews his vow to obtain revenge: "I'll inflict personal chastisement on him in addition to the exposure he richly merits" (*PP* 260).

As good as his word, Pickwick proceeds to Ipswich "to expose the treachery and falsehood of an individual upon whose truth and honour," he states, "I placed implicit reliance" (*PP* 342). He enlightens Nupkins, a humbug of a magistrate whose daughter Jingle is pursuing.[6] Jingle "preys upon society and makes easily deceived people his dupes," Pickwick charges (PP 384). Seducing women who have money seems less heinous than Montague Tigg's insurance scam (*Martin Chuzzlewit*) or Merdle's crooked finances (*Little Dorrit*), but it does deprive society of eligible females and investment capital, thereby tainting both love and money. Hence, the heat in Pickwick's assertion that exposure is "leniency" and that he "might [. . .] have taken a much greater revenge" (*PP* 393, 394).

A pattern has been established: thwarted with Rachel Wardle at Dingley Dell, Jingle outwits Pickwick at Westgate House, only to be blocked again at Nupkins's. Sports metaphors disclose the Sisyphean nature of this pattern. Prior to Ipswich, Sam Weller looks forward to a "return match" with Jingle and Job Trotter, proclaiming, "It's my innings now" (*PP* 352), after which, presumably, the other side bats again. The title of chapter 25 promises that the reader will learn "how Mr. Weller returned Job Trotter's shuttlecock as heavily as it came" (*PP* 376). If the contest between right and wrong, good and evil, boils down to a game of cricket or badminton, there can be no terminus, just back and forth in never-ending repetition, an unbreakable sequence.

Pickwick's epiphanic realization of this unfortunate state of affairs is doubly ironic. By chapter 18, Jingle has already disrupted Dingley Dell and Winkle has been accused of dallying with Mrs. Pott. "Beneath whatever roof they locate," Pickwick laments, his followers "disturb the peace of mind and happiness of some confiding female" (*PP* 278). These observations are interrupted by Sam's arrival with a communication from Dodson and Fogg: their client, Mrs. Bardell, is suing Pickwick for "breach of promise of marriage" (*PP* 278), a repetition with a twist of Jingle's behavior and Winkle's. This time, the innocent Pickwick, not "the diabolical Jingle" (*PP* 277), is accused of taking advantage of a woman.

The second ironic development unfolds shortly thereafter: putting up at Ipswich, Pickwick enters the wrong bedroom and is surprised by Miss Witherfield, "a middle-aged lady in yellow curl papers" (*PP* 346). Again Pickwick unsettles a woman. The next morning, Miss Witherfield denounces Pickwick to her suitor, Peter Magnus. The ensuing melee brings everyone before Nupkins, where Pickwick's testimony results in Jingle's expulsion from the gullible magistrate's family circle. Undesirable repetitions are so deeply embedded in the life process, Dickens demonstrates, that even blameless individuals such as Pickwick, who is actually fighting against them, are caught up.

Finally, in chapter 42, Pickwick breaks the comic yet ultimately depressing cycle whereby revenge follows trickery but is quickly nullified by fresh deception. In the novel's first genuine reversal, instead of turning victimizers into victims, he repays deceit with an act of charitable forgiveness. It marks his transformation from gullible buffoon into an angel of mercy.[7] Although Pickwick, Jingle, and Job Trotter have all been imprisoned for nonpayment of debt, the first mentioned is still affluent whereas the latter two, being destitute, are also defenseless. The Fleet, it turns out, is a repetition of society at large with its "poor side" where have-nots live separately from haves. Mr. Alfred Jingle's features have been "changed by suffering and pinched by famine" (*PP* 647).

Fortunately, Pickwick undergoes a change of attitude; he refrains from administering the "personal chastisement" with which he threatened Jingle (*PP* 260). "Take that, sir," says Pickwick. Job Trotter shrinks from an anticipated "blow [. . .] a sound hearty cuff" from the person he has "duped, deceived, and wronged"; instead, he is the surprised recipient of several coins from Pickwick's "waistcoat pocket" (*PP* 650). Cleverly, Pickwick imparts to his act of charity an ironic twist. Like the novel's deceivers, who thrive on the confusion they create, Pickwick deliberately invites misunderstanding here, not unintentionally as he did when asking Mrs. Bardell if two could live as cheaply as one. While saying one thing and intending another, he reverses the meaning of "Take that" from negative to positive; in place of impending harm, he dispenses unexpected largess.[8]

At the Bardell–Pickwick trial, Pickwick, having often been deceived, is found guilty of being a deceiver, a most unfortunate role reversal. Sergeant Buzfuz goes so far as to call him a "serpent" (*PP* 517), an unjust repetition of Pott's epithet for Winkle. Sentenced to incarceration in the Fleet, Pickwick takes a more adamant vow than his previous one to punish Jingle: "not one farthing of costs or damages do you get from me," he swears to Dodson and Fogg, "if I spend the rest of my existence in a debtor's prison" (*PP* 534). Repeating his "unalterable determination" in chapter 31 "to pay no damages whatsoever" (*PP* 470), Pickwick becomes the epitome of irreversibility, that is, of repetition as continuance without change. But Dodson and Fogg also have committed Mrs. Bardell to the Fleet for failure to pay costs of the trial. This is a repetition because the same injustice overtakes her as befell Pickwick, and yet it is a cruel reversal of legal procedure in that the victorious plaintiff is jailed along with the defendant. Perker informs Pickwick that Mrs. Bardwell's "speedy liberation or perpetual imprisonment rests on [him] and [him] alone" (*PP* 714).

Pickwick does the humane thing: he agrees to pay £750 in damages. Thus he goes back on his oath more dramatically than he did by not following through on his promise to chastise Jingle. In effect, he reverses himself by breaking a promise, by not keeping his word— precisely the offense of which he was found guilty. Perker declares that his client has taken a "very magnanimous revenge" (*PP* 716); the oxymoron underlines a change of heart as the archetypal reversal, a repairing of harm done instead of perpetuating it by getting even. Pickwick discharges his debt to society by forgiving his enemies and relieving their sufferings. Thus the second major reversal in Pickwick outstrips the first. Having reversed the behavior of Jingle and Job from wrongdoing to repentance and his behavior toward tricksters from vindictiveness to pardon, Pickwick rises above principle to reverse himself again. He triumphs over repetition even as he repeats his kindness to Jingle on a larger, more expansive scale with Mrs. Bardell.[9]

Not long afterwards, Pickwick announces that his "rambles [. . .] are over" (*PP* 851), but Sam refuses to leave his service. "My mind is made up," he swears, "and nothin' can ever alter it" (*PP* 851). This is a praiseworthy repetition of Pickwick's oath never to pay damages. Justifiably unalterable, it is also an acceptable reversal of Pickwick's breaking his promise never to pay. In any case, Pickwick's change of heart regarding Jingle and Job and his relenting toward Mrs. Bardwell shatter the pattern of endless repetitions of injustice and revenge. That there is "no scene of forgiveness or reconciliation" (Bowen 59) between Pickwick and Mrs. Bardell does not lessen the value of the novel's second genuine reversal.[10]

Dickens's picaresque novel revised the picaresque pattern of reversal. Traditionally, the *picaro*, younger but no more worldly-wise than

Pickwick, is repeatedly taken advantage of until, fed up, he retaliates. In one episode of the novel named after him, Lazarillo de Tormes serves a miserly blind man who beats him unmercifully and almost starves him to death. Finally, to cross a rivulet in the street, the vengeful servant sets his master opposite a pillar and urges him to "jump as hard as [he] can" (*Lazarillo* 40). The blind man splits open his head and falls back "half dead" (41). However, this turning of the tables fails to make the world a nicer place. True Pickwickian reversal, Dickens remonstrated, requires behavior different from revenge, which merely perpetuates the amount of misery in society. When Pickwick forgives Jingle and liberates Mrs. Bardell, treating both charitably, his generosity increases the sum of good in the world, if ever so slightly.[11]

George Orwell accused Dickens of lacking "constructive" suggestions (5). Dickens, Orwell noted, "attacks the law, parliamentary government, the educational system, and so forth, without ever clearly suggesting what he would put in their places" (5). Yet Orwell often speaks both for and against Dickens's preference for piecemeal change. On the one hand, Orwell complained, "there is no clear sign that [Dickens] wants the existing order to be overthrown, or that he believes it would make very much difference if it *were* overthrown" (5). Orwell thought that a change of heart was merely the "alibi of people who did not wish to endanger the *status quo*" (22). On the other hand, he could not simply disparage Dickens's call for "a change of spirit rather than a change of structure" (22). Honesty compelled him to admit that expecting "decent" behavior to produce a decent world, as Pickwick does, was more than a resort to "platitude" (23).

Instead of belaboring *Pickwick Papers* with Orwellian reservations, one should credit Dickens for consistently maintaining that it is pointless to alter the system before human nature has been improved significantly. No matter how dystopic the socialist in Orwell became, he inclined towards systemic change. "Useless to change institutions without a 'change of heart'—that, essentially, is what [Dickens] is always saying," Orwell griped (22).[12] Indeed, reversal, not revolution, is the primary pattern to emerge from *Pickwick*. The pattern for structuring the novel and for achieving social change is the same. The method for making the novel go and for improving society seems virtually identical. Dickens endorsed repetitions corrected by reversal in hopes that it would become the new rhythm of life, replacing the picaresque pattern of an eye for an eye. Except for the briefly held delusion that

America might be the ideal republic he had often imagined, Dickens eschewed wholesale change no matter how dark the latter novels became.[13] Satiric metaphors for the life process itself—an unending law case, an exercise in circumlocution—overshadowed but never totally eclipsed the patterns from *Pickwick*.

Scrooge's vow to compensate Bob Cratchit handsomely makes the former miser the quintessential paradigm for reversal as reform, a switch from unfairness to fairness that transpires independently of politics and legislation. Were England willing to reform itself as Scrooge does himself, no obstacle to the general improvement could remain standing, Dickens believed. Pickwick set the example. Later, Martin Chuzzlewit experiences a heartfelt change of outlook in Eden as intense as David Copperfield's in the Alps. *Great Expectations* furnishes yet another prime instance. Forgiveness replaces revenge when Pip acknowledges Magwitch, compassionates Miss Havisham, reconciles with Estella, and starts to mentor his namesake, little Pip. The novel begins again in the final chapter with a virtual repetition of its opening scene that is actually a reversal: "I took [little Pip] down to the churchyard," Mr. Pip writes, "and set him on a certain tombstone there" (*GE* 356).[14] Perhaps the supreme reversal would have occurred when John Jasper reenacted his murdering of Drood, this time apprehending his darker second self as the culprit (see Meckier 171–79).

Critics such as Orwell overlook a second pattern for social change in *Pickwick Papers*, one that equates catastrophic reversal with providential retribution. Thus the Wellers, father and son, accomplish the "exposure" of "the red-nosed man" when they have the intoxicated reverend thrust into the monthly meeting of the local Temperance Association (*PP* 502). The title of chapter 33 calls Stiggins's public humiliation "a small installment of retaliation." Then, in chapter 52, soon after Pickwick has relieved Mrs. Bardwell, Tony Weller seizes the unsuspecting Stiggins and begins "kicking him most furiously"—out of the bar of the Marquis of Granby and into the street, where he immerses the head of the deputy shepherd "in a horse-trough full of water" (*PP* 798–99).

Throughout *Pickwick Papers*, reappearance counts as repetition. Religious hypocrite and inebriated freeloader, Stiggins plagues the Wellers, father and son, in chapters 27, 33, and 45.[15] Night after night, he drinks "hot pine-apple rum and water" at Mrs. Weller's expense, while castigating her husband for an "obderrate" sinner (*PP* 406, 408). When the elder Weller is widowed a second time, Stiggins asks if the late Mrs. Weller left him a "little token" in her will. His audacity provokes Tony's attack. The same omniscient narrator who praises Pickwick's kindness to Jingle and Mrs. Bardwell calls Tony's administration of kick after kick "a beautiful and exhilarating sight," followed by the "still more exciting spectacle" of Stiggins's head being held under water "until he was half suffocated" (*PP* 799).

Stiggins and Jingle plague their respective targets, Tony and Pickwick, similarly, but they are dealt with differently. Pickwick treats Jingle kindly in chapter 42, then rescues Mrs. Bardell in chapter 47; the Wellers expose Stiggins in chapter 33, and Tony assaults him in chapter 52. Far from not controlling the novel's form, Dickens fashioned a structural parallel into a thematic counterpoint involving repetitions and reversals. In chapter 47, Pickwick repeats his act of kindness from chapter 42; his actions reverse the pattern of retaliation and revenge he was adhering to previously. In chapter 52, Tony completes the overthrow of Stiggins begun in chapter 33; this repetition is also a reversal in that it marks the end of Stiggins's domination of the Weller household. The red-nosed gentleman is not only overthrown but is literally thrown out of Mrs. Wellers's establishment as well. Dickens's narrator, one must reiterate, endorses equally Pickwick's benevolent treatment of Jingle and Tony's violent discomfiture of Stiggins, one of the novel's funniest scenes.

Dickens's tolerance for religious humbugs like Stiggins was limited.[16] In the same vein, Pickwick refuses "the hand of reconciliation" that Dodson and Fogg extend (*PP* 801). Along with religious hypocrisy, legal chicanery remains beyond the pale. To be reconciled with unreformed villainy, Dickens realized, would not constitute legitimate reversal. Crying "Robbers!" instead of shaking hands, Pickwick feels "perfectly comfortable and happy" (*PP* 812). Dickens approved of Pickwick's moral indignation just as he sanctioned Tony Weller's physical outburst.[17]

One should emphasize the difference between Lazarillo de Tormes's revenge on his skinflint master and the Wellers' trouncing of Stiggins. Instead of merely settling a personal score, as the *picaro* did, the Wellers rid society of a genuinely despicable pest. If Pickwick is an angel of mercy, they are avenging angels, comical agents of retribution. When Tony holds Stiggins's head under water, he performs a reversed baptism: the red-nosed reverend is not being cleansed so much as society is being cleansed of him. Here is perhaps the earliest appearance, albeit in comedic form, of Dickens the sensational realist who later explodes Chancery by proxy in the person of Krook and publishes a novel about the French Revolution the same year that Darwin's *Origin of Species* appeared. Evolution might be a continuous, mostly gradual progress, Dickens, in effect, pointed out, but history is punctuated by catastrophic blowups and society-wide reckonings that take the unwary by surprise.

In both *Bleak House* and *A Tale of Two Cities*, the melodramatic realist demonstrated that disastrous upheavals only appear to occur spontaneously. In retrospect, sudden reversals can be seen as the inevitable, long overdue outcome of complex procedures whereby the life process periodically purges itself.[18] Such reversals can seem providential, either badly needed societal corrections or richly deserved divine punishments. Each time Stiggins reappears, one can feel the wrath of the Wellers, father and son, simmering until Tony, free of wifely constraints, administers a timely comeuppance in what may be called the novel's third climax. Throughout Dickens's novels, two patterns of change from his first novel vie for paramountcy. On the one hand, Dickens shows readers how change best comes about, that is, in the Pickwickian way or through Scrooge's conversion, another nonviolent internal form of reversal; on the other hand, he used events such as Krook's combustion and the French Revolution to remind readers of what could happen if it did not. Which will it be, Dickens repeatedly asked, who will furnish the societal paradigm—Pickwick and Scrooge or Krook and Monsieur the Marquis?[19]

If reappearance in *Pickwick Papers* amounts to repetition, disappearance connotes reversal. After repeated intrusions, Stiggins is expelled from the late Mrs. Weller's bar and Dickens's novel simultaneously. In chapter 53, Jingle and Job make their final reappearance before emigrating to the West Indies. Their departure reverses the manner of Stiggins's expulsion in the previous chapter, dignified departure as the opposite of an ignominious heave-ho. Mr. Lowten, Perker's clerk, calls Job "a soft chap"; Mr. Pickwick replies, "I always thought him the reverse" (*PP* 802–03). Who will prove to be correct remains unsettled. Mr. Pickwick asks his lawyer if Jingle's will be a "permanent reformation" (*PP* 806) or just a temporary reversal. Perker's opinion, namely that Pickwick has behaved well no matter what the outcome, must suffice.

Pickwick Papers begins with its protagonist, heretofore retired, sallying forth; it ends two years later with Pickwick's withdrawal from the world to a house in Dulwich. No place name could more strongly suggest the cessation of adventure. However, not even this final reversal can erase the lessons Pickwick has learned or the good he has done. Initially, he was a good-natured innocent, even a bit of a humbug. Now he has every right to take credit for two accomplishments on which societal change depends. Neither Marcus's enthusiasm for the novel's language nor Orwell's qualms about its politics can do these accomplishments justice: Pickwick exults in what he calls "the enlargement of my mind and the improvement of my understanding" (*PP* 858).

NOTES

1   In the "Afterword" to the Signet edition, the text cited throughout this essay, Marcus stopped short of calling Pickwick "automatic writing" but added that, "in this one work," Dickens's "conscious mind" was not exercising its customary "formal control" (*PP* 868).
2   Interpolated tales, one may argue, are answers to a neophyte serial novelist's exigencies. Valiant attempts have been made to assimilate them. Robert L. Patten maintained, in three separate essays, that the tales are thematically connected to the main narrative, were written expressly for the numbers in which they appear, and teach lessons relevant to Pickwick's education. Garrett Stewart suggested that the tales exorcise the darker side of human nature so as not to upset Pickwick's world (32), yet the chapters set in the Fleet prison certainly do so. Stewart's admiration for the novel's linguistic exuberance rivals Marcus's.
3   According to James Phelan and Peter J. Rabinowitz, most commentators on prose narrative now "find the search for organic unity a decreasingly rewarding critical pursuit" (5–6). On the contrary, discovery of a pattern in *Pickwick* continues to be a priority.
4   In the 1837 "Preface," Dickens may have been thinking of this pattern when he remarked that "the whole twenty numbers [. . .] should form one tolerably harmonious whole" (*PP* vii). On the other hand, there is the disclaimer in the 1847 preface to the Cheap Edition of *Pickwick*: "no ingenuity of plot was attempted, or even at that time considered very feasible by the author in connexion with the desultory mode of publication adopted." Consensus has gone heavily against the 1837 statement. G. K. Chesterton set the tone in 1907, dubbing *Pickwick* "splendid" but "shapeless" (15). Archibald C. Coolidge said its "incidents [were] arranged like beads on a string" (61). Butt and Tillotson contended that *Pickwick* "discovers its shape" after a quarter of the way but is always "a miscellany" (71–72). Only with the trial, Jonathan H. Grossman stipulated, does *Pickwick* move "from loosely linked narrative sketches" towards the complexly plotted Victorian novel" (84). Even after Mrs. Bardell misunderstands Pickwick, Paul Schlicke decided, *Pickwick Papers* never ceased to be "episodic" (452). For Juliet John, *Pickwick*

was "originally conceived" not as a novel but as a "periodical" (127–28). William F. Axton attempted to organize the novel around the ambiguity of appearance and reality but his has long remained a solitary voice. Recently, Barry Tharaud argued for a novel unified by Dickens's efforts to measure "the shortcomings of both reason and feeling as a basis for morality" (157).

5   Even Pickwick, alleged expert on Tittlebats, is called "a humbug"; supporters of the Pickwick Club are dismissed as "so many humbugs" (*PP* 27, 180).

6   Pickwick is guilty of a perhaps unintentional pun: he informs Nupkins that the magistrate has been "harbouring" a "gross imposter" disguised as a naval officer (*PP* 383, 384).

7   Marcus found Pickwick "quasimythical [. . .] as if he were a kind of demigod come to visit the earth" (*PP* 867).

8   To make a case for integrating the interpolated tales, one should begin with "a queer client" in chapter 21. Perhaps Pickwick befriends Jingle and Job in chapter 42 because he benefited from hearing the old man's story about Heyling. He reduced his father-in-law to abject poverty in order to obtain "revenge" for the death of his wife and child. They perished after Heyling was cast into debtors' prison, thanks to his father-in-law, who disapproved of him. Unlike Heyling, whose conduct he reverses, Pickwick never swears, "I will have life for life" (*PP* 327).

9   W. H. Auden identified this reversal as the novel's climax: "In order to do his duty, [Pickwick] has to do in fact what he had falsely been accused of doing, commit a breach of contract by breaking his vow and putting money into the pockets of Dodson and Fogg; for the sake of charity, he has to sacrifice his honor" (428).

10 The desired note of reconciliation can be found in the flurry of marriages in the final pages, all of these unitings facilitated or supported by Pickwick—Winkle and Arabella Allen, Snodgrass and Emily Wardle, Sam Weller and Mary. Dickens reversed Pickwick's breaking of promises, no matter how commendable, with three vows certain to be kept.

11 To argue that, at the conclusion of Pickwick, "benevolence has not been able to change the world, to remake it to correspond to Mr. Pickwick's original innocent conception of it," seems unduly harsh (Hornback 13). There is nothing sacrosanct about Pickwick's "original innocent conception." Nor should he be required to reverse the consequences of the fall.

12 In 1937, T. A. Jackson credited Dickens with a progressive "Radicalism" that "deepened" into something akin to "Socialism or Communism" (7). Two years later, Orwell took the opposite view, deploring "change of heart" as an alternative to more radical solutions.

13 Dickens was always more radical in utterance than in practice. Urania Cottage typifies his style when it came to doing rather than ranting. This 1847 experiment remains something of a Pickwickian enterprise. Besides Mrs. Bardell, Pickwick must deal with Rachel Wardle, Jingle's imaginary heiress, and the lady in yellow curlers; he can barely cope with one case at a time. Although fundamentally of a different order, Dickens's interchanges with residents such as Jemima Hiscock, Mary Joynes, and Frances Cranstone, to name just three, left him feeling as put upon as Pickwick. Hiscock and Joynes were found "dead drunk"; Cranstone, an "evil-doer," might have "corrupted the whole house" (Bodenheimer 140–41). Dickens never dreamed of stamping out prostitution all across London. His asylum modestly aspired to give a few "fallen women" a lift.

14 For Robert A. Stein, there are no reversals in the last three chapters of *Great Expectations*, just a "confluence of repetitions" (152); he is skeptical of their value. Stanley Friedman found numerous "duplicating devices" in Dickens's fiction, such as "repetition" involving similar characters, parallel plots, and recurrent motifs both within individual novels and between them (xi). For example, he cites numerous instances of parents in *Pickwick Papers* interfering with their children's marital choices (Friedman 31–32). See J. Hillis Miller for a sevenfold discussion of "the way repetition works in fiction" (17). In *Pickwick Papers*, however, repetition, although useful as a structural device, has no positive moral or ethical ramifications. Indeed, quite the opposite. Julian Wolfreys decontextualizes *Pickwick* as an ahistorical novel structured around "various types of vision" which must themselves be viewed "from several perspectives" (16); most of these are provided not through examination of Dickens's novel but by postmodern literary theorists. To rescue *Pickwick* from Wolfreys, see Parker (202–12).

15 Reappearance can also be salutary repetition. For example, Bob Sawyer and Benjamin Allen from chapter 30, who reappear in chapters 38, 48, and 50, are always welcome. In contrast, when Pickwick reencounters Pott and Slurk in chapter 51, thirty-eight chapters after the Eatanswill election, the rural editors of the *Eatanswill Independent* and the *Eatanswill Gazette* come to blows immediately. In between them trying to keep the peace, Pickwick absorbs all their punches. Dickens peppered his novel with numerous minor repetitions that, mostly harmless, augmented pattern and theme. In chapter 54, for instance, Jo the fat boy, walks in on Mr. Snodgrass embracing Emily Wardle just as he once surprised Tupman and Rachel Wardle. Over the last three installments, Dickens reintroduced many of his leading characters for a curtain call.

16 The narrator rails against "those false prophets and wretched mockers of religion, who, without sense to expound its first doctrines or hearts to feel its first principles, are more dangerous members of society than the common criminal" (*PP* 690). His tone, strident for a comic novel, anticipates the irate narrator's in chapter 47 of *Bleak House*. After Jo dies, the narrator excoriates "Right Reverends and Wrong Reverends" (*BH* 572).

17 Michael Slater has stated that Dickens uses Pickwick and the Wellers "to distribute rewards and punishments" but "the law in the form of Dodson and Fogg is beyond Pickwick's power to reform or punish" (134). Contrary to Kathryn Chittick, who found the "question of structure" in *Pickwick* "difficult" because no one is eager to see how the story turns out (70), ongoing struggles between Pickwick and Jingle, Tony Weller and Stiggins, cry out for resolution.

18 For a discussion of the conflict between catastrophism in sensational or melodramatic realists such as Dickens and Wilkie Collins, on one side, and the gradualism whereby changes occur in George Eliot's domestic realism, on the other, see Meckier (250–52, 248–54, and 256–58).

19 No matter how sensational a realist Dickens became, he continued to inflict comical yet devastating humiliations on humbugs in his novels. Old Martin thrashes Pecksniff at the resolution of *Martin Chuzzlewit* (*MC* 882); Orlick and his ruffians pummel Pumblechook in the antepenultimate chapter of *Great Expectations* (*GE* 346); and Sloppy pitches Silas Wegg into a scavenger's cart at the end of *Our Mutual Friend* (*OMF* 862). But Stiggins's seminal comeuppance is structurally unique. Although exposed and discredited, Pecksniff exits forgiving his enemies.

BIBLIOGRAPHY

Auden, W. H. "Dingley Dell and the Fleet." *The Dyer's Hand and Other Essays*. New York, 1962.
Axton, William F. "Unity and Coherence in *The Pickwick Papers*." *SEL* 5 (1965): 663–76.
Bodenheimer, Rosemarie. *Knowing Dickens*. Ithaca, 2007.
Bowen, John. *Other Dickens*. Oxford, 2000.
Butt, John, and Kathleen Tillotson. *Dickens at Work*. 1957. London, 1968.
Chesterton, G. K. *Chesterton on Dickens*. London, 1992.
Chittick, Kathryn. *Dickens and the 1830s*. Cambridge, 1990.
Coolidge, Archibald C. *Charles Dickens as Serial Novelist*. Ames, 1967.
Dickens, Charles. *Bleak House*. Ed. George Ford and Sylvère Monod. New York, 1977.
———. *Great Expectations*. Ed. Edgar Rosenberg. New York, 1999.
———. *Martin Chuzzlewit*. London, 1986.
———. *Our Mutual Friend*. Harmondsworth, 1971.
———. *The Pickwick Papers*. Afterword by Steven Marcus. New York, 1964.
Friedman, Stanley. *Dickens's Fiction: Tapestries of Conscience*. New York, 2003.
Grossman, Jonathan H. *The Art of the Alibi: English Law Courts and the Novel*. Baltimore, 2002.
Hornback, Bert. *Noah's Arkitecture: A Study of Dickens' Mythology*. Athens, 1972.
Jackson, T. A. *Charles Dickens: The Progress of a Radical*. 1937. New York, 1987.
John, Juliet. *Dickens's Villains: Melodrama, Character, Popular Culture*. Oxford, 2001.
Lazarillo de Tormes. *Masterpieces of the Spanish Golden Age*. Ed. Angel Flores. New York, 1957.
Marcus, Steven. "Language into Structure: Pickwick Papers." *Representations: Essays on Literature and Society*. New York, 1975. 224–46.
Meckier, Jerome. *Hidden Rivalries in Victorian Fiction: Dickens, Realism, & Revaluation*. Lexington, 1987.
Miller, J. Hillis. *Fiction and Repetition: Seven English Novelists*. Cambridge, 1982.
Orwell, George. "Charles Dickens." 1939. *Dickens, Dali & Others*. New York, 1946.
Parker, David. "The Topicality of *Pickwick*." *The Dickensian* 105 (2009): 202–12.
Patten, Robert L. "The Art of *Pickwick*'s Interpolated Tales." *ELH* 34 (1967): 349–66.
———. "The Interpolated Tales in *Pickwick Papers*." *Dickens Studies* 1

(1965): 86–89.
———. "The Unpropitious Muse: Pickwick's Interpolated Tales." *Dickens Studies Newsletter* 1(1970): 7–10.
Phelan, James, and Peter J. Rabinowitz. *Understanding Narrative*. Columbus, 1994.
Schlicke, Paul, ed. *Oxford Companion to Dickens*. New York, 2000.
Slater, Michael. *Charles Dickens*. New Haven, 2009.
Stewart, Garrett. *Dickens and the Trials of the Imagination*. Cambridge, 1974.
Stein, Robert A. "Repetition during Pip's Closure." *Dickens Studies Annual* 21 (1992): 143–56.
Tharaud, Barry. "Form as Process in *The Pickwick Papers*: The Structure of Ethical Discovery." *Dickens Quarterly* 24 (2007): 145–58.
Wolfreys, Julian. *The Old Story, with a Difference: Pickwick's Vision*. Columbus, 2006.

Three Revolutions: Alternate Routes to Social Change in *Bleak House*

Joel J. Brattin
Worcester Polytechnic Institute

In Dickens's *Bleak House* (serialized between 1852 and 1853), many characters are deeply concerned with the idea of revolution. Not only Sir Leicester Dedlock, Mr. Gridley, Lawrence Boythorn, and the Ironmaster, but both narrators also focus our attention on the issue, which was, of course, topical for Dickens, writing in the aftermath of the European revolutions of 1848. Dickens explores three different paths or routes to social change, and in one crucial moment, he allows all three routes to converge at once, in a single misspelled word of three letters. I will dangle that critical juncture (and the misspelled word) as a little puzzle while I briefly discuss each of the three alternative routes or paths to social change.[1]

The first type of revolution is scientific or technological, with profound economic and social implications; it is what we now call the Industrial Revolution. In general, Dickens has little faith in technology as a solution to social problems, but he attempts to consider the Industrial Revolution fairly and embodies that type of revolution most powerfully in the equivocal but generally positive figure of the Ironmaster, Mrs. Rouncewell's son and George Rouncewell's elder brother. (Strangely, Dickens never identifies the given name of the Ironmaster. I refer to him here as "Mr. Rouncewell.") Mr. Rouncewell is what Dickens's friend and contemporary Thomas Carlyle would call one of the "Captains of Industry" (IV. 4: 361), and although he is not a fully developed character, he is an important one, embodying for

Dickens an important feature of the rapidly changing conditions in the nineteenth century.

The Ironmaster reveals his technological bent early in life, "constructing," we are told,

> steam-engines out of saucepans, and setting birds to draw their own water, with the least possible amount of labor; so assisting them with artful contrivance of hydraulic pressure, that a thirsty canary had only, in a literal sense, to put his shoulder to the wheel, and the job was done. (*BH* 7: 60)[2]

He goes on to construct "a model of a power-loom" and eventually takes employment in some "Works" in the "iron country farther north" (*BH* 7: 60).

As an adult, and a captain of industry, Mr. Rouncewell is clearly transforming the country. His transformation of his own landscape is obvious from the description in the chapter "Steel and Iron," in which we learn that "coalpits and ashes, high chimneys and red bricks, blighted verdure, scorching fires, and a heavy never-lightening cloud of smoke, become the features of the scenery" (*BH* 63: 600). But Dickens emphasizes that the Ironmaster is also in the business of *spreading* this revolution, travelling constantly throughout England: he tells Sir Leicester, "in these busy times, when so many great undertakings are in progress, people like myself have so many workmen in so many places, that we are always on the flight" (*BH* 28: 278).

Mr. Rouncewell's Industrial Revolution may be based primarily on scientific and engineering developments, but it has profound economic and social implications, as Sir Leicester Dedlock intuitively understands. He says with evident dismay, shortly before we first meet the Ironmaster, that he has heard from Mr. Tulkinghorn that Mr. Rouncewell "has been invited to go into Parliament" (*BH* 28: 277). Sir Leicester Dedlock, the voice of conservative landowners all over Britain, resists the Industrial Revolution as he must resist all social change. Dedlock's last name, of course, effectively forecasts his reactionary impulse: he is firmly resistant to any kind of change whatsoever.

The Ironmaster names his only son Watt, no doubt after the engineer James Watt; James Watt was a vitally important figure in the Industrial Revolution that transformed both the nation and the world, first by steam power in the eighteenth and nineteenth centuries, and then by electric power (which we measure in Watts) in the twentieth and twenty-first centuries. James Watt offered revolutionary improvements to the efficient functioning of the steam engine; in naming his son "Watt," the Ironmaster honors a leading industrialist, and may be recalling his own early years in Lincolnshire, when he constructed "steam engines out of saucepans" (*BH* 7: 60).

Before moving on to the second path to social change, I want to note Dickens's continuing interest in the power of the Industrial Revolution to shape and distort our lives. Dickens published many articles about science and technology in the 1850s, considering the Industrial Revolution (especially the railroads, and the transformations wrought by them) extensively in his journals *Household Words* and *All the Year Round*. Henry Morley's leading article, "Need Railway Travellers Be Smashed?," offers one early example: this piece considers the high cost of railway accidents to society, in destruction of life and property, and the absurdly low cost of a simple mechanical device, designed and built by Mr. C. F. Whitworth, to prevent these accidents. In the months of 1852 and 1853 during which *Bleak House* was serialized, Dickens published three more articles about railroads and technology, as well as articles about the manufacture of buttons, pottery, cloth, playing cards, coaches, brass founding, adhesive paste, gold refining, and opium.[3] In Dickens's next novel after *Bleak House*, *Hard Times*, he again turned his attention to the Industrial Revolution by looking at the world it shapes (or distorts) in Coketown and by a close examination of the repellant "self-made" captain of industry Josiah Bounderby. Another piece published by Dickens at the same time as *Hard Times* takes a grim, unblinking look at industrial accidents in mills.[4] Dickens's view of the Industrial Revolution after *Hard Times* is certainly not all dark. In his next novel, *Little Dorrit*, Dickens paints an unambiguously positive figure of an industrial revolutionary: the engineer and inventor Daniel Doyce.

The second type of revolution in *Bleak House* is organized social and political action, often accompanied by at least an implied threat of violence. Sir Leicester Dedlock fears political revolution will stem from the industrial one: he thinks of "the people in the iron districts who do nothing but turn out by torchlight," and he "stirs with indignation" (*BH* 28: 278). In no less than three chapters, he voices his fear of revolution, using his own particular metaphor: that the floodgates will open. Sir Leicester tells his sycophantic relative Volumnia:

it is a remarkable example of the confusion into which the present age has fallen; of the obliteration of landmarks, the opening of floodgates, and the uprooting of distinctions [. . .] that I have been informed [. . .] that Mrs. Rouncewell's son [the Ironmaster] has been invited to go into Parliament. (*BH* 28: 277)

Later in this same chapter, Sir Leicester learns that the Ironmaster expects his son's wife to have more education than she can get in the Lincolnshire village school:

From the village school of Chesney Wold, intact as it is this minute, to the whole framework of society; from the whole framework of society, to the aforesaid framework receiving tremendous cracks in consequence of people (ironmasters, lead-mistresses, and what not) not minding their catechism, and getting out of the station unto which they are called— necessarily and for ever, according to Sir Leicester's rapid logic, the first station in which they happen to find themselves; and from that, to their educating other people out of *their* stations, and so obliterating the landmarks, and opening the floodgates, and all the rest of it; this is the swift progress of the Dedlock mind. (*BH* 28: 280)

In the next chapter, Sir Leicester reads a Tory newspaper and feels "particularly complacent, because he has found in his newspaper some congenial remarks bearing directly on the floodgates and the framework of society" (*BH* 29: 283). And later in the novel, after Sir Leicester learns from Mr. Tulkinghorn that both the Ironmaster and his son Watt Rouncewell were "uncommonly active" against Sir Leicester's conservative interests in the recent election—Mr. Tulkinghorn says the Ironmaster is "a very good speaker. Plain and emphatic. He made a damaging effect, and has great influence" (*BH* 40: 402)—Sir Leicester's rhetoric attains a paranoid and slightly incoherent crescendo: "upon my honor, upon my life, upon my reputation and principles, the floodgates of society are burst open, and the waters have—a—obliterated the landmarks of the framework of the cohesion by which things are held together!" (*BH* 40: 403).

The man from Shropshire, Gridley, is introduced in the first chapter of the novel, in opposition to the Chancery court system. He freely admits that he is "violent" and has "been in prison for threatening the solicitor" (*BH* 15: 153); later, the narrator speaks of Gridley's "condition of resentment and violence" (*BH* 24: 243), and Tulkinghorn calls him a "threatening, murderous, dangerous fellow" (*BH* 27: 274). Although

Gridley is in fact no revolutionary, his violent criticism of and antipathy toward the existing system suggests a revolutionary possibility.

Lawrence Boythorn, the irascible friend of John Jarndyce, speaks with even greater ferocity than usual when he talks about Chancery, and he uses the language of violent revolution, if not of terrorism:

> "There never was such an infernal cauldron as that Chancery, on the face of the earth!" said Mr. Boythorn. "Nothing but a mine below it on a busy day in term time, with all its records, rules, and precedents collected in it, and every functionary belonging to it also, high and low, upward and downward, from its son the Accountant-General to its father the Devil, and the whole blown to atoms with ten thousand hundred-weight of gunpowder, would reform it in the least!" (*BH* 9: 83)

As Boythorn sees it, liberal "reform" of Chancery is an impossibility; the only possible route to social change to which he gives voice is violent revolution.

The third-person narrator hints at the possibility of such a violent revolution several times, perhaps most strikingly in the final sentence of the first chapter of the novel: "If all the injustice [the court] has committed, and all the misery it has caused, could only be locked up with it, and the whole burnt away in a great funeral pyre,—why, so much the better for other parties than the parties in Jarndyce and Jarndyce!" (*BH* 1: 5).

Later in the novel, the third-person narrator warns us that if we do not heed the cause of the poor, embodied in the crossing-sweeper Jo and the many other residents of the slum Tom-all-alone's, we may suffer violent repercussions ourselves. The narrator notes that on market day,

> blinded oxen, over-goaded, over-driven, never guided, run into wrong places and are beaten out; and plunge, red-eyed and foaming, at stone walls; and often sorely hurt the innocent, and often sorely hurt themselves. Very like Jo and his order; very, very like! (*BH* 16: 157)

The narrator goes on to compare Jo's existence to a street dog's and points the moral of that comparison thus: "Turn that dog's descendents wild, like Jo, and in a very few years they will so degenerate that they will lose even their bark—but not their bite" (*BH* 16: 158).

In November of 1605, a would-be revolutionary named Guy Fawkes conspired with a group of others in an attempt to blow up the Houses of Parliament in what is now known as the Gunpowder Plot. As if in commemoration of that day in November, Dickens evokes the figure of Guy Fawkes in the November 1852 installment of the novel, describing Grandfather Smallweed as a "limp and ugly figure," "at first sight scarcely reconcilable with any day in the year but the fifth of November" (*BH* 26: 261)—an allusion to the effigies of Guy Fawkes burned on Guy Fawkes Day. Later in the novel, Mr. Guppy again describes Grandfather Smallweed in the same terms, asking if Lady Dedlock has had a visit from "a person without the use of his lower extremities, carried up-stairs similarly to a Guy" (*BH* 55: 537).

Dickens treats the Gunpowder Plot in another work published at almost precisely the same time as *Bleak House*: he discusses the revolutionary plot in the sixth paragraph of chapter 34 of *A Child's History of England*, originally published in *Household Words* on July 16, 1853, a few months before the final installments of *Bleak House* appeared. Dickens writes that one of the conspirators, Robert Catesby,

> formed one of the most desperate and terrible designs ever conceived in the mind of man; no less a scheme than the Gunpowder Plot. His object was, when the King, lords, and commons, should be assembled at the next opening of Parliament, to blow them up, one and all, with a great mine of gunpowder. (478)[5]

Dickens evinces no sympathy with the plotters, and explicitly characterizes the plan as a "horrible idea" (478). But it is interesting how closely Dickens's language here mirrors the sympathetic character Lawrence Boythorn's violent fantasy in chapter 9 of *Bleak House*.

Spontaneous combustion may be closely related to this type of violent revolution: the character who suffers this fate at the precise midpoint of the novel (*BH* 32: 320) is Mr. Krook. Miss Flite tells us that Krook is also known as "the Lord Chancellor" (*BH* 5: 36) and that his shop is informally known as "the Court of Chancery" (*BH* 5: 36). As noted earlier, violent fantasies of the destruction of the Court of Chancery figure in the narrator's imagination as early as the first chapter. "The Lord Chancellor's" self-destruction here surely reflects these narrative fantasies of violent revolution, specifically those targeting the court of Chancery.

Another revolutionary event that finds entrance into Dickens's novel is the fourteenth-century Peasants' Revolt whose leader Wat Tyler figures in *Bleak House* repeatedly. Sir Leicester Dedlock, opposed to the Ironmaster's Industrial Revolution, fears a social and political one as well, and often links what he fears to the Peasants' Revolt. He thinks sanctioning complaints about the court of Chancery "would be to encourage some person in the lower classes to rise up somewhere—like Wat Tyler" (*BH* 2: 9), and when he meets the Ironmaster for the first time, he once again feels all his "old misgivings relative to Wat Tyler" (*BH* 28: 278). Sir Leicester "refers back in his mind to Wat Tyler" again in chapter 40, which treats the electoral defeat of his party, partly due to Mr. Rouncewell's influence (*BH* 40: 404).

Dickens discusses the Peasants' Revolt, too, in *A Child's History of England*. In chapter 17, published in *Household Words* on 12 June 1852, a few months after the first installment of *Bleak House* was published, Dickens does not shrink from relating the violent acts committed by Tyler, saying "Wat Tyler himself [. . .] broke into the Tower of London and slew the archbishop and the treasurer" (305). But Dickens seems sympathetic to Tyler, saying, "Wat was a hard-working man, who had suffered much, and had been foully outraged" (306). He notes that the rebellion was in part a reaction to "a certain tax, called the Poll-tax," forced on the people by the government of King Richard II (304) and tells of a tax collector who "behaved in a savage way, and brutally insulted Wat Tyler's daughter," who was "under the age of fourteen" (305). Wat "did what any honest father under such provocation might have done—struck the collector dead at a blow" (305). Dickens notes that "[i]nstantly the people of that town uprose as one man" (305). Dickens goes on to say that Tyler probably had "a much higher nature and a much braver spirit than any of the parasites who exulted [. . .] over his defeat" (306). Dickens creates sympathy for the rebels by noting that "some fifteen hundred of the rioters were tried [. . .] and executed with great cruelty" (306), and he offers a final comparison which casts Tyler in a very favorable light: "The king [Richard II]'s falsehood in this business makes such a pitiful figure that I think Wat Tyler appears in history as beyond comparison the truer and more respectable man of the two" (306). Although Dickens comes short of praising Tyler, riot, and revolution, he certainly seems to have sympathy and understanding for Tyler and for his sufferings.

A Child's History of England appeared in *Household Words* at irregular intervals; generally, Dickens would publish one chapter (rarely, two) in every fourth installment of the weekly magazine. It is interesting, however, perhaps just a coincidence, that the weekly issue of *Household Words* describing the Peasants' Revolt is the one dated

12 June 1853. No installment of *A Child's History of England* had appeared since 15 May 1853, so it almost seems as though Dickens were celebrating the anniversary of the Revolt, which took place on 13–14 June 1381, by choosing to publish this installment of *A Child's History of England* on a date so close to the anniversary of Wat Tyler's actions and his death.

Before moving on to the third type of revolution Dickens models in *Bleak House*, I would again like to suggest that Dickens's interest in treating the second type continues in later works of the 1850s. Dickens alludes to Guy Fawkes in both *Hard Times* and *Little Dorrit*. In an early installment of *Hard Times*, the young whelp Tom Gradgrind voices his resentment at his mode of utilitarian education in particularly Boythornian language, telling his sister Louisa, "I wish I could collect all the Facts we hear so much about, [. . .] and all the Figures, and all the people who found them out; and I wish I could put a thousand barrels of gunpowder under them, and blow them all up together!" (*HT* 8: 216).[6] And near the middle of the same novel, James Harthouse begins to plot for Louisa Gradgrind, now married to Mr. Bounderby— that is, he "began to think it would be a new sensation, if the face which changed so beautifully for the whelp, would change for him" (*HT* 23: 429). There is no specific allusion to Guy Fawkes here, but it is perhaps telling that Dickens eventually gave this chapter, so concerned with plotting, the title "Gunpowder."[7] Dickens's next novel, *Little Dorrit,* contains two brief allusions to Guy Fawkes. The loquacious Flora Finching alludes to "Mr. F's Aunt brought home like the fifth of November in a rush-bottomed chair" (*LD* 1. 24: 209),[8] reminding us of Grandfather Smallweed. Later, when the swindler Mr. Merdle meets Fanny Dorrit (now Mrs. Sparkler), Mr. Merdle's "hand seemed to retreat up his sleeve [. . .] and he gave her such a superfluity of coat-cuff that it was like being received by the popular conception of Guy Fawkes" (*LD* 2. 16: 461). Certainly Dickens's fascination with violent political revolution is manifest throughout much of his next novel, *A Tale of Two Cities*.

The third type of revolution in *Bleak House* is the type embodied by the first-person narrator, Esther Summerson: a gentle and personal revolution of love, social commitment, and social responsibility. In the first chapter narrated by Esther, she tells us that early in her life, she resolves "to be industrious, contented, and kind-hearted, and to do some good to some one, and win some love to myself" (*BH* 3: 13). Thirty-two chapters later, she recalls this early prayer, using virtually identical language (*BH* 35: 348); the only verbal difference is that this time, she says "true-hearted" in place of "kind-hearted." Dickens emphasizes these two prayers, not only by the verbal repetition but also by the rigorous symmetry of their placement within the novel: the first prayer appears in the third chapter of the first half of the novel (installment 1), and the second appears in the third chapter of the second half of the novel (installment 11).

Esther's revolution is a quiet and gentle one. She says she thinks it best "to be as useful as I could, and to render what kind services I could, to those immediately about me; and to try to let that circle of duty gradually and naturally expand itself" (*BH* 8: 74). Her tender love for those in her circle of duty includes devoted and kind service to John Jarndyce, Ada Clare, Richard Carstone, Miss Flite, Caddy Jellyby, Charley Neckett, and many others, finally including her mother, Lady Honoria Dedlock. And it is interesting to consider how that circle of love and duty does indeed "gradually and naturally expand itself": many of these characters, learning from Esther, behave in loving and generous ways themselves.

John Jarndyce might be considered a proponent of this type of loving revolution; a few others, such as Caddy Jellyby Turveydrop, Charley Neckett, and George Rouncewell, belong in this group, as does Esther's husband Alan Woodcourt, the hero of the novel. Alan Woodcourt is a brave man. His kindness and generosity involves exposing himself to mortal danger, yet he does not shrink from hardship and is willing to suffer privations in order to "be as useful as [he can]." Miss Flite tells Esther of his heroism in the "shipwreck over in those East-Indian seas": "Death in all shapes. Hundreds of dead and dying. Fire, storm, and darkness. Numbers of the drowning thrown upon a rock. There, and through it all, my dear physician was a hero" (*BH* 35: 351).

At the end of the novel, Alan Woodcourt chooses to serve as "a medical attendant for the poor" in Yorkshire (*BH* 60: 579), "an appointment to a great amount of work and a small amount of pay" (*BH* 60: 579–80). Woodcourt is an ambitious young man—but he is ambitious not for money or status, but for doing good work where it is needed. John Jarndyce tells Esther that "[a]ll generous spirits are ambitious, I suppose; but the ambition that calmly trusts itself to such a road [of usefulness and good service], instead of spasmodically trying to fly over it, is of the kind I care for. It is Woodcourt's kind" (*BH* 60: 579).

If a generous and imaginative love that looks first outside of or beyond one's self is the third route to social change in *Bleak House*, little need be said about Dickens's treatment of that type of revolution in the rest of the 1850s; love is a constant theme throughout Dickens's career. But Sissy Jupe in *Hard Times* (identified as the "Power of affection" in his working notes for that novel)[9] and the loving and self-sacrificing Amy Dorrit and Sydney Carton in *Little Dorrit* and *A Tale of Two Cities* are revolutionary in their effects on those around them.

Perhaps the minor character Watt Rouncewell, the Ironmaster's son, belongs among these loving revolutionaries, too. The convergence of the three paths to social change I mentioned earlier appears in the forty-eighth chapter of the novel. In this chapter, the Ironmaster, representative of the Industrial Revolution, confronts Sir Leicester Dedlock, antagonistic to both that Industrial Revolution and the political revolution he associates with Wat Tyler. Sir Leicester, listening to Mr. Rouncewell speak of his son's attachment to Rosa, Lady Dedlock's protégée, thinks "that there may be a hidden Wat Tylerish meaning in [the Ironmaster's] expression" (*BH* 48: 463). On the next page, when Lady Dedlock has (under duress) stated that she intends to part with Rosa, the latter sobs and expresses her gratitude to Lady Dedlock. The Ironmaster chides Rosa, "in a low voice, though not angrily," and says, "[H]ave a spirit, if you're fond of Wat!" (*BH* 48: 464). The last word the Ironmaster speaks here, "Wat," refers to Mr. Rouncewell's own son, and it should be spelled with four letters, as it invariably is everywhere else in the novel: young Rouncewell is, after all, named after the engineer and industrial revolutionary James Watt, and of all people, his father should know how to spell it. But the name appears in the first edition as "Wat," with just three letters, as if Watt were named after Wat Tyler, the leader of the Peasants' Revolt.

> says the ironmaster, checking her in a low voic
> " have a spirit, if you're fond of Wat ! " My Lac
> with indifference, saying, " There, there, child ! Yc

Detail from the first edition of *Bleak House*, chapter 48, page 464. Courtesy of the Robert D. Fellman Collection, Gordon Library, WPI.

When I first saw the spelling "Wat" in the first edition (regularized to four letters in the Penguin edition [*BH* 742], but retained as three letters in the Norton Critical edition [*BH* 578]), I thought this misspelling must be a compositor's error, likely arising from the close proximity of the phrase "Wat Tylerish," just a single page earlier in the text. But on checking Dickens's manuscript, I was surprised to discover that Dickens himself misspelled the name, penning only "Wat" on his page.[10]

Although it is not, strictly speaking, a typographical error (the compositor faithfully recorded the spelling his author gave him, and Dickens had ample opportunity to correct the spelling in the proof stages), it is still unquestionably an error: the Ironmaster, who speaks the words, could hardly be confused about which revolutionary was his son's namesake. But that confusion—in not only Sir Leicester's mind but also in his creator Charles Dickens's—is highly suggestive.

Is Watt Rouncewell a spiritual descendent of James Watt, as his father hopes—the new voice of the Industrial Revolution? Or is he a spiritual descendent of Wat Tyler, as Sir Leicester fears—a future political revolutionary, destined to obliterate floodgates and destroy the framework of society? Or is he essentially a lover, such as Esther Summerson Woodcourt is?

We do not know whether Watt will turn out to be like either James Watt or Wat Tyler, but we do know that his love for Rosa is already transformative—and ultimately revolutionary. Late in the novel, Watt's father the Ironmaster tells his brother, Trooper George,

> I make an agreement with my son Watt to-day, that on this day twelvemonth he shall marry as pretty and as good a girl as you have seen in all your travels. She goes to Germany tomorrow [. . .] for a little polishing up in her education. (*BH* 63: 602)

Watt's love for Rosa has resulted in changes in his father, in his beloved—who will get a far better education in Germany than she could ever have received in the village school in Lincolnshire—and in himself.

NOTES

1 My grateful thanks go to Kathleen Markees, who prepared the illustration from the first edition of *Bleak House* for me. See p. 26.
2 Unless otherwise noted, all quotations from *Bleak House* are to the first edition of 1852–53. Parenthetical references are to chapter and page.
3 Henry Morley's "A Novelty in Railway Locomotion" appeared in the 6 March

1852 issue; William Howard Russell's "Belgian Briskness" (considering railway regulations) appeared in the 2 October 1852 issue; and Henry Morley's "Self-Acting Railway Signals" appeared in the 12 March 1853 issue. For an index to other articles treating manufacture and industry in *Household Words*, see Anne Lohrli's useful volume *Household Words* (1973). (Note that a few weeks before the first installment of *Bleak House* was published—on 7 February 1842, Dickens's fortieth birthday—the lead article in *Household Words* considered the manufacture of "Gunpowder.")

4 Henry Morley's "Ground in the Mill" appeared in *Household Words* on 22 April 1854. This same issue of *Household Words* contains chapters 7 and 8 of *Hard Times*.

5 All quotations from Dickens's *A Child's History of England* are to the first edition, as originally serialized in Dickens's journal *Household Words*. The issue and date of publication are given in the body of the text; parenthetical references are to the relevant page number.

6 All quotations from Dickens's 1854 novel, *Hard Times*, are to the first edition, as originally serialized in Dickens's journal *Household Words*. Parenthetical references are to chapter and page; there was no division into books in the original serial publication.

7 No chapter titles appear in the original serial installments; the title "Gunpowder" appears for the first time in the first book edition of *Hard Times* (1854).

8 All quotations from Dickens's 1855–57 novel *Little Dorrit* are to the first edition. Parenthetical references are to book, chapter, and page.

9 The manuscript and notes for *Hard Times* are in the Forster Collection at the Victoria and Albert Museum in South Kensington. Dickens's notes are reproduced in facsimile in Stone (254).

10 The manuscript and notes for *Bleak House* are also in the Forster Collection at the Victoria and Albert Museum in South Kensington.

BIBLIOGRAPHY

Carlyle, Thomas. *Past and Present*. London, 1843.
Dickens, Charles. *A Child's History of England*. London, 1852–54.
———. *Bleak House*. London, 1852–53.
———. *Bleak House*. Ed. George Ford and Sylvère Monod. New York, 1977. Norton Critical Edition.
———. *Bleak House*. Ed. Nicola Bradbury. London, 1996. Penguin Edition.
———. *Hard Times*. London, 1854.
———. *Little Dorrit*. London, 1857.
Lohrli, Anne. *Household Words*. Toronto, 1973.
Morley, Henry. "A Novelty in Railway Locomotion." *Household Words* 6 Mar. 1852: 568–69.
———. "Ground in the Mill." *Household Words* 22 April 1854: 224–27.
———. "Need Railway Travellers Be Smashed?" *Household Words* 1 Dec. 1851: 217–21.

———. "Self-Acting Railway Signals." *Household Words* 12 Mar. 1853: 43–45.

Russell, William Howard. "Belgian Briskness." *Household Words* 2 Oct. 1852: 70–72.

Stone, Harry. *Dickens' Working Notes for His Novels*. Chicago, 1987.

Dickens, Society, and Art: Change in Dickens's View of Effecting Social Reform

Robert Heaman
Wilkes University

In his recent biography of Dickens, Michael Slater argues that after chapter 38 of *The Old Curiosity Shop* (1840–41), Dickens's appeal "to the nation's rulers to 'turn aside from the wide thoroughfares [. . .] and strive to improve the wretched dwellings in bye-ways where only Poverty may walk'" (157) becomes the dominant theme in his writing. This appeal earns him "that unique public status as deeply compassionate champion of the poor, accorded to him alone among all the writers of the age" (157). David Paroissien points out that Victorian novelists "agreed that fiction should provide a paradigm to show people how to behave more decently in the future and offer what Dickens called 'an occasional refuge to men busily engaged in the toils of life'" (*Selected Letters* 284). This "reform tradition of the Victorian novel, in which novelists committed themselves to trying to improve nineteenth-century society" (284) culminates, for Dickens, in *David Copperfield* (1849–50).

In that novel, Bert Hornback indicates, Dickens finds the way

> for goodness and wisdom to influence this world for the better [. . . Dickens] finds it first [. . .] in the "growing reputation" which comes from David's "Story . . . of [his] experience," in his "growing reputation and success" which "enlarge [his] power of doing good." [. . .] David begins, for Dickens, to make this world a better world. (62–63)

After *David Copperfield*, Dickens writes "condition-of-England" novels, according to Slater (362), until *A Tale of Two Cities* (1859). I would include *A Tale of Two Cities* as a condition-of-England novel warning of what would happen to English society if conditions in England did not change.

With *Great Expectations,* however, Dickens's notion of the nature and role of the artist takes precedence over his focus on social reform. Dickens reread *David Copperfield* before he wrote *Great Expectations* "to be sure [he] had fallen into no unconscious repetition" (qtd. in Slater 489). In Dickens's revisiting of the story of a young man's development, it is noteworthy that Pip does not share David's vocation as a writer, perhaps in part because Dickens's notion of how to improve society is no longer to write novels that address the condition-of-England question, as David evidently does. Instead, as I argue in the following, Dickens suggests that to be true "reformers," agents of change need not become artists themselves, but must assume distinctive qualities of an artist: the imaginative capacity to perceive reality truly, to love, to forgive, and to accept the "eternal shape" of the past (*GE* 339).

David Copperfield writes novels that, as Agnes says, allow him "to teach others" (*DC* 795), allow him to become part of the "reform tradition of the Victorian novel." Dickens, too, assumed this mantle. His next novel, *Bleak House* (1852–53), is a tightly wrought, deeply symbolic work of art whose pages, according to Robert Tracy, "are Dickens's Great Exhibition of 1852, reminding England that all is not well" (384). In the Introduction to his edition of *Bleak House*, Stephen Gill observes that

> Slum houses, without sanitation or pure water, the breeding ground for disease; the lack of even basic medical provision for the poor; the noisome, pestilential state of many city graveyards; the inhuman treatment of pauper children; the unwanted offspring of a rapidly growing but unknown underclass—such topics, so rebarbative in themselves, struck Dickens as full of meaning, portentous signs of the times. (viii)

Although the omniscient narrator in *Bleak House* appeals to the "nation's rulers" in the memorable chapter-ending peroration upon Jo's death, the first-person narrator, Esther Summerson, responds to these overwhelming conditions by vowing "to be as useful as I could, and to render what kind of services I could, to those immediately about me; and to let that circle of duty gradually and naturally expand itself" (*BH* 117).

Dickens's own "circle of duty" involves addressing the social problems plaguing England at this time through his writing.

After *Bleak House*, Dickens addresses the problems raised by an insensitive political/economic philosophy, an education system based wholly on facts, and a utilitarian approach to complex social issues. *Hard Times* (1854) is the novel F. R. Leavis famously identified as a "moral fable," in which Dickens is "possessed by a comprehensive vision, one in which the inhumanities of Victorian civilization are seen as fostered and sanctioned by a hard philosophy [utilitarianism], the aggressive formulation of an inhumane spirit" (341). Bernard Shaw goes further: for him, *Hard Times*

> is Karl Marx, Carlyle, Ruskin, Morris, Carpenter, rising up against civilization itself as against a disease, and declaring that it is not our disorder but our order that is horrible; that it is not our criminals but our magnates that are robbing and murdering us; and that it is not merely Tom All Alone's that must be demolished and abolished, pulled down, rooted up, and made forever impossible so that nothing shall remain of it but History's record of its infamy, but our entire social system. (33)

How does Dickens hope to have an effect on this horrible, destructive order? In August of 1854, Dickens wrote to Henry Carey explaining his notion of the purpose of the novel:

> To interest and affect the general mind in behalf of anything that is clearly wrong—to stimulate and rouse the public soul to a compassionate or indignant feeling that it must not be—without obtruding any pet theory of cause or cure, and so throwing off allies as they spring up—I believe to be one of Fiction's highest uses. And this is the use to which I try to turn it. (Qtd. in Slater 363)

By the time he was writing *Little Dorrit* (1855–57), Paroissien points out, Dickens "[f]eared that concerns over Britain's military setbacks during the Crimean War (1854–56) would divert attention from much needed social reform" (*Selected Letters* 263). His original title for the novel, *Nobody's Fault*, "was no doubt meant as an ironic comment on how Britain's ruling class managed to deny or evade responsibility for national disgraces and disasters," according to Slater (391), and in a letter to Macready in October of 1855, Dickens admits that "in No. 3 of my book [*Little Dorrit*] I have been blowing off a little of indignant steam, and with God's leave I shall walk in the same all the days of my life; but I have no present political faith or hope—not a grain" (*Letters* 7: 716).

Dickens blows off more "indignant steam" in *A Tale of Two Cities* (1859), a novel, "[i]n its own distinctive way, as pointed a critique of Benthamism as *Oliver Twist* and *Hard Times*," according to Andrew Sanders (*Charles Dickens* 155). Dickens had written to Austen Henry Layard in April of 1855 about "the alienation of the people from their public affairs":

> And I believe the discontent [in England] to be so much the worse for smouldering, instead of blazing openly, that it is extremely like the general mind of France before the breaking out of the first Revolution and is in danger of being turned by any one of a thousand accidents—a bad harvest—the last strain too much of aristocratic insolence or incapacity—a defeat abroad—a mere chance at home—into such a devil of a conflagration as never has been beheld since. (*Letters* 7: 587)

A Tale of Two Cities gives us a glimpse of what might happen if the nation does not address these problems, problems that go beyond glib Benthamite solutions that seek to fulfill man's best self-interest. But Dickens now has "not a grain" of faith or hope in the workings of government and the "nation's rulers." Sydney Carton's sacrifice suggests an alternative hope. He demonstrates the extent to which humans are capable of acting against their own self-interest in favor of an interest larger than the self. According to Sanders, "[b]y exploring the vital interconnection of the private and the public, the personal and the social, in fiction [Dickens] was attempting to suggest that even history itself was subject to a greater law than that of utility" (*Charles Dickens* 155).

By the time Dickens was preparing to write *Great Expectations* (1860–61), he seemed no longer confident in "the reform tradition of the Victorian novel in which novelists committed themselves to improve nineteenth-century society" (Paroissien, *Selected Letters* 284) by addressing the condition-of-England question. When he reread *David Copperfield* to avoid unconscious repetition, did he respond as Gareth Cordery does in examining Forster's response?

> Forster and his fellow readers [according to Cordery] shared David's rather complacent view of the world expressed from his comfortable position at the end as successful public figure and happily married man, and they subscribed to the means by which he achieved it. (374)

Or did he feel the "contrast between his elaborate description of David's domestic bliss at the end of the novel and the subsequent shipwreck of his own real-life marriage," by which, as Slater points out, he must have been "strongly [. . .] affected" (489)? Dickens surely must have wondered if his own "growing reputation and success" (*DC* 821) would necessarily "enlarge his power of doing good" (*DC* 821), as Agnes tells David his must, particularly given Dickens's suspicion of those who were in power. According to Hugh Cunningham,

> Dickens shared with many radicals in Britain a deep suspicion of the state and of office-holders. Look at the state, many said, and ask what it does; it gets Britain engaged in numerous wars, it subjects people to the indignities of the Poor Law, it taxes knowledge, it, until 1846, gives a privileged financial position to aristocratic farmers, and so on. And who makes up the state? Aristocrats and their hangers-on. (172)

If the condition of England cannot be improved through the good work of the state and its officeholders, where is Dickens to look for improvement? Sanders's claim that Dickens perceives history as the product of a force greater than utility is borne out in a letter to Wilkie Collins: Explaining why he did not indicate to the reader the connection between Dr. Manette's Bastille ordeal and Darnay's family's involvement before that relationship is revealed at Darnay's trial, Dickens observes:

> I think the business of Art is to lay all that ground carefully, but with the care that conceals itself—to shew by a backward light, what everything has been working to—but only to SUGGEST, until the fulfillment comes. These are the ways of Providence—of which ways, all Art is but a little imitation. (Qtd. in Slater 477)

Further, in a letter to Bulwer-Lytton, Dickens defends on aesthetic grounds his having disposed of Mme. Defarge in an accidental discharge of her gun during the struggle with Miss Pross:

> Where the accident is inseparable from the passion and emotion of the character, where it is strictly consistent with the whole design, and arises out of some culminating proceeding on the part of the character which the whole story has led up to, it seems to me to become, as it were, an act of divine justice. (*Letters* 9: 259)

Here Dickens anticipates modernists who would claim a godlike creative power for the artist. As Andrew Sanders points out in his reading of this letter,

> [t]he story, of which Dickens was so proud, is a "design" which has to be read and understood as a pattern. That pattern can represent a human ordering which offers some meaning amid a sequence of historical events which seemed to Carlyle to teeter on the edge of Chaos. (Introduction xiii)

Dickens, the designer of *A Tale of Two Cities*, sees himself in the late 1850s as responsible not only for trying, as an artist, to figure out how to deal with the multitude of social and economic problems besetting Victorian England, but also for trying to understand those problems in the pattern of a larger historical context. What is to prevent an England in the stranglehold of the bureaucratic morass represented by the Circumlocution Office in *Little Dorrit* (1857) from exploding as France did under the stranglehold of the old order at the end of the previous century? In analyzing the events in France, he, as an artist, perceives a pattern quite contrary to the pattern of embittered vengeance knitted by Mme. Defarge. If all art is a "little imitation" of providence, if accident can be strictly consistent with the whole design, then the work of the artist is to perceive the order, to discover and reveal that larger design. Dickens now sees that the very qualities that allow for artistic vision allow for social redemption: love, sacrifice, and the imaginative capacity to perceive design and order amidst apparent disjunction and chaos.

No novel of Dickens explores the pattern of accident, chance, coincidence, and fate more relentlessly than the novel that follows *A Tale of Two Cities, Great Expectations* (1860–61). Indeed, the narrator of that novel, reflecting on events many years after they occurred, interrupts the narrative to exhort the reader: "Pause you who read this, and think for a moment of the long chain of iron or gold, of thorns or flowers, that would never have bound you, but for the formation of the first link on one memorable day" (*GE* 60). This pattern is often read as suggesting that Pip's life is determined by those events that followed from his "first link." But the thrust of Dickens's narrative as well as the narrative perspective complicate such a reading. By using a reflective narrator who reviews events long past, Dickens suggests that by contemplating the complete design and pattern of one's life, one is able to gain perspective on the significance of the pattern. Now older and wiser, Pip sees the importance of getting beyond feeling the sense of injustice and entrapment he suffered as a result of the manipulation Miss Havisham and Magwitch inflicted upon him in their attempts, in their different ways, to make up for the wrongs Compeyson had done them. He learns to discover the truth that Sanders claims the plot of *A Tale of Two Cities* demonstrates to its readers: that "individuals possessed the power to free themselves from historical conditioning and from an imposed uniformity of response" (*Charles Dickens* 154).

When Pip tells Jaggers that he supposed Miss Havisham was his benefactor, Jaggers responds, "Take nothing on its looks; take everything on evidence" (*GE* 251). This, Jaggers would have Pip believe, is how to deal with reality. But later, Jaggers asks Pip where he is headed, and Pip responds,

"For the Temple, I think."
"Don't you know?" said Mr. Jaggers.
"Well," I returned, glad for once to get the better of him in cross-examination, "I do *not* know, for I have not made up my mind." (*GE* 290)

And here begins Dickens's analysis, through Pip's mental processes, of how we are to sift through bits of evidence and facts to sort out and perceive truly the world around us and to shape that world into a meaningful pattern. Significantly, Pip has dinner with Jaggers later that day and notices "a certain action" of Molly's fingers and is reminded by her eyes and hands of "exactly such eyes and hands, on a memorable occasion very lately" (*GE* 292):

> I thought of the inexplicable feeling that had come over me when I last walked—not alone—in the ruined garden, and through the deserted brewery. I thought how the same feeling had come back when I saw a face looking at me, and a hand waving at me, from a stage-coach window; and how it had come back again and had flashed about me like Lightning, when I had passed in a carriage—not alone—through a sudden glare of light in a dark street. I thought how one link of association had helped that identification in the theatre, and how such a link, wanting before, had been riveted for me now, when I had passed by a chance, swift from Estella's name to the fingers with their knitting action and the attentive eyes. And I felt absolutely certain that this woman was Estella's mother. (*GE* 292)

This intuitive leap hardly shows Pip working toward knowledge on empirical evidence alone. In recalling a chain of incidents sparked by a flash of recognition, Pip is working out links through feeling, instinct, memory, association, and imagination to get at truth. And Pip is able to confront Jaggers with this information, along with the fact that he knows who Estella's father is as well, having pieced that evidence together through inquiries to Wemmick and Miss Havisham.

But Pip is not merely able to see a pattern or design in reality as it is, he is also able to perceive beyond the temporal and spatial limitations of our time/space dimension. When Pip first goes to Satis House,

> It was in this place, and at this moment, that a strange thing happened to my fancy. I thought it was a strange thing then, and I thought it a stranger thing long afterwards. I turned my eyes—a little dimmed by looking up at the frosty light—towards a great wooden beam in a low nook of the building near me on my right hand, and I saw a figure hanging there by the neck. A figure all in yellow white, with but one shoe to her feet; and it hung so, that I could see the faded trimmings of the dress were like earthy paper, and the face was Miss Havisham's, with a movement going over the whole countenance as if she were trying to call to me. In the terror of seeing the figure, and in the terror of being certain that it had not been there a moment before, I at first ran from it, and then ran towards it. And my terror was greatest of all, when I found no figure there. (*GE* 55)

This hallucination is revealed as a vision when Pip returns years later to Satis House to perfect the only good thing he has ever done with his supposed inheritance, secure Herbert's partnership. At this point Miss Havisham asks Pip if he can forgive her when she dies. After telling her he can do so now, Pip goes out into the ruined garden and turns to look back:

> A childish association revived with wonderful force in the moment of the slight action, and I fancied I saw Miss Havisham hanging to the beam. So strong was the impression, that I stood under the beam shuddering from head to foot though I knew it was a fancy—though to be sure I was there in an instant. (*GE* 299)

Acting on this "fancy" of Miss Havisham's being in danger and distress and her calling on him for help, Pip returns to Miss Havisham and "saw a great flaming light spring up. In the same moment, I saw her running at me, shrieking, with a whirl of fire blazing all about her, and soaring at least as many feet above her head as she was high" (*GE* 299). Pip's having anticipated this horrible event in his childhood "fancy," and his recollecting the memory of that "fancy" precisely at the time that it occurs in reality, indicate that Pip, like a visionary artist, has the imaginative capacity to perceive reality beyond the limitations of time and space.

This capacity is accompanied by the ability to forgive those who have wronged him and to love. The imaginative capability to order the world in some way allows us to perceive a design beyond the appearance of actuality surrounding us. It is also the means of liberating Pip from an irrevocable chain of iron or gold.

"Was there ever such a Fate!" Pip exclaims to Herbert upon discovering the truth about his benefactor (*GE* 256). But the Pip who is able to forgive Miss Havisham now has all his repugnance for Magwitch

> melted away, and in the hunted, wounded, shackled creature who held my hand in his, I saw only a man who had meant to be my benefactor, and who had felt affectionately, gratefully, and generously, towards me with great constancy through a series of years. (*GE* 332)

While reflecting on the pattern of the past and acting with generosity and imagination, Pip rejects the role that others have embraced and sought to impose on still others. Pip now sees beyond the constraints of fate, sees beyond the limitations of human and social manipulation; he sees beyond the confused welter of reality without embracing the paranoid vision of victimhood that perceives a world designed by forces outside his control.

Miss Havisham, like Mrs. Clennam before her, in her solitary exclusion, has allowed her mind to grow "diseased, as all minds do and must and will that reverse the appointed order of their Maker" (*GE* 394). And Pip forgives her, as Little Dorrit forgives Mrs. Clennam. "Was there ever such a Fate!" Miss Havisham, like Mrs. Clennam, like Mme. Defarge, attempts to control reality, to impose her "diseased" version of order on lives and events. They try to "bend the past out of its eternal shape" (*GE* 339). Pip's imaginative sensibility, the same force in him that inspired his poor dreams and allowed him to see Miss Havisham hanging to the beam, allows him to forgive Miss Havisham and to love Magwitch, his second father. The circumstances of life, the links of the chain, can only bind Pip if he, like Miss Havisham, Mrs. Clennam, and Mme. Defarge, is imaginatively incapable of getting beyond himself and his personal grievances. He is ensnared by fate only insofar as he is limited by the actual events he experiences. But Pip's efforts to understand the pattern or design of what has happened to him and to assume responsibility for his own actions, his revised judgments and self-criticism, suggest his capacity to gain control and independence. His selfless generosity to Herbert allows the opportunity to make his way in the world without bitterness and without regret. He works hard at Clarriker and Pocket and eventually becomes a partner in Clarriker, Pocket, and Pirrip.

Gareth Cordery is suspicious of these mid-Victorian, middle-class values that Forster claims are celebrated in *David Copperfield*: "self denial, and patience, quiet endurance of unavoidable ills, strenuous efforts against ills remediable; and everything in the fortunes of the actors warns us, to strengthen our generous emotions and to guard the purity of the home" (374). Pip eventually learned these very values. But, unlike David, Pip does not become "a successful public figure and a happily married man" whose "rather complacent view of the world" "Forster and his fellow readers shared" (Cordery 374). I do not think David achieved success and happiness through the mid-Victorian, middle-class values Forster celebrates, however. I think David becomes David by becoming an artist.

My argument here is not that David does not become a successful artist, but that Dickens no longer believes that the kind of art David makes, the writing of condition-of-England novels, is the kind of art through which Dickens can fulfill himself as artist, nor perhaps, the kind of art that England needs at this time. Hornback points out that

> David creates "characters" in his novel, and in his life he meets and comprehends the world through those characters. What this says is that, for Dickens, the artist is—or should be—everyman. Only through the use of the comprehending imagination, he says, can everyman become free, and wise. (47)

The Dickens who refers to Providence and divine justice as he justifies his aesthetic, the Dickens who "carefully placed [Carton's sacrifice] within a Christian context" (Sanders, *Charles Dickens* 155), is making large claims for the capacity of the imagination. Pip, like David Copperfield who sees Little Emily's future as he watches her teetering on the timbers over the sea, sees Miss Havisham struggling with death in his fancy even as she is on the verge of struggling with death in reality. Dickens comes to believe that such stuff as artists are made of is what every man must cultivate, and he comes to have greater faith in the powers of the imagination than in the workings of the state and its officeholders.

The pattern that Dickens is working through from *David Copperfield* to *Great Expectations* is finally apparent in his last completed novel, *Our Mutual Friend*. Here Dickens revisits many of the social problems he has dealt with in the past—the poor law and workhouses with Betty Higden, children's hospitals with Our Johnny, poverty, squalor, and crime. And he returns to his major character types and themes: John Harmon, like Arthur Clennam and Pip—even David, after Dora's death—is dispirited and alienated and finds redemption and earns his inheritance through the virtues Dickens has always celebrated, earnestness, discipline, hard work, perseverance. And like David and Clennam, John Harmon works through the confusion and vicissitudes of romantic love to win Bella and to help her discover that she is "true golden gold at heart" (*OMF* 821). But the other plot of *Our Mutual Friend*, the Lizzie Hexam/Eugene Wrayburn story, is not at all similar to what Dickens has been doing all along. Eugene, in fact, starts out as very much an antihero, for Dickens, a Steerforth, Harthouse, Henry Gowan figure: a bored, useless, decadent, and dangerous member of the upper class. Dickens had intended him to die, in fact; he told Stone that "'One of the strongest features of the story . . . will be the death of Eugene after the assault of the schoolmaster.' Dickens added, 'I think it will be one of the best things I have ever done'" (Slater 525).

But instead of killing Eugene, Dickens has him redeemed. As a result of his near-death experience after Bradley's assault, Eugene recognizes the worth of Lizzie and is able to become a good husband and a useful member of society. Like Pip, who on reflecting on the events of his life is able to alter an apparently determined pattern, Dickens alters what he has determined to do with Eugene. As Pam Morris points out, the marriage of Lizzie and Eugene combines "patrician disaffection" with the "dialect speaking class" in such a way as to provide cultural renewal in a society that has "devalued its own expressive currency" through the degeneration of language (187). I have argued elsewhere that

> their marriage offers something larger than a palliative to the degeneration of language in Victorian England. The union of Lizzie and Eugene represents, for Dickens, an emblem of what Matthew Arnold believes must be done to correct the misdirection of culture in Britain at this time. (Heaman 4)

In "Hebraism and Hellenism," Arnold argues that, after the liberating aestheticism of the Renaissance, Britain in its adoption of the Reformation had embraced the Hebraic ethical tradition of "conduct and obedience" and "strictness of conscience" (109). This was the wrong course for England to take at that time, according to Arnold:

> For more than two hundred years [since the Renaissance] the main stream of man's advance [in the rest of the western world] has moved towards knowing himself and the world, seeing things as they are, spontaneity of consciousness [Hellenism]; [whereas] the impulse of a great part, and that the strongest part, of our nation has been towards strictness of conscience. (119)

Arnold believes that England must again embrace Hellenism to address the cultural crisis of nineteenth-century England. He insists "not that Hellenism is always for everybody more wanted than Hebraism, but that [. . .] at this particular moment [. . .] for the great majority of us [. . .] it is more wanted" (126). In this context, as Dickens is returning to what he refers to in a letter to Wilkie Collins as the "big brush and the large canvass" (*Letters* 9: 346) of his large novels and, reflecting on his own career and the effects his writings have had on the condition of England, he may no longer believe that Eugene's fate is determined any more than Pip comes to believe his has been. The aesthetic sensibility that initially attracted Eugene to Lizzie may itself provide the "spontaneity of consciousness" that allows Lizzie's love to redeem him. Surely, the Dickens who flouted Victorian standards to the extent that he allowed himself to become intimate with a young actress no longer believed that the nation's salvation lies in "strictness of conscience." Like Steerforth, Harthouse, and Gowan, Eugene has not been guided by his conscience. But Dickens has come to believe that Eugene's aesthetic sensibility itself can become his means of redemption, and so he has changed his mind about killing him. He allows his pursuit of Lizzie's beauty to become the basis of redemption.

At the end of *Our Mutual Friend*, the England of the Podsnaps and the Veneerings and Weggs and Riderhoods is in greater need of Hellenism than of Hebraism. The stuff artists are made of is the stuff that must be awakened if what is beautiful and promising in the world of Dickens's England is to be preserved, and it must be awakened "for the great majority of us" (Arnold 126). Lizzie awakens it in Eugene, and that is why Dickens realized that the schoolmaster must not destroy him.

Dickens is pursuing a more ambitious transformation of society than the nation's leaders are capable of producing. As Joel J. Brattin points out in the Introduction to his edition of *Our Mutual Friend*, Dickens is "completely serious about the power of love to move the world—and to transform it utterly" (xxiii). This love is identified with the imagination, with the creation and perception of beauty, with the capacity to order the world and see it whole, with renewal and forgiveness. At one with the art that Blake insists is charity, it allows the artist to enable those with eyes that can see and ears that can hear to bring about a new Earth and a new Heaven.

BIBLIOGRAPHY

Arnold, Matthew. *Culture and Anarchy*. Ed. Ian Gregor. New York, 1971.
Brattin, Joel J. Introduction. *Our Mutual Friend*. By Charles Dickens. London, 2000.
Cordery, Gareth. "*David Copperfield*." Paroissien, *Companion* 369–79.
Cunningham, Hugh. "Dickens as a Reformer." Paroissien, *Companion* 159–73.
Dickens, Charles. *A Tale of Two Cities*. Ed. and introd. Andrew Sanders. New York, 1998.
———. *Bleak House*. Ed. George Ford and Sylvère Monod. New York, 1977. Norton Critical Edition.
———. *David Copperfield*. Ed. Nina Burgis. Oxford, 1999.
———. *Great Expectations*. Ed. Edgar Rosenberg. New York, 1999. Norton Critical Edition.
———. *The Letters of Charles Dickens*. Ed. Madeline House, Graham Storey et al. 12 vols. Oxford, 1965–2002. Pilgrim Edition.
———. *Little Dorrit*. Ed. Harvey Peter Sucksmith. Oxford, 1999.
———. *Our Mutual Friend*. Ed. Joel J. Brattin. London, 2000.
Ford, George, and Sylvère Monod, eds. *Hard Times*. By Charles Dickens. 2nd ed. New York, 1999. Norton Critical Edition.
Gill, Stephen. Introduction. *Bleak House*. By Charles Dickens. Oxford, 1999. vii–xxi.
Heaman, Robert J. "Hebraism and Hellenism in *Our Mutual Friend*." *Dickens Quarterly* 21 (2004): 3–11.
Hornback, Bert. *The Hero of My Life*. Athens, 1981.
Leavis, F. R. "*Hard Times*: An Analytic Note." *The Great Tradition*. London, 1948. 227–48. Rpt. in Ford and Monod 340–60.
Morris, Pam. "A Taste of Change in *Our Mutual Friend*." *Rethinking Victorian Culture*. Ed. Juliet John and Alice Jenkins. Handsmill, 2000. 179–95.

Paroissien, David, ed. *A Companion to Charles Dickens*. Oxford, 2008.
———, ed. *Selected Letters of Charles Dickens*. Boston, 1985.
Sanders, Andrew. *Charles Dickens*. Oxford, 2003.
———. Introduction. *A Tale of Two Cities*. By Charles Dickens. New York, 1998. vii–xx.
Shaw, Bernard. Introduction to *Hard Times*. London, 1912. v–xvi. Rpt. in Ford and Monod 333–40.
Slater, Michael. *Charles Dickens*. New Haven, 2009.
Tracy, Robert. "*Bleak House*." Paroissien, *Companion* 380–89.

The World Changing Dickens, Dickens Changing the World

Bert Hornback
Universität des Saarlandes

The first time the world changed for Charles Dickens was in *Pickwick Papers*, when Sam Weller took Mr. Pickwick on a tour of the Fleet Prison and showed him the "poor side," where the real debtors lived. Dickens had seen debtors' prisons—had known the Marshalsea, when his father was incarcerated there; he had seen poverty and homelessness in London, and had described such in *Sketches by Boz*.[1] But he seems first to have imagined it, seriously, when he decided to show it to Mr. Pickwick.

Mr. Pickwick, a "benevolent" sixty-five-year-old innocent who pretends to be an "observer" of this world, is shocked by what he sees and retreats. "Henceforth," he tells Sam, "I will be a prisoner in my own room" (*PP* 599). And in effect, Mr. Pickwick "retires" as an adventurer in the world at that point in his story.

In his contribution to this volume, Jerome Meckier has argued convincingly that Dickens does something more, and more important than this, with Mr. Pickwick, and that although Mr. Pickwick is shocked into retirement from this rough and brutal world, he has also learned something important from his various picaresque confrontations and defeats. Meckier sees Mr. Pickwick's early comic attempts to avenge wrongs by fighting back replaced by merciful acts of kindness and forgiveness. Meckier sees these as acts of what Dickens's Mr. Perker calls "magnanimous revenge" (*PP* 716). And this change, he argues, is important for Dickens.

Mr. Pickwick's forgiving charity to Mr. Jingle and Job Trotter does in fact result in their "permanent reformation" (*PP* 693) in the end, and Mr. Pickwick never has "occasion to regret his bounty" to them (*PP* 742). In the final pages of the novel, Dickens reports Bob Sawyer and Benjamin Allen reformed and soberly working in Bengal, and Mrs. Bardell back to letting rooms and earning "great profit" without engaging "sharp" lawyers (*PP* 742). But Dodson and Fogg remain in business as "mean, rascally, pettifogging robers" (*PP* 697), and as Mr. Pickwick retires to Dulwich, his wise magnanimity has done nothing to alleviate the suffering of impoverished debtors, let alone change this ill-organized world.

Dickens did—could not—retire, at age twenty-six, and he did not retreat. Instead, he started over. In the same month that Mr. Pickwick heroically announced his intention to go to prison rather than pay an unjust judgment against him in the case of *Bardell vs. Pickwick*, Dickens began *Oliver Twist*. By the time Mr. Pickwick had seen the horrors of the Fleet prison and retreated to his prison room, Oliver, "badged and ticketed" from birth as an "orphan of the workhouse [. . .] to be cuffed and buffeted through the world" (*OT* 5), had arrived in London.

Pickwick Papers started out as anything but a novel of social criticism. Then, halfway through writing it—and almost by accident—Dickens invented the novel of social criticism. And in the second chapter of his new novel, he let little Oliver utter, on behalf of all the starving children in the workhouse, the Ur-cry of all revolutions, "Please Sir, I want some more" (*OT* 12). By this novel's end, however, Dickens had removed Oliver from the real world without changing either it or the people who govern it. Mr. Brownlow—Dickens's second "benevolent" gentleman—is perhaps magnanimous in forgiving Monks, a gentleman by birth, for his crimes and allowing Monks to escape justice, but then Mr. Brownlow seeks—with Dickens—brutal revenge on Sikes and Fagin.

With Fagin dead, the boys he fed and housed are on their own, with no one to care for—or about—them. And Mr. Brownlow, retired now with his one saved child, has proved to be no better than the feeding fat board member in the white waistcoat at the workhouse: the one who is certain that Oliver "will be hung" (*OT* 17). And that Christian gentleman is no better than Mr. Bumble in his Christian-buttoned beadle's coat.

But Dickens could not afford to see such, and instead, at the end of the novel, he relied on Mr. Brownlow—and God—and forgot about this world. Mr. Brownlow is never a particularly good man, and not an observant man: he is lost to the world around him, reading a book, when the Artful Dodger steals his snuffbox. He is impotent before Mr. Fang and would let Oliver be sentenced to "three months—hard labour of course" (*OT* 67). In the end, he claims to have done "all that [he] could hope to do" in arranging to save Oliver's inheritance and sets out, then, "in a fever of excitement wholly uncontrollable," his "blood boil[ing] to avenge" Nancy's murder (*OT* 328).

Dickens joined Mr. Brownlow, losing himself in the violence of Sikes's and Fagin's deaths. Then Dickens turned to God and fabricated a supposedly happy ending to the novel, invoking "that Being whose code is Mercy and whose great attribute is Benevolence" (*OT* 360) and forgetting all about this troubled real world. The social critic disappeared, retired with Mr. Brownlow and Oliver to a safe but unreal place "whose condition approached as nearly to one of perfect happiness as can ever be known in this changing world" (*OT* 357)—which is to say that it is not *in* this changing world.

Of all the characters in *Oliver Twist*, only the refreshingly skeptical Mr. Grimwig is left living in the real world at the end. But already Dickens had his third novel under way, and Nicholas Nickleby—nineteen years old, not nine—has arrived in London, wanting to work there. And Dickens, aware surely that the conclusion to *Oliver Twist* was not satisfactory, was trying yet again.

Dickens was not and never would have been a systematic social philosopher. He was not so at age twenty-four, when beginning *Pickwick Papers*, or a year later, in *Oliver Twist*. He was not such at twenty-six, as he started *Nicholas Nickleby*. "Benevolence" is not a social philosophy. Pickwickian benevolence fails to save anyone, and Mr. Brownlow's benevolence is directed only at Oliver—and at saving Oliver's inheritance. The Cheeryble brothers' benevolence is better, because they actually go about seeking to do good, but Dickens has given them seemingly infinite wealth with which to pursue their charities.

Dickens is a novelist, not a philosopher, though his goal is similar to that of the social philosopher. But Dickens's method is different from the philosopher's. Dickens is more creator than analyst; he works with his imagination, through his characters. And although many critics have complained that Dickens was not a "thinker," not a Bentham or a Malthus, they do not mention that those social philosophers were not imaginative artists and that their philosophical ideas were neither sound nor sane. Dickens's imagination is of much more value than are their philosophies. Dickens's knowing their works would not have made him a better novelist. But had they known Dickens well, they might have been better social philosophers.

Of course, Dickens was not simply writing novels; only in *Pickwick Papers* did he set out with such a simple goal. Because Mr. Pickwick went to prison, Dickens had been trying to figure out—trying to imagine—how to save this world. The overlap of his first three novels is significant, not just of his outrageous creative energy but also, more importantly, of what it is he was doing, and his impatience to get it done. He was trying to figure out how to change the world.

William Faulkner wrote to Malcolm Cowley, in 1944, that his work was in a sense one long novel: "I am telling the same story, over and over. [. . .] I am trying to say it all in one sentence, between one Cap and one period" (Cowley 14). Dickens did the same thing—but his one novel is much, much longer and is finally much more ambitious than is Faulkner's. Its intention is to work out in the lives of his characters how to make this world a better place.

Dickens learned early on in *Pickwick Papers* that the world needed changing, and he wanted to work for that change. "If any man ever was so, he was a radical at heart," Trollope wrote at Dickens's death (Collins 325). That's true, but for the first half of his career, Dickens's radicalism was fragmentary and sporadic. He attacked evils—the workhouse, Yorkshire schools—and various vices—vanity, selfishness, greed, and hypocrisy. But he could not see or imagine yet the whole of the problem, let alone its solution. He came close to a full diagnosis in *Martin Chuzzlewit,* on both sides of the Atlantic. His disappointment at finding the United States just like England, but worse, may have inspired him to write *A Christmas Carol*—which is indeed a radical story. Although Scrooge's conversion does not change the world, this kind of conversion could begin to change it, and when Dickens elaborates rhetorically on Scrooge's change, he lets that change infect his own response to our situation:

> Scrooge became as good a friend, as good a master, and as good a man, as the good old city knew, or any other city, town, or borough in this good old world. (*CC* 95)

Good is a good word, and as Dickens rang the changes on that good word, in honor of Scrooge, he was proposing to us the radical idea of society.[2]

Dickens was not himself truly or fully a radical, however, until he wrote *David Copperfield*. Not only is *David Copperfield* a radical novel; in writing it, Dickens taught himself to be a much more genuine radical than Trollope meant that he was or thought that he was. Dickens is most fully and deeply an agent of change in *David Copperfield*, and all his work thereafter—as well as the influence which that work has had upon this world of ours—came from *David Copperfield*.

A radical is not an extremist. A radical is someone who wants to get back to *root* values. As a lexicographer, Dr. Strong is a radical of sorts, working on his "root" dictionary, but even with David's industry to assist him, he would never finish it. And David's radical project is not just a dictionary. David's project has more in common with Mr. Dick's than with Dr. Strong's.

As the man who would "memorializ[e] the Lord Chancellor, or the Lord Somebody or other" (*DC* 175), Mr. Dick is a central character in *David Copperfield*, and a central character for Dickens's career.

As Mr. Pickwick set out to "enlarg[e] his sphere of observation, to the advancement of knowledge, and the diffusion of learning" (*PP* 5), he is "aware," he asserts, of troubles in this world: "Stage coaches were upsetting [. . .] horses were bolting [. . .] boats were overturning [. . .] boilers were bursting" (*PP* 9). But Mr. Pickwick is not afraid to take his chances in the midst of such perils. When he discovers what is really wrong with this world, what its serious troubles are, he is utterly overwhelmed and retires. Mr. Brownlow lives in London but stays insulated from it in his library; in the end he runs away to the country and takes Oliver with him. Barnaby Rudge sees—and is involved in—the Gordon riots and is so frightened by the experience that he can never again be "tempted into London" (*BR* 648). Old Martin Chuzzlewit knows the world—and what he knows makes him cynical; Dickens needed Mark Tapley to give himself hope at the end of that novel.

Mr. Dick knows the world and its madness; Miss Betsey gives him refuge from it. But even in the safety of Miss Betsey's protection, Mr. Dick is not in retirement or retreat. He is trying to write the Memorial, petitioning "the Lord Chancellor, or the Lord Somebody or other"—by kite—to do something about the madness. When the omniscient narrator in *Bleak House* warns us against Chancery—"Suffer any wrong that can be done you, rather than come here!" (*BH* 4)—he is speaking, in a sense, for Mr. Dick. Mr. Boythorn, who wants to blow up Chancery with "ten thousand hundredweight of gunpowder" (*BH* 102), speaks for Mr. Dick as well. Stephen Blackpool's evidence in *Hard Times* about the "muddle" is like Mr. Dick's, as are Stephen's warning that Bounderby's ways will never make this world a better place "till th' sun turns t' ice [. . .] till God's work is onmade" (*HT* 119) and the narrator's warning of "the Writing on the Wall" (*HT* 234) at the end of that novel. Dickens's attack on the Circumlocution Office in *Little Dorrit* is a chapter from Mr. Dick's Memorial. And Dickens's addresses to "my lords and gentlemen and honourable boards" in *Our Mutual Friend* (188ff., 308ff., 476ff.) are all part of the Great Memorial called social criticism, the execution of which Dickens takes over from Mr. Dick.

Only in a society gone mad, a society that has lost its *root* values—a society, that is, which no longer is a society—could a radical be called an extremist. Mr. Dick tells young David that this is "a mad world. Mad as Bedlam, boy!" (*DC* 172). As Miss Betsey explains, Mr. Dick's sister married a man who "made her wretched." This cruelty "had such an effect upon the mind of Mr. Dick (*that's* not madness, I hope!) [. . .] that it threw him into a fever" (*DC* 175). According to Miss Betsey, to be upset by antisocial conduct is not madness—and we should agree with her. *Not* to be so disturbed is madness.

Mr. Dick tries to explain what has gone wrong, but cannot manage the logic and rhetoric of exposition well enough to do so effectively. In the end, David—and Dickens—take over the job of addressing this mad world's madness, and Mr. Dick is free to fly kites. And as Agnes tells her novelists, both David and Dickens, "Your growing reputation and success enlarge your power of doing good" (*DC* 721). The work Mr. Dick does, in the end—entertaining David's children—is good work, too, of course, and Mr. Dick does it well.

Mr. Dick knows, when David is but a child, that this world is "mad as Bedlam." But Mr. Dick cannot write his Memorial. He has the symbol—"the figure, or the simile, or whatever it's called" (*DC* 175)—but he cannot write it all out. Nor could Mr. Dick write *Bleak House* or *Hard Times* or any of the rest of Dickens's novels, but the boy whom Mr. Dick called "Phoebus" could do so and did.

When David returns from his "Absence" in the Alps, he is working on his third novel. His "growing reputation and success," Agnes tells him, "enlarge [his] power of doing good" (*DC* 721). And he keeps on writing. When he closes "these leaves" at the end of *David Copperfield*, he must go on writing. David is Dickens's age now—and like Dickens, he must go on writing.

We do not know what David's other novels are, but Dickens's later novels do not sound like—are not like—*David Copperfield* at all. Or so it seems. As a narrator, Esther Summerson is in some ways like David; however, she is writing her "portion" of *Bleak House*, not for herself but presumably for the author of the rest of the novel. And the author of the rest of *Bleak House* was angry and wanted to blow up this mad world. The paragraph that follows the death of Jo could be from Dickens's version of Mr. Dick's Memorial—as could the Man from Shropshire's anger, or Mr. Krook's combustion.

Esther has the ambition to "do some good to those immediately around [her], and let that circle of endeavor gradually and naturally expand itself" (*BH* 91). That ambition leads to her having, like David, a "power of doing good," and in the end of the novel, she and her husband—whose "hopes and aims [. . .] should prove to be a way of usefulness and good service" (*BH* 689)—are working in this world for change. The angry omniscient narrator has—like Mr. Dick—retired.

All of the novels after *David Copperfield* are novels about work and workers, and for the most part, the characters who work in this world keep the Mr. Dick in Dickens pacified. The only one of the last seven novels that fails to find central characters ready and willing to work to change this world is the one most directly concerned with work and workers, *Hard Times*. Dickens's depiction of the industrial world was strong and well focused. Stephen Blackpool understands its problems, and Dickens gave him the appropriate mythic language to describe them: this world is "aw a muddle" and will remain so until "God's work is onmade" (*HT* 119). But in the end, Dickens the novelist surrendered. He let Mr. Sleary—whose "philosophical" authority is undermined by Dickens's giving him a lisp, a wandering eye, and a drinking problem—offer only "amuthment" to ameliorate the suffering of the working class (*HT* 230). And Louisa spends her life "trying hard to know her humbler fellow-creatures, and to beautify their lives of machinery and reality with [. . .] imaginative graces" (*HT* 234). Neither Mr. Sleary nor Loo will change this world. Their answers to the problems of the poor are as unsatisfactory as is Marie Antoinette's.

Perhaps it is because Dickens himself could not figure out how to change this world significantly that he could not describe—realize or make real—Daniel Doyce's great "invention" in *Little Dorrit*. Doyce, of course, does not claim to have "invented it," but rather says that he simply "happened to find it" (*LD* 488). The Europeans consider it useful, however, and in the end, Doyce has brought it back to England. As the novel closes, "How Not to Do It" is being answered by Arthur Clennam and both of his partners—Doyce and Amy Dorrit—with work. Arthur works for and with Doyce, and Dickens sent Arthur and Amy "down" to work in this world, among "the arrogant and the forward and the vain, [who] fretted and chafed, and made their usual uproar" (*LD* 778). Maybe work itself is the invention that is not an invention, which Doyce wants to give us, wants to persuade us to.

Between *Little Dorrit* and *A Tale of Two Cities*, Dickens wrote a letter to Wilkie Collins, proposing this understanding of the world and one's responsibility in it:

> Everything that happens [. . .] shews beyond mistake that you can't shut out the world—that you are in it to be of it—that you get into a false position the moment you try to sever yourself from it—and that you must mingle with it, and make the best of it, and make the best of yourself into the bargain. (*Letters* 8: 650)

Since *David Copperfield*, Dickens often focused on being "happy and useful." It is usefulness, for Dickens, that enables happiness: Agnes is wrong when she keeps "every thing as it used to be when we were children. For we were very happy then, I think" (*DC* 719): happiness is not something to be kept. For Dickens, *happy* is not an adjective but an active verb.[3] Mr. Dick is "happy" when he can be useful to Miss Betsey and, in the end, as the master kite flyer for David and Agnes's children (*DC* 748). Esther, Jo, Allan, Sissy Jupe, Little Dorrit, Pancks, Doyce, and Arthur all want to be useful—not violent revolutionaries, but usefully "in the world, and of it" (*NN* 97).[4]

The opening sentence of *A Tale of Two Cities* gives us two views of this world. The one is something like Conversation Kenge's—we have "a very great system" (*BH* 712) and this is "the best of times" (*TTC* 3); the other is Mr. Dick's. In this "mad world," however, King Charles is not the only one who loses his head.

Although *A Tale of Two Cities* pretends to be an historical novel, as its opening sentence tells us, the referenced historical time is remarkably "like the present period" (*TTC* 3). At the end, as Sydney Carton mounts to the guillotine, the world is indeed mad. But Dickens fabricated an amelioration, and Carton's act of love allowed him, hypothetically, a prophetic vision. That prophesy is—unintentionally, I think—an ironic one. Dickens imagined what "prophetic" words Sydney might have uttered, had he spoken before he died, and let him see ahead through two generations: to Lucie and Darnay's son and to that son's son, bearing Carton's name and being told Carton's story. By then, "the evil of this time and of the previous time of which this is the natural birth," has "gradually [made] expiation for itself," and Paris has been restored (*TTC* 320). Carton's dream takes us almost to the present—but as the opening sentence of the novel tells us, the time in which the novel is set is desperately "like the present period" (*TTC* 3). So the present—despite Sydney's prophecy—is not so idyllic. There is still much work to be done.[5]

By the beginning of *Great Expectations*, visions of King Charles's head have almost disappeared. Magwitch is not a beast, but a hungry human who can cry, and Pip's small kindness—"I hope you enjoy it, sir" (*GE* 17)—can make him happy. Joe Gargery's threat to Jaggers for proposing to pay for Pip almost brings King Charles back momentarily, but only momentarily. And when Orlick threatens to kill Pip—he will never see Joe and Biddy and Herbert again—suddenly these three are with Pip, in his imagination, and even before his actual rescue, the tension is relieved. Mr. Dick and Mr. Boythorn might have been delighted by the justice Pumblechook receives from Orlick—but Pumblechook's hypocrisy is not stuff for the Memorial. And, otherwise, *Great Expectations* is a quiet novel.

In *Our Mutual Friend*, Dickens's attacks on "My lords and gentlemen and honourable boards" are written in Memorial language—and Dickens repeats Pumblechook's comically violent end in disposing of Silas Wegg. The rest of *Our Mutual Friend* is told as though it were written by Mortimer Lightwood, Dickens's chief observer in the novel. And though Mortimer can be "allegorical"—another of Miss Betsey's words for the Memorial (*DC* 175)—in describing old Harmon's mounds, he is not driven mad by the mad world. Rather, in the end, Mortimer challenges and infuriates it, and having shaken hands with his new ally, Mr. Twemlow, "fares to the Temple gaily" (*OMF* 775).

Toward the "end" of *The Mystery of Edwin Drood*, a character obviously in disguise arrives in Cloisterham. Dick Datchery has come to the city, he says, to end his days there (*MED* 177, 178). He is ready to retire. But his retirement is not as Mr. Pickwick's was, or Mr. Brownlow's. He is not opting out of responsible life. And though he says he has come to Cloisterham to die—and though Dickens was to die that night—Dick Datchery "falls to with an appetite" in the novel's last words (*MED* 236). Present tense: *falls to*.

Datchery is an observer and a scorekeeper. All the characters in this novel, except for the Dean, Mr. Crisparkle, and Edwin Drood himself, are close observers. Datchery, however, is an observer's observer, Dickens's observer. He is watching to see who has been paying attention. And I suspect that the person under Datchery's wig is observing us as well as the characters in the novel. In the end, he marks up a good score for the Princess Puffer and Deputy and for us, as observers. Like Mr. Grewgious, we know Jasper for what he is: a wicked man, a hypocrite, and a murderer—whether Edwin actually has been murdered or not. We have learned to pay attention, to observe; we can judge Jasper. And thus, for Dick Datchery—who has *known* Jasper all along, it seems—everything is in order. The "end" is similar to the end of *Our Mutual Friend*.

It is safe, now, for Mr. Grewgious to die—he was afraid of dying with anything left unfinished (*MED* 97)—and safe for Dick Datchery to do so as well. And it is safe for Charles Dickens, who, having finished his last novel, was to go inside to his dinner and collapse. He finished his novel but knowingly left this *world* unfinished, and still in need of change, to us.

Mr. Pickwick sets out to observe the world, sees it, retreats, and retires. Mr. Brownlow takes Oliver out of the world with him. Nicholas enters the world, to work in it; in the end, he still works, but lives in Devon. Scrooge changes—thanks to ghostly visitors or indigestion—and becomes a good man, and he finds as he looks at the world that "everything could yield him pleasure" (*CC* 93).

In *David Copperfield*, we get the story of two writers: Mr. Dick, and David. Both are stand-ins for Dickens, as he tries to imagine how he can change this world. At the end of the novel, Mr. Dick is not working on his Memorial any more: he will finish it when he has "nothing else to do" (*DC* 748)—but for now he is busy. And David closes this novel, but continues to write—as Charles Dickens.

The omniscient narrator retires in *Bleak House*—but Esther does not end the novel. She and Allan, in a real Victorian Yorkshire of "streams and streets, town and country, mill and moor" (*BH* 689), have work yet to do. At the end of *Little Dorrit*, Dickens sends Amy and Arthur "down" into the world, "happy and useful," to work among "the arrogant, and the forward, and the vain, who shouted and chafed and made their usual uproar" (*LD* 778).

At the end of *Great Expectations,* we know that Pip is still working, a partner now in Clarriker's, in Cairo. Mortimer closes *Our Mutual Friend* and goes home to the Temple, in London, where he lives and works. Dickens must have been happy with him—and proud of him. And at the end of *Edwin Drood,* Dick Datchery—the strange retiree who has come to Cloisterham to die—pleased with what he observes, confidently adds "a thick line to the score [. . .] then falls to with an appetite" (*MED* 236).

And Dickens retired. But not the way Mr. Pickwick did.

NOTES

1 See, for example, "A Visit to Newgate," "Criminal Courts," "Shabby-Genteel People," "A Passage in the Life of Mr. Watkins Tottle," and "Brokers' and Marine-Store Shops."
2 *Good* comes from the same Germanic root as *gather* and *together.* It is a social word. "Little Jack Horner," thus, must be an ironic nursery rhyme.
3 Dickens's inspiration in this direction may have come from Mark Tapley, in *Martin Chuzzlewit,* who can only be "jolly" when busy: "if there's a Werb alive, I'm it" (*MC* 704).
4 When, in 1858, Dickens proposed to Collins that "you can't shut out the world—you are in it to be of it," he was quoting himself, from *Nicholas Nickleby,* nearly twenty years earlier. There, young Nicholas thinks appreciatively of little Miss LaCreevy as "living in the world, and of it"—as Nicholas himself wants to.
5 France in the mid-nineteenth century was hardly what Dickens has Sydney Carton prophesy. The years between 1848 and 1860—the Second Republic and the first years of the Second Empire—were not peaceful, free, and untroubled times in France. Nor were social conditions in England anything near ideal, as Dickens's own journalism and fiction had shown.

BIBLIOGRAPHY

Collins, Philip. *Dickens: The Critical Heritage.* London, 1971.
Cowley, Malcolm. *The Faulkner-Cowley File.* London, 1966.
Dickens, Charles. *Bleak House.* Ware, Hertfordshire, 2001.
―――. *A Christmas Carol.* Ware, Hertfordshire, 1993.
―――. *David Copperfield.* 1849–50. MS. Victoria and Albert Museum, London.

———. *David Copperfield*. Ed. Nina Burgis. 1981. Oxford, 2003.
———. *Great Expectations*. Ware, Hertfordshire, 2007.
———. *Hard Times*. Ware, Hertfordshire, 1995.
———. *The Letters of Charles Dickens*. Ed. Madeline House, Graham Storey et al. 12 vols. Oxford, 1965–2002.
———. *Little Dorrit*. Ware, Hertfordshire, 2002.
———. *Martin Chuzzlewit*. Ware, Hertfordshire, 1997.
———. *Nicholas Nickleby*. Ware, Hertfordshire, 1995.
———. *Oliver Twist*. Ware, Hertfordshire, 2000.
———. *Our Mutual Friend*. Ware, Hertfordshire, 2002.
———. *The Mystery of Edwin Drood*. Ware, Hertfordshire, 2005.
———. *Pickwick Papers*. Ware, Hertfordshire, 2000.
———. *A Tale of Two Cities*. Ware, Hertfordshire, 1999.
Trollope, Anthony. "Charles Dickens." *St. Paul's Magazine* 6 (July 1870): 370–75.

ance # II. Dickens and Changes of Power

Parrots, Birds of Prey, and Snorting Cattle: Dickens's Whig Agenda of the 1840s

David Paroissien
University of Buckingham

Attempts to generalize about a writer's political outlook face obvious difficulties. Views tend to fluctuate over time. New ideas push old ones aside, and fresh perspectives emerge in response to unforeseen events and developments. Dickens's attitude to change proves no exception and holds true for opinions he expressed about other issues such as education, public health, and criminal law. My response to the challenge the topic of "Charles Dickens as an agent change" poses therefore is deliberately restrictive and will concentrate on the first stage of his career—roughly 1834 to 1844—when he made the transition from journalist to novelist. Those years and the decades immediately following his birth in 1812 cover a crucial period of English history. They coincide with England's slow emergence from political stasis—the legacy of the wars against revolutionary France—set against a growing call for reform and social legislation, both delayed by governments inclined to view change as a threat, an attitude that prevailed until the ascendancy of the Whigs in 1832. The son of a civil servant appreciative of his newly won respectability, Dickens struggled to find his political bearings at a time when England experienced social and cultural transformation at a rate never previously experienced.

A letter addressed to Douglas Jerrold on 3 May 1843 serves to introduce what I would like to describe as Dickens's Whig agenda. Jerrold, a close friend and popular journalist committed to attacking injustice and oppression, had sent Dickens a copy of his new periodical, the *Illuminated Magazine*, whose first essay had caught his attention.

"I am greatly pleased with your opening paper" (*Letters* 3: 481) he wrote, referring to "Elizabeth and Victoria." The paper stood out, Dickens thought, for several reasons. The topic, an ironical description of the "good old days," illustrated the journal's intention, announced in the preface, to expose "our social abuses and social follies" and speak with "boldness" to "the masses of the PEOPLE" (Preface, *Illuminated Magazine*). Equally commendable, Dickens thought, was Jerrold's sustained ridicule of those who looked on bygone days as "the lost Paradise of another age," convinced that "[w]e shall never see such times again!" (4). "Elizabeth and Victoria," Dickens concluded, was written with "the finest end of that iron pen of yours." It was also "witty," "wise," and full of much needed "Truth" (*Letters* 3: 481).

Dickens's praise, I suggest, is far from perfunctory. Rather the energy apparent in his reply originates in shared preoccupations. Foremost among them—one of the "signs of the times" noted by Carlyle in 1829—was concern over the growing tendency to look to the past for guidance, rather than forward to an age that welcomed change and progress. By way of illustration, Dickens referred Jerrold to a "Hospital Dinner" he had recently attended. The occasion had a commendable objective, an anniversary banquet to raise funds for a charitable foundation. The "loyal" and "patriotic" rhetoric of the speechmaking, however, made Dickens's blood boil.[1] "Oh Heaven, if you could have been with me," he writes, recalling the overblown oratory delivered after dinner was over:

> There were men there—your City aristocracy—who made such speeches, and expressed such sentiments, as any moderately intelligent dustman would have blushed through his cindery bloom to have thought of. Sleek, slobbering, bow-paunched, overfed, apoplectic, snorting cattle—and the auditory leaping up in their delight! (*Letters* 3: 481–82)

The specificity of Dickens's attack on London's "City aristocracy" and their auditors—described in a deleted phrase as "Bankers and sheriffs and aldermen"[2]—contrasts with an earlier comment in the same letter. It was not just overfed and snorting "cattle" who were prone to lavish praise on the past. Equally guilty were those he characterizes as "Birds of Prey" and their fellow travelers, "the Parrots of Society." The latter, popular on account of their ability to mimic whatever they were taught, struck Dickens as "the more intolerable and mischievous" (481). Extol "those merry, golden days of good Queen Bess," as Jerrold had written in "Elizabeth and Victoria," and "parrots" would swell the chatter of people eager to portray all change as a decline "and a further lapse from Paradise" (7). In the face of such obdurate nonsense, Dickens resolved that he must act to prevent the young from getting hold of ideas he associated with "conservative or High church notions." And the best way to do that, he added, is "to wring the parrots' necks" while children are still in their cradles (*Letters* 3: 482).[3]

Dickens's reaction to "Elizabeth and Victoria" raises questions I would like to explore. What is the "truth" that Dickens sees in Jerrold's essay and how seriously should we take the attack he makes on snorting cattle, parrots, and birds of prey? Are the animal and ornithological metaphors exaggerations indulged in by two friends?[4] Or is Dickens's anger directed at genuine political enemies, those who saw all reform and legislation as an attack on the laws and customs that had kept England secure from "the whirlwinds" Benjamin Disraeli saw toppling down "crowns in less fortunate countries" (*Runnymede* 179)? Two years earlier, Dickens had contributed "The Fine Old English Gentleman" to the *Examiner*.[5] "By Jove, how radical I am getting!" he remarked at the time to Forster. "I wax stronger and stronger in the true principles every day" (*Letters* 2: 357). This satirical ballad had appeared on 7 August 1841, a fierce squib directed at the Tories, whose victory at the next election seemed almost certain:

> The bright old day now dawns again; the cry runs through the land,
> In England there shall be—dear bread! In Ireland—sword and brand!
> And poverty, and ignorance, shall swell the rich and grand,
> So, rally round the rulers with the gentle iron hand,
> Of the fine old English Tory days,
> Hail to the coming time!

In what follows, I want to confine my analysis of Dickens's political ideology to the first decade of his career, beginning with the publication of an essay in the *Morning Chronicle* on 18 December 1834. This period serves as the setting for an increasingly sharp struggle between the interventionist policies of the Whigs, unleashed by the triumph of the Reform Bill in 1832, and the determination of Tories and Conservatives to resist further legislative change. Against this contentious background Dickens sought to define himself politically in three interrelated ways:

as a professional novelist who had produced five novels in six years,[6] as an engaged writer seeking an audience among the readers of newspapers and periodicals, and as a public intellectual anxious to turn his "social knowledge" to good practical account in some extraliterary way. All three strands of his career evolved during a decade dominated by an intense debate over the role of government. Did the conditions and disposition of "the Working Classes," described by Carlyle in *Chartism* (1839) as "ominous" (151), demand further intervention? Or was the nation in danger of being condemned to live "in a perpetual vortex of agitation," as Sir Robert Peel warned voters five years earlier, with the government promising "the instant redress of anything which anybody may call an abuse"?[7] These two questions, opposite sides of the same political coin, define the principal issues Dickens confronted during the first decade of his life as a public figure.

The publication of "'The Story without a Beginning' (Translated from the German by Boz)" marks Dickens's entrance into the world of partisan journalism. Occasioned by a specific event—William IV's abrupt dismissal of Prime Minister Melbourne and the Whigs on 15 November 1834—Dickens adapts a German moral-allegorical tale to comment on the King's action.[8] The story tells of a child who discovers the world about him represented by a small flower garden next to the cottage where he lives. In Dickens's version, the child stands in for William IV, who, similar to the child in the story, delights in the flowers around him. William's flowers grow and flourish under the ministrations of his majesty's gardeners, refigured in the political allegory as bees, "active" and "hard-working" ("Story without a Beginning" 12). They set to in earnest, expose roots threatened with corruption, let in streams of water and pull up weeds festering in "close and rotten" (12) burrows. But the child, "tender-hearted" (12) and easily frightened, becomes alarmed. The insects living in the burrows start to cry, "like slimy crocodiles" (12), and prompt him to overreact. He turns the bees "out of their hive, and put[s] the insects in their places," thus consigning the flowers to "their new masters" (12).

The mildness of the satire[9] should not distract from the political alignment the allegory reveals. Dickens nails his colors to the Whig mast of intervention: government should assume an active role and initiate legislation to improve the lives of those in need of assistance. England in the 1830s offered plenty of scope for politicians committed to building a more inclusive society, one less based on privilege and ancient rights.[10]

Dickens's public engagement two years later, *Sunday under Three Heads*, a pamphlet published in June 1836, has the bite the earlier piece lacks.[11] The attack on the absurdity of attempting to legislate what people do on the Sabbath makes plain his exasperation at this assault on the poor, "a bill of blunders," "a piece of deliberate cruelty," whose blatant class bias deserved nothing but contempt (Sparks [Dickens] 22). The whole "of the saintly venom," Dickens argued, was not only foolish and coercive; it was also dangerous (25). "[L]et those who advocate the cause of fanaticism, reflect well, upon the probable issue of their endeavours" (32), he counseled. A nation will treat with patience delay on some political questions. But tamper with people's liberty and freedom, he warned, and you may "rouse a feeling abroad, which a king would gladly yield his crown to quell, and a peer would resign his coronet to allay" (32–33).

Language resonant with the earlier Jacobinism of William Hazlitt and Thomas Paine should not distract us from a second concern, initially one more indirectly expressed. While it was the Evangelical branch of the Church most harshly exposed in *Sunday under Three Heads*, Dickens held no illusions about mischief arising from its opposite wing. We see hints of trouble in the description of two Sunday services in the pamphlet's first section, "Sunday as It Is." One is held in a fashionable London church attended by worshippers holding "richly-bound prayer-books," the other "in a less orthodox religious place of worship," a small close chapel with plain deal pews and a pulpit (Sparks [Dickens] 8). The differences deepen as the two ministers go to work. In the chapel, the preacher warms to his task, swinging his arms violently and clenching his fists. The Anglican clergyman, by contrast, young, "of noble family and elegant demeanour," reads in a soft voice and applies his white hand, "studded with brilliants, to his perfumed hair" (7). Eton and Cambridge educated, he had picked up some of the affectations soon to spread from the senior common rooms of the two ancient universities into the public arena under the guise of Tractarianism, Ritualism, Puseyism, or, more inclusively, the Oxford Movement. Existing records reveal no evidence of a visit to Oxford before Dickens wrote *Sunday under Three Heads*. His description of the Anglican minister nevertheless suggests awareness of the attraction Rome held for some members of the Church of England.

Seven years later, distaste for this development finds open expression in a contribution to the *Examiner*, a liberal weekly with impeccable radical credentials. Published on June 3, 1843, as the leading article, Dickens's "Report" makes the pretence of investigating "the darkness of Colleges as compared with the Mines" (Slater, *Dickens' Journalism* 2: 60). The findings, presented in a format parodying the 1842 commission into the conditions of children employed in mines and manufactories, were equally alarming, with respect to both the conditions of employment and the ignorance that prevails. Reminding readers that the University of Oxford "was first established for the Manufacture of Clergymen" (61), Dickens notes that the colleges, since their foundation, "have stood still" (61), or if they have moved at all, "have moved backward" (61). The consequences for the undergraduates, he explains, are "extremely pernicious" (61), making them deaf and blind to the world around them. Condemned to an atmosphere rife with "ignorance and superstition" (60), they lapse into a melancholy state, trained to engage in doctrinal debates, and to argue about what priests should wear, which way they should turn when they said their prayers, and how many candles should decorate the altar. It must not be forgotten, he reminded readers, that "in the minds of the persons employed in the University of Oxford," the source of all "Clerical degrees," "such comprehensive words as justice, mercy, charity, kindness, brotherly love, forbearance, gentleness, and Good Works, awaken no ideas whatever" (62).

The move backward Dickens detected in Oxford looked even more ominous in London. The same spirit, for example, lay at the heart of Tory ideology and informed Conservative opposition to the ameliorative agenda Dickens sought to promote. If England were to maintain the order and civilization that had evolved over the course of centuries, it was imperative, Tories argued, to halt the Whig assault on the constitutional monarch, the Church of England, the peerage, and the Commons. Disraeli, leader of the Young England party and vocal theorist of Conservative principles, stated this case in public, simultaneously seeking office to promote the cause in Parliament. When he succeeded after four attempts to obtain a safe seat as MP for Maidstone in 1837, he gathered round him a group of young idealists, all recently elected and motivated by an attachment to a romantic version of chivalry, paternalism, and religious orthodoxy fashionable in university circles and in parts of the country among Tory landowners.

Two publications by Disraeli and one by Kenelm Digby offer insight into the kind of nonsense the narrator of *Bleak House* later ridiculed as "Dandyism in Religion" (*BH* 156). Motivated in part by the belief that "the Vulgar" wanted faith in things in general, Young England idealists like Digby and his clique offered a version of English history that in the eyes of the narrator willfully put back "the hands on the Clock of Time," canceling in the act "a few hundred years of history" (*BH* 156). This incisive comment, similar to Dickens's attack on "the red-faced gentleman" in *The Chimes*, who yearns for "the good old times" (*TC* 101), fits perfectly Digby's *Broadstone of Honour*, a polemical manifesto published and expanded over several years (1822–27), whose subtitle lays bare its curious contents: "The True Sense and Practice of Chivalry." Truth in this instance can only be rendered by deliberate falsification, for how else can one take seriously such a flawed and elitist view of the past? In this "book of ensamples and doctrines" designed for consultation by "the gentlemen of England" anxious to learn the "obligations of duties" their status confers (Preface), Digby presents an idealized version of life in the Middle Ages as the appropriate template for redressing the injustice and oppression associated with the explosion of industrialism in early nineteenth-century England. One's object, he argues, should be to "to combine the most amiable, the most exalted sentiments of which human nature is susceptible, with the faith and practice of Christianity" (xiv). According to Digby and other Young Englanders, an elite group of Tory aristocrats who venerated the Stuart monarchy and high Anglicanism, England's three classes had not met in amity and good will since "the palmiest days of feudalism," when the rich and the poor sat at the same table and partook of "the same fare with those beneath them."[12]

Disraeli's *Vindication of the English Constitution* (1835) and his *Letters of Runnymede* (1836) offer prescriptions for action if less bizarre then no more out of touch with all that had happened over several centuries. Post-Waterloo England invited solutions to problems long suppressed by a nation at war for nearly two decades (1793–1815). To expect Tory squires, protected by the patently discriminatory Corn Laws, country magistrates and the three traditional Estates of the realm to solve the nation's problems was to lose touch with reality. "The Tory party in this country is the national party; it is the really democratic party of England" (*Vindication* 182), Disraeli asserted, unlike the Whig opposition, which he characterized as aggressive and unprincipled, a collection of power-hungry bandits, who had gained power in 1834 by an oligarchical "*coup-d-état*" (189). The Tories, he continued, support "the institutions of the country because they have been established for the common good" (182–

83). In the eyes of Disraeli, England's best hope lay in obeisance to the sound principles that had guided our forefathers, hitherto "dignified by the venerable title of the Wisdom of our Ancestors," a phrase, he noted, now lamentably "the object of scorn" (61).[13]

With ideas like these seeding the mainstream of English political discourse, Dickens needed allies. Forster and his colleagues working for the *Examiner* provided early support, as we have seen. But if Dickens were to have greater impact, he would have to do more. Two options opened, one he set his mind to before his literary star had risen, the other evolved as a consequence of his early success as a novelist. Both played into the ambition I referred to earlier as a wish to make himself useful in some extra-literary way, an intellectual committed to pro bono work infused with his "social knowledge."

The first evidence we have of this aspiration is a letter dated 13 November 1834 and addressed to the Steward of New Inn, one of the old Inns of Chancery. Ostensibly, a request for information about taking "a set of rooms" for immediate occupation, the letter points to another objective. "I am not a member of the legal profession," Dickens explains, as the whole of his time is currently devoted "to literary pursuits" (*Letters* 1: 43). But nevertheless, "I intend entering at the bar, as soon as circumstances will enable me to do so" (43). Engagement to Catherine Hogarth the following May, marriage in February 1836, the publication of *Sketches by Boz* (first series) and the contract to write *The Pickwick Papers* evidently compelled Dickens to sideline that ambition, only to revive it five years later when he became a student of the Middle Temple, one of the four more prestigious Inns of Court, in December 1839. This commitment, as later correspondence reveals, was a serious one made at some financial cost. After paying the Treasurer of the Middle Temple £33. 8s ("First Fees on Entrance," *Letters* 1: 646) and making a substantial deposit to secure his place (£100), Dickens continued to pay regular fees to ensure his right to keep terms and dine. "Will you pay the enclosed £10.0.10 at your convenience," he instructed W. H. Wills, writing from holiday in France on September 29, 1854, "and ask at the same time how many Terms I have to keep before being qualified to be called?" (*Letters* 7: 427). In the same letter, Dickens expressed the view that he would, now, never keep that intention, but he nevertheless continued paying fees to the Middle Temple for one more year before petitioning the Benchers of that "Honourable Society" to make final his separation (569).

Dickens knew enough about England's legal system not to take this intention lightly. He also understood that by being called to the bar he would have the opportunity to exercise forensic skills he unquestionably possessed. It is perhaps fortunate for literary students that Dickens's efforts to undertake professional legal work failed, despite applications he made to influential people. "I would that I were a Police Magistrate," he wrote to Lord Brougham in September 1843, hoping that something might be done on his behalf to secure a position as an extra magistrate eligible under new legislation. "I have often had this desire in my mind, but never so strongly as now" (*Letters* 3: 570). Nothing came of Dickens's importuning[14] though the intention persisted, prompting an even more pressing declaration to Lord Morpeth three years later:

> I wish to confide to you, a very earnest desire of mine, [. . .] I have an ambition for some public employment—some Commissionership, or Inspectorship, or the like, connected with any of those subjects in which I take a deep interest, and in respect of which the Public are generally disposed to treat me with confidence and regard. (*Letters* 4: 566)

Continuing to press his case, Dickens went further to reveal how he had hoped, for years, "to become at last a Police Magistrate, and turn my social knowledge to good practical account from day to day" (567). Forster records how he learned of this inquiry with "some surprise" (1: 328). The response Dickens received, which has not been preserved, was negative and, Forster adds, discouraged Dickens from making similar applications.

Efforts elsewhere, however, began to pay off as Dickens's social life expanded in proportion to his rising literary fame. Deemed "presentable" by Lady Holland (*Letters* 1: 412n), he was invited to Holland House in August 1838, an opening that introduced Dickens to a circle of writers and politicians whose commitment to reform and government intervention he shared. Soon at ease among a circle Disraeli characterized as "an old clique of pure Whiggery" (*Letters* 2: 63n), he found a responsive audience. Here were people with whom Dickens could exchange ideas and make plans, both immediate and more far-reaching. Once Dickens had made up his mind to visit North America, for example, he asked Lady Holland in December 1841 if she would help him make contact with Lord Morpeth, who, defeated by what Disraeli termed "the great Conservative triumph in 1841" (Preface, *Coningsby*), was already in the country. She agreed to do so and offered advice about his intention to "ascertain by personal inspection the condition of poor slaves" (*Letters* 2: 447n). Don't divulge this intention on the other side of the Atlantic, she counseled. "[Your] life might be endangered" (447n).

A more remarkable request followed seven months later. On this occasion, Dickens sought Lady Holland's "kind influence" to help him with a proposal to which he felt strongly inclined: "to establish a new evening paper" to replace the recently defunct *Courier* (*Letters* 3: 262). A former Whig paper whose allegiances had swung back and forth, the paper returned to Whig control in 1830 and flourished under S. L. Blanchard, until its proprietors changed again in 1839. The paper struggled on for another two years before publishing its last issue on 6 July 1842. The fact that the premises "and types and so forth" were all to be disposed of, Dickens thought, presented the Liberals with an excellent opportunity (262). If funds could be raised and backing from "the Members of the late Government, or from the Reform Club" obtained (262), here was an opportunity to throw their resources into the breach and open a new enterprise dedicated to reform. Closing his case to Lady Holland, Dickens signed off gracefully: "Knowing how strongly you sympathize with the views I am so earnestly desirous of advocating, I can scarcely think that I need offer you any lengthy apology—even for this long trespass on your time and patience" (262–63). The idea, however, failed to raise interest among those able to supply financial backing, leaving Dickens with no alternative other than to emphasize the purity of his own motives. "Please assure all those to whom you spoke," he wrote five days later, that "my idea originated in no thought of personal advantage; and that at the very best, I should have been, in a pecuniary sense, a loser for many years" (265).

Three years later, Dickens's ambition to take charge of a newspaper with an agenda committed to administrative reform took a more positive turn. This time sufficient funds were available, money generated by speculation in railway shares and secured by Joseph Paxton working in conjunction with several railway proprietors willing to set up a new paper, advertised on 1 December 1845 to be of "Liberal Politics and thorough Independence" (Schlicke 143). Dickens was secured as the editor and reporters recruited from established papers. Appearing for the first time on 21 January 1846, the *Daily News* sold 10,000 copies, and the venture seemed destined for success.[15] But not with Dickens as its editor. He resigned on 9 February after only seventeen issues, recognizing he was unsuited to the stress of daily editorial work. Forster took over for nine months until Charles Wentworth Dilke put the paper on a firmer course, one that continued into the twentieth century.

This short span in the editorial chair of a daily paper taught Dickens something about his limitations. It failed, however, to dampen his desire for some kind of public service beyond his commitment to writing fiction. He continued his association with the *Daily News*, contributing articles consistent with his Whig agenda: five powerful letters stating his unequivocal opposition to the death penalty and the practice of hanging offenders in public,[16] and a persuasive paper, "Crime and Education," in which he argued for the need for schools as the first step in the reformation of child offenders. Similarly hard-hitting pieces on social issues also continued to appear in the *Examiner*,[17] journalistic work that he also supplemented in yet another, more immediately practical sphere: a cooperative effort undertaken in conjunction with Angela Burdett Coutts to rehabilitate prostitutes. This asylum opened in November 1847, a project Dickens committed to for the next ten years, active as an administrator and supervisor of the day-to-day operation (Hartley 2009).

When asked if in confidence if he would stand for election in May 1842 as the Liberal candidate for Reading, Dickens replied that he was "much obliged and flattered" by the query (*Letters* 2: 288) "My principles and inclinations would lead me to aspire to the distinction you invite me to seek," he explained to his addressee (288). But he was bound to add that with little "reasonable chance of success" and his inability to afford "the expense of a contested election," he had no hesitation in putting the suggestion aside (288). In the face of the almost certainty of a Conservative victory in the forthcoming election, the Pilgrim editors note that Dickens's "chances of success at Reading would have been minimal" (288n). Confronted with such odds, Dickens took the right course. But in abandoning an opportunity, albeit a distant one, to stand for his beliefs from inside, he never slackened in his commitment to reforming and improving public life, an agenda for change that shaped his entire career.

NOTES

1 "Public Dinners," (*Evening Chronicle*, 7 April 1835), provides a full though more tolerant description of these early- and mid-century charitable occasions, public

dinners for male patrons only, to which ladies were invited to listen to the speeches from a gallery, after the banquet had concluded. See Slater, *Dickens' Journalism* (1: 162–67).

2   "[H]eavily deleted by CD," write the editors. See *Letters* (2: 482n). A fictional attack on these figures appears a year later during the composition of *The Chimes*, when Dickens also introduced a character designed to satirize the Young England Movement. But since Forster disliked "the Young England gentleman," Dickens agreed to "knock him out," intending to replace him with another who "recognizes no virtue in anything but the good old times, and talks of them, parrot-like, whatever the matter is" (*Letters* 4: 209).

3   Convinced of the need for action, Dickens had already embarked on "a little history of England" for Charley, his six-year old son, written to correct such misrepresentations of England's past (*Letters* 3: 482n). This project, he explained three months later to Miss Burdett Coutts, had been undertaken to counter any "tender-hearted notions of War and Murder" Charley might have absorbed and to teach him to see not only "the bright side of Glory's sword" but also its "rusty one" (539). The letter to Jerrold contains the first recorded reference to *A Child's History of England*, which appeared serially in *Household Words* (1851–53).

4   For an earlier instance of moralizing imagery, see "'The Story without a Beginning' (Translated from the German by Boz)" (*Morning Chronicle*, 18 Dec. 1834), in which Dickens characterizes the Tories as "insects and reptiles" and the Whigs as industrious garden bees anxious to promote growth and share the good life with others.

5   This was one of three squibs Dickens published in the *Examiner* in August 1841. For the full text of each, see Forster (bk. 2, ch. 12) and Kitton (59–76).

6   All five of Dickens's novels attacked a range of specific abuses, including: the plight of debtors and the conditions of prisons (*The Pickwick Papers*); the inadequacies of the New Poor Law (*Oliver Twist*); the Yorkshire boarding schools (*Nicholas Nickleby*), and more generally the vulnerability of children and the poor (*The Old Curiosity Shop* and *Barnaby Rudge*). The focus of this study is limited to his nonfictional writing.

7   See the Tamworth Manifesto, 18 December 1834, a statement of principles reissued on 28 July 1841 setting out views that brought Peel to the fore for a second time in September 1841. Peel campaigned as one not hostile to reform when it was undertaken in a friendly manner, but he was no believer in committing the government to a program of ameliorative legislation if it meant living in "a perpetual vortex of agitation." Although no defender of abuses, he made clear his conviction that 1832 was "a final and irrevocable settlement of a great constitutional question."

8   Friedrich Wilhelm Carové, *Das Märchen ohne Ende*, trans. Sarah Austin in 1834 as "*The Story without an End*."

9   Dickens's first, as Michael Slater (*Dickens' Journalism* 2: 10) notes.

10 Dickens's call for legislation, however, requires qualification. On 6 January 1870, Dickens described his "political creed" in a single sentence: "My faith in the people governing, is, on the whole, infinitesimal; my faith in The People governed, is, on the whole, illimitable" (*Speeches* 407).

11 Published under the name of "Timothy Sparks," Dickens vigorously attacked the Sunday Observance legislation proposed by Sir Andrew Agnew, who sought, among other restrictions, to close bakers' shops on Sundays. The legislation had an obvious class bias, denying to the poor leisure activities the rich could easily enjoy. Despite the bill's defeat, Sundays nevertheless retained what Dickens characterized as penitential gloom. Michael Slater terms Dickens's entrance into this debate his "first piece of crusading journalism" (*Charles Dickens* 70).

12 Lord John Manners, Seventh Duke of Rutland, speaking at Birmingham Athenic Institution, 26 August 1844. See also Manners's *England's Trust* (1843) and *A Plea for National Holy Days*, both rich sources of well-intended but absurdly paternalistic celebrations of an integrated, hierarchical society, a fancy version of "Merrie England" such as never existed.

13 When Dickens moved into Tavistock House in November 1851, he instructed his carpenter to install a series of shelves in his library designed to complete the illusion of an unbroken line of imitation books bearing fictional titles. Among them was *The Wisdom of Our Ancestors*, a set of seven imaginary volumes each with its own title: *Ignorance*, *Superstition*, *The Block*, *The Stake*, *The Rack*, *Dirt*, and *Disease*. Next to these bulky tomes sat a single volume so narrow the title—*The Virtues of Our Ancestors*—had to be printed sideways.

14 An Act for regulating the Police Courts in the Metropolis (2 & 3 Vict., cap. 71), whose offices had recently been expanded, set out the qualifications for the vacancies the new legislation created in the following terms: "fit persons shall have practised as a Barrister during at least seven years then last past, or who shall have practised as a Barrister for four years then last past, having previously practised as a certified Special Pleader for three years below the Bar, to be Magistrates of the said Courts." Lord Brougham, one assumes, must have drawn Dickens's attention to his lack of qualifications.

15 A good start, Drew notes, but a long way off from the *Times*'s 25,000 copies (79).

16 For the text of the letters, see Paroissien (213–48).

17 Particularly noteworthy are the eviscerating attacks on the administrative failings of Bartholomew Drouet, master of the "Infant Pauper Asylum" in Tooting, where more than 100 children died following an outbreak of cholera in 1848. See Slater, *Dickens' Journalism* (2: 147–56).

BIBLIOGRAPHY

An Act for Regulating the Police Courts in the Metropolis. 2 & 3 Victoriae, Cap. 71. 24 Aug. 1839. *legislation.gov.uk*. The National Archives. Web. 7 Mar. 2012. <http://www.legislation.gov.uk/ukpga/1839/71/pdfs/ukpga_18390071_en.pdf >.

Carlyle, Thomas. "Signs of the Times." 1829. *Thomas Carlyle: Selected Writings*. Ed. Alan Shelston. Harmondsworth, 1986. 61–85.

———. *Chartism*. 1839. *Thomas Carlyle: Selected Writings*. Ed. Alan Shelston. Harmondsworth, 1986.
Carové, Friedrich Wilhelm. *The Story without an End*. Trans. Sarah Austin. London, 1834.
Dickens, Charles (see also Sparks, Timothy). *Bleak House*. Ed. Duane DeVries. New York, 1971.
———. *The Chimes*. 1844. *A Christmas Carol and Other Christmas Books*. Ed. Robert Douglas-Fairhurst. Oxford, 2006.
———. *The Letters of Charles Dickens*. Ed. Madeline House, Graham Storey et al. 12 vols. Oxford, 1965–2002.
———. *The Speeches of Charles Dickens*. Ed. K. J. Fielding. Oxford, 1960.
———. "The Story without a Beginning." *Dickens' Journalism*. Ed. Michael Slater. Vol. 2. London, 1996. 10–13.
Digby, Kenelm. *The Broadstone of Honour: or, Rules for the Gentlemen of England*. London, 1822.
Disraeli, Benjamin. *The Letters of Runnymede*. London, 1836.
———. *Vindication of the English Constitution in a Letter to a Noble and Learned Lord*. London, 1835.
———. Preface. *Coningsby; or The New Generation*. London, 1844.
Drew, John M. L. *Dickens the Journalist*. Basingstoke, 2003.
Forster, John. *The Life of Charles Dickens*. 1872–74. 2 vols. London, 1969.
Hartley, Jenny. *Charles Dickens and the House of Fallen Women*. London, 2009.
Jerrold, Douglas. "Elizabeth and Victoria." *Illuminated Magazine* 1 (May–Oct. 1843): 3–8.
———, ed. *Illuminated Magazine* 1 (May–Oct. 1843).
Kitton, Frederick G., ed. *The Poems and Verses of Charles Dickens*. London, 1903.
Manners, Lord John. *Addresses*. London, 1845.
———. *England's Trust and Other Poems*. London, 1841.
———. *A Plea for National Holy Days*. 2nd ed. London, 1843.
———. *What are the English Roman Catholics to Do? The Question Considered in a Letter to Lord Edward Howard*. London, 1841.
Mitchell, Leslie. *Holland House*. London, 1980.
Paroissien, David, ed. *Selected Letters of Charles Dickens*. Basingstoke, 1985.
Peel, Robert. "The Tamworth Manifesto." *Victorian Web*. N.p., 22 Jul. 2002. Web. 19 Mar. 2012.
Schlicke, Paul, ed. *Oxford Reader's Companion to Dickens*. Oxford, 1999.
Slater, Michael, ed. *Charles Dickens: A Life Defined by Writing*. New Haven, 2009.
———. *The Dent Uniform Edition of Dickens' Journalism*. 4 vols. London, 1994–2000.
Sparks, Timothy [Charles Dickens]. *Sunday under Three Heads. As it is; as Sabbath bills would make it; as it might be made*. London, 1836.

"The Tremendous Potency of the Small": Dickens, the Individual, and Social Change in a Post-America, Post-Catastrophist Age

Nancy Aycock Metz
Virginia Tech

Dickens's first trip to America exposed him to a view of historical process analogous to geological "catastrophism." According to democratic apologists, the American Revolution, like the biblical deluge, had "wiped the slate clean," washing away the sins and traces of the past,[1] permitting a momentous new start (Martin 192). To Dickens, however, the American landscape seemed as much "old" as "new"— a place blind to its position in a history with no beginning or end. In writing about America, Dickens emphasized the past *in* the present and the operation of identical processes across vast reaches of history. As a corollary, he viewed with skepticism a historical narrative dominated by "remarkable" men and their decisive interventions. In these ways, Dickens aligned himself with a view of historical process analogous to what became known as uniformitarianism, the theory of actual causes given brilliant and influential expression in Lyell's 1833 *Principles of Geology*. In this essay, I want to tease out the implications of these contrasting models to Dickens's thinking about agency in the period just following his first American tour as he was composing *Martin Chuzzlewit*.

As much as Dickens scorned American claims to have turned the tide of history, in his own life, and in the context of his own passionately felt sense of urgency about the particular historical moment, he himself longed to intervene in similarly decisive, high-impact ways. Again and again during this period, we find him promising and deferring what was to be a single, heavy blow from his own hand—a blow mighty enough to change hearts and minds and mighty enough, perhaps, to alter the course of a nation bent on widening the dangerous gulf between rich and poor. We see him troubled and vacillating over the best means of making such an impact. With Southwood Smith, he follows up an unfulfilled pledge to compose "An appeal to the People of England, on behalf of the Poor Man's Child" with a proposal to write something that will have "twenty times the force—twenty thousand times the force—I could exert by following out my first idea" (*Letters* 3: 461, 459; see also Dickens's earlier letter to Edward Fitzgerald, after a visit to the Manchester cotton mills: "I mean to strike the heaviest blow in my power for those unfortunate creatures" [*Letters* 1: 484]). All the while carrying on a campaign of reform-minded journalism in such periodicals as *The Morning Chronicle* and *The Daily News*, Dickens seems to be struggling over issues of agency and means. A skilled "skirmisher and sharpshooter" for liberal causes,[2] Dickens longed to make a deeper and more permanent impact on the course of current events.

In a very personal way, Dickens was brooding over issues of "trace" and legacy in the years surrounding the composition of *Martin Chuzzlewit*. His visit to America was in part planned explicitly with a view to his "future fame and station," which he felt would be enhanced by temporary removal from ephemeral modes of publication (*Letters* 2: 365). In explicit and intentional ways, he was reflecting on the after-life of his art and its impact on a world from which he himself would one day disappear. Dickens's famous comment to Forster about his intentions for Mrs. Gamp—"I mean to make a mark with her"—revealingly signals this new stage of awareness in Dickens, the novelist (*Letters* 3: 520). Later, touring monumental Venetian palaces in 1844, he would write feelingly to Forster of his desire "to leave [his] hand upon the time, lastingly upon the time, with one tender touch for the mass of toiling people that nothing could obliterate" (Forster 328). A note of plangency plays beneath the determined surface of this letter to Forster, reminding us that Dickens's trademark confidence notwithstanding, neither the certainty of making a permanent mark on his world nor the best means of doing so were altogether clear to him at this time. But the determination to do so was never so fiercely felt.

What does *Martin Chuzzlewit* itself have to say about these issues of individualism, authorship, and agency so central in the 1840s to new scientific understandings and to a newly perceived urgency—urgently shared by Dickens—about "The Condition of England"? The answer, I want to argue, is not at all clear, but the *question* is central to much that is interesting and generative about this conflicted text. Notwithstanding the novel's preoccupation with the dark prospect of oblivion,[3] it is also centrally focused on the art of *being in* and *making a difference to* the world. A revised set of understandings about the conditions within which human beings enact and exert their full humanity seems to operate in and through the narrative. Among so much that is excessive or exaggerated, a new note of restraint enters the novel—a chastened and disciplined sense of what one person—even a heroic or "remarkable" person—can accomplish. And related to this reconsideration of heroic possibility, the text sharply and explicitly critiques the "catastrophist" paradigm of history, with its emphasis on great men and cataclysmic events. New in Dickens's fiction as well is an emphasis on the special, spiritual challenge of laboring on without the certainty of end or reward and—in the ultimate case—without the sustaining faith that comes from the belief that the individual's life participates in a divine plan. I want to briefly unpack these features of the *Chuzzlewit* world, which periodically trouble its more traditional comic surface, before proposing the new forms of agency toward which they point.

Not only for young Martin but also for his selfless sidekick Mark, the events of the novel prove humbling to individual ambition. The "clever, dashing youth who might cut his way through the world as if it were a cheese" must learn that the world is not so malleable and does not so readily receive his imprint (*MC* 89). His companion, obsessed with the more benign fear that "nobody never will know half of what's in me, unless something very unexpected turns up" (*MC* 66) must also undergo sharp discipline, learning to content himself with a life lived out in ordinary time, among unremarkable people and events, a life unknown and uncredited beyond his small circle of care. As would-be "great men," Martin and Mark participate in the novel's larger reconsideration of the "great man" theory of history, with its narrow focus on the decisive impact of "divers slaughterous conspiracies and bloody frays" (*MC* 1)—man-made equivalents of the earthquakes, floods, and eruptions that punctuated the catastrophist plot line. Interestingly, Dickens's plans for (and perhaps even a partial draft of) *A Child's History of England* roughly coincide with the publication of *Martin Chuzzlewit*. In August 1843, Dickens was to write to Angela Burdett Coutts of his intentions to write this revisionist history "to the end that [Charley] may have tender-hearted notions of War and Murder, and may not fix his affections on wrong heros, or see the bright side of Glory's sword and know nothing of the rusty one" (*Letters* 3: 539).

Although the formal distribution of rewards and punishments in the penultimate chapter brings a superficial closure to the novel, the text maintains a counterbalancing interest in effort unrecognized and unrewarded, in work without outcome or acknowledgment. Hopelessness remains a viable possibility in this novelistic world. Despite steady application, Mark can make no progress in domesticating Eden to his own uses. In an image that speaks memorably to one of the fundamental anxieties of the novel, Dickens describes how, "as his foot-prints sunk into the marshy ground, a black ooze started forth to blot them out" (*MC* 378). When Martin and Mark do leave, hopelessness remains—in the landscape and in the countenances of the thin figures on the bank. Similarly, although Tom listens expectantly for every rustle and footstep outside the library, no one ever appears to congratulate him on a job well done. And no combination of ardent love and faithful service will ever win him Mary as his wife. As Tom tells Ruth firmly, the universe is large, and "it does not order events [. . .] for [our] individual accommodation" (*MC* 763).

One could, of course, take the comforting position that suffering, disappointment, and loss become ultimately meaningful as part of the divine plan, but in this novel the argument from design is decisively coopted, and therefore rendered toxic, by Pecksniff himself in a series of memorably hilarious homilies on the "legs of the human subject," the exquisite machinery of his own digestion, and the "quite natural, and [. . .] very beautiful arrangement" by which some are cold and hungry so that others can admire "the fortitude with which certain conditions of men bear cold and hunger" (*MC* 153–54, 116). At the same time that the novel decisively rejects the argument from design, it invites us rather provocatively to enter into and empathize with a complete loss of faith experience. What if the problem were more complicated than discerning God's design? How would the world—and one's place in it—look if there were no "superintending intelligence" (Fulweiler 51)? What principles would govern action in such a world? "Secularity," George Levine reminds us, "was not simply an epistemological argument of the radical intellectuals; it was also a way of living and imagining the moral life within the day-to-day world" (15), and the Victorian novel "tends toward the secular even as it so often insists on the providential order of things" (13). Tom's worship of Pecksniff as a false God, and Pecksniff's subsequent fall, give Dickens a safe scenario within which to frame questions that the text could not otherwise authorize. After the presiding deity of Tom's world is unceremoniously dethroned,

> The star of his whole life from boyhood, had become, in a moment, putrid vapour. [. . .] From the lofty height on which poor Tom had placed his idol it was tumbled down headlong, and
>   Not all the king's horses nor all the king's men
>   Could have set Mr. Pecksniff up again.
> [. . . Tom's] compass was broken, his chart destroyed, his chronometer had stopped, his masts were gone by the board; his anchor was adrift, ten thousand leagues away. (*MC* 491)

In a tone oddly vibrating between playfulness and radical questioning, Dickens tests the case of the good man suddenly deprived of foundational spiritual beliefs. Lacking tools to identify his position in limitless time and space, with no firm footing in the midst of flux, and no means of setting a course, Tom finds himself helpless even to seek help in the usual ways. He can scarcely even pray. But with this unwelcome disillusionment comes a strange and subversive form of power. Against his will, the doors of perception momentarily open, and innocence hangs in the balance:

> An uneasy thought enters [his] head; a shadowy misgiving that the altered relations between himself and Pecksniff, were somehow to involve an altered knowledge on his part of other people, and were to give him an insight into much of which he had had no previous suspicion. (*MC* 580)

In fact, nothing comes of this interesting misgiving. After hanging in the balance, Tom's innocence remains intact; his faith that "all will be well in time" is unshakeable to the end (*MC* 99). But the metaphors used to describe Tom's crisis float free in the text and are not so easily dismissed. They seem to come from a set of concerns larger than Pinch and Pecksniff. It is perhaps worth remembering that Dickens's own disillusionment with the magical thinking and complacency of organized religion was at its lowest ebb during this period. It was at this time that he joined the Unitarians who, he wrote to Felton in March 1843, "practise Charity and Toleration" and "would do something for human improvement, if they could" (*Letters* 3: 455–56).[4]

In its restrained phrasing and tone of modest understatement, this tribute to Unitarian religious practice accords well with the fictional world I have been describing—a world where would-be "remarkable men" recognize the limits of individual agency, and where neither the scale of human suffering nor the partial, conditional nature of the difference even kind-spirited people can make constrains effort, discipline, and salutary struggle. A novel without a satisfactory hero, where grand architectural ambitions are exposed as plagiarisms or foundationless castles in the air—a novel whose very structure mocks the conventions of "first" and "last," *Martin Chuzzlewit* invites readers to share a compensating optimism in the value of small, often unacknowledged deeds of helpfulness or generosity. These go by various names—"this simple act" (*MC* 194), "these simple means" (*MC* 691), "little acts of tenderness" (*MC* 249), "little household offices" (*MC* 249), or even "jollity"—and the text multiplies examples of them—there are literally dozens, from Tom's uncompensated organ playing and repair of the harpsichord key to Mark's unpretending services to the emigrant family.

More than just illustrations of individual character or grace notes to the novel's critique of selfishness, these gestures constitute a significant part of the novel's argument and belief system. As such, they participate in a larger cultural conversation about agency influenced by scientific findings. Virginia Zimmerman describes how "nineteenth-century excavators," who were both "observers of small actions and actors themselves," brought about a new appreciation for "the tremendous potency of the small": "If the minute actions of a water drop could carve a canyon, then the seemingly insignificant actions of a man or woman might also have great effect" (19). "Very small actions" performed by "individuals who had formerly appeared to be absolutely insignificant" could over time "affect great change" (19). The point is made in reverse by Mercy Pecksniff to Tom when she reflects on the consequences of small gestures *withheld*. Recalling Old Martin's brief and unproductive interview with her before her marriage, she says,

> Tell him that if he could know how my heart trembled in the balance that day, and what *a very little* would have turned the scale, his own would bleed with pity for me. [. . .] I]f he had relented *but a little more*; if he had

thrown himself in my way *but one other quarter of an hour*; if he had extended his compassion for a vain, unthinking, miserable girl *in but the least degree*; he might, and I believe he would, have saved her! (*MC* 582, emphases added)

But, of course, consequences can seldom be predicted, and the afterlife of a deed may never even be known by its author. Thus the novel ascribes to a philosophy of effort as a present progressive practice undertaken for its own sake and so is immune from the potentially paralyzing rewards or disappointments of ambition. Dickens wants his readers to be like Mark Tapley—embodied verbs: "always a-bein, sometimes a-doin, and continually a-sufferin" (*MC* 730). In such practices, in such daily discipline, lie "amazing power[s] of self-sustainment" (*MC* 517).

There is a wonderful exchange between Martin and Mark after the discovery of Pecksniff's plagiarism when both seem to have arrived at this understanding. Young Martin, at first petulant at the discovery of the fraud, is corrected by Mark:

> "Compare that fellow's situation to-day with ours!" said Martin bitterly.
> "Lord bless you, sir!" cried Mark, "what's the use! Some architects are clever at making foundations, and some architects are clever at building on 'em when they're made. But it'll all come right in the end, sir; it'll all come right!"
> "And in the meantime," began Martin.
> "In the meantime, as you say, sir, we have a deal to do, and far to go. So sharp's the word, and Jolly!" (*MC* 555)

Mark's linguistic intervention here—the way he interrupts Martin's throwaway "in the meantime" and reinvests it with meaning—brings to the foreground an important dimension of the narrative. Whatever we might say about the novel's time scheme and setting, from the characters' point of view, life is always lived and action always taken in this bracketed, provisional space, this "meantime" positioned between origins we cannot discern and ends we cannot predict. In the situation of the passengers on board the *Screw*, Dickens offers his most focused and concentrated exploration of this universal human condition. Similar to the unnamed inhabitants of this human ark, Dickens seems to say, we, all of us, pass our lives largely unconscious of "unfathomable depths," unaware of how small and vulnerable a position we occupy in a world of vast and elemental forces. Under these conditions, a willed forgetting, a perhaps necessary unconsciousness permits action in the present, a constant striving admirable in itself, regardless of odds or ends. "On, on, on [. . .] onward she comes [. . .] Still she comes striving on." There were "people there asleep; as if no deadly element were peering in at every seam and chink, and no drowned seaman's grave, with but a plank to cover it, were yawning in the unfathomable depths below." More than any other group of characters in the novel, this stalwart band, whose fates are analogically linked to the fate of England — "that small island sleeping a thousand miles away so quietly in the midst of angry waves" — embody the ideal of living "in the meantime" (*MC* 246–47). The idiot snapping his fingers to amuse a crying child, the old men engaged in maladroit but well-intentioned acts of housework, the poor woman burdened with her infant but mending another child's clothes — each one, acting in the present and testing by modest measures the limits of individual capacities, in different ways proves "the tremendous potency of the small."

And yet — and here I arrive at the fundamental contradictions at the heart of *Martin Chuzzlewit* — these small gestures do not finally add up to a solution to "the Condition of England." Moreover, the novel itself averts its gaze from the scenes of suffering, injustice, and radical inequality Dickens knew to be features of his sentimentally inscribed landscape. Wiltshire, the home to which America is away — the embodiment of a threatened way of life represented here as beautiful in proportion to its fragility — is a case in point. Wiltshire was the first county to cite a decrease in population during the first half of the century when the population was increasing dramatically elsewhere. By 1842, according to Jane H. Berard, 500 people had emigrated from eighteen Wiltshire villages (75; Burnett 556; Prince 17). Summarizing these conditions in an 1843 article, the *London Medical Gazette* concluded, "the condition of our farm apprentices approaches far nearer to that of slaves or serfs than it is pleasant to acknowledge" ("Employment" 490). Less than two years after the publication of *Martin Chuzzlewit*, Dickens published his own cauterizing exposé of rural suffering, "The Hymn of the Wiltshire Labourers," but in the novel itself, Wiltshire's history of rick-burning and poverty-induced violence is safely quarantined in a single allusion spoken by the narrator ex cathedra.

"Awake the present!" (Slater 210). Dickens sounded this keynote in the prologue to John Marston's *The Patrician's Daughter* composed just as the contours of *Martin Chuzzlewit* were taking shape in his mind. He wanted readers of the novel to feel the urgency and relevance of this imperative to their lives, and one can safely assume, I think, that he was calling for bold and immediate undertakings, in addition to small acts of kindness, undertaken "in the meantime." In an epigram adapted from the prologue, ultimately removed at Forster's urging, Dickens turned the text on its readers in an apparent call to action aimed at their assumed inertia and complacency: "*Your* homes the scene. Yourselves the Actors, here" (Slater 210). And periodically speaking with his own outraged voice, he interrupts the flow of narrative, urging action only tangentially related to the characters and events of the story: "Go [. . .] Teachers of content and honest pride, into the mine, the mill, the forge, the squalid depths of deepest ignorance and uttermost abyss of man's neglect" (*MC* 226). "Beneath the Pickwickian/Nicklebeian surface of *Chuzzlewit*," Michael Slater comments, Dickens's "anger about contemporary social issues burns away [. . .] sometimes bursting through" (213).

Dickens had yet to bring topical, contemporary concerns into the fabric of a narrative reaching outward in time and space, as he did so brilliantly in the *Carol* through the figures of Ignorance and Want, but in *Martin Chuzzlewit*, he begins to expand the scale of past, present, and future and to imagine how "the Spirits of all Three," living within the humbled, striving human being, could impact a suffering world. Tom's role as dreamer is important in this regard. As his hands wander over the keys of the old piano in the Furnival's Inn apartment, as Ruth begins to sing "words of old poets" in the darkening chamber, as "the shadows deepened; deepened" and outside the window "the city's hum and stir" and "the chiming of the old church clocks" are felt as presences and emanations (*MC* 691), there is that suggestion so familiar in Dickens's later fiction of a great tide of urban humanity past and present that connects the moment and the individual living within its exigencies with all those who have come before and with a starry cosmos beyond the human realm. If the rapidly darkening room evokes "the flight of time" (*MC* 690) on a smaller scale, the figures at the window and at the piano model a way of being *in time*—of suspending its rapid flow through the spiritual self-hypnosis of music and of bringing the scale of a vast city down to the intimacy of lovers' looks. Such moments matter in their power to liberate human beings from selfishness and to direct empathy outward. As for the "Sledge hammer" blow, when Dickens does deliver it in the form of *A Christmas Carol*, both its message and the miniature, gemlike textual artifact itself affirm "the tremendous potency of the small" and the power of the socially engaged writer to "make a mark" "lastingly upon the time."

NOTE

1 For an extended discussion of the U.S. historical narrative as a "divine ordering of events" proceeding from known origins and blank slates, see Martin (3–16).
2 Macaulay's phrase, quoted by Drew (53) and Slater (168).
3 See, for example, Dickens's description of how death swallows up all traces of Old Anthony's life, reducing him to the status of "next" in an unending sequence of such obliterations—"one new mound [. . .] another heap of earth" in the cemetery: "Time, burrowing like a mole below the ground, had marked his track by throwing up another heap of earth. And that was all" (*MC* 327).
4 Robert Newsom's analysis of Dickens's *The Life of Our Lord*, written for Plorn in the late 1840s, is interesting in this regard. Acceptance of miracles and of the resurrection notwithstanding, "there is often ambiguity about Jesus's divinity" in Dickens's version of the *New Testament*. Indeed, his account approaches Unitarian "adoptionism (the heresy that Jesus *became* God's son), and Christ is presented here simply as a model of good behavior and the best of teachers" (44–45).

BIBLIOGRAPHY

Berard, Jane H. *Dickens and Landscape Discourse*. New York, 2007.
Burnett, John. "Country Diet." *The Victorian Countryside*. Vol. 1. Ed. G. E. Mingay. London, 1981. 554–65.
Dickens, Charles. *The Letters of Charles Dickens*. Ed. Madeline House, Graham Storey et al. 12 Vols. Oxford, 1965–2002.
— — —. *Martin Chuzzlewit*. Ed. Margaret Caldwell. Oxford, 1982.
Drew, John M. L. *Dickens the Journalist*. New York, 2003.
"Employment of Women and Children in Agriculture." Rpt. from *The London Medical Gazette*. *The Boston Medical and Surgical Journal* 28 (1843): 489–92.
Forster, John. *The Life of Charles Dickens*. Ed. J. W. T. Ley. London, 1928.
Fulweiler, Howard W. "A Dismal Swamp: Darwin, Design, and Evolution in *Our Mutual Friend*." *Nineteenth-Century Literature* 49.1 (1994): 51–74.
Levine, George. "Dickens, Secularism, and Agency." *Contemporary Dickens*. Ed. Eileen Gillooly and Deirdre David. Columbus, 2009. 13–34.
Martin, Terence. *Parables of Possibility: The American Need for Beginnings*. New York, 2005.
Newsom, Robert. "Dickens and the Goods." *Contemporary Dickens*. Ed. Eileen Gillooly and Deirdre David. Columbus, 2009. 35–52.
Prince, Hugh. "Victorian Rural Landscapes." *The Victorian Countryside*. Vol. 1. Ed. G. E. Mingay. London, 1981. 17–29.
Slater, Michael. *Charles Dickens*. New Haven, 2009.
Zimmerman, Virginia. *Excavating Victorians*. Albany, 2008.

MONEY, POWER, AND APPEARANCE IN *DOMBEY AND SON*

Michael Hollington
Clare Hall, University of Cambridge

[Introductory note: The financial upheavals of recent years have certainly had the effect of reviving interest in Dickens's portrayal of nineteenth-century capitalism, in particular its shadier, even criminal features. The temptation to link Madoff and Merdle, for instance, has proved irresistible, and indeed on more plausible grounds than mere alliteration. Whilst not a believer in simple linkages of fiction and reality (Vaihinger's *Philosophie des Als Ob* [*The Philosophy of As If*] seems helpful here to convey that such comparisons can never offer compelling truth, merely suggestive provocation for further thought), the present author nonetheless seeks to deepen understanding of Dickens's representation of capitalism and capitalists, fraudulent and otherwise, with the help of the magnum opus of the German sociologist Georg Simmel, *The Philosophy of Money* (*Philosophie des Geldes*).]

Dombey sat in the corner of the darkened room in the great arm-chair by the bedside, and Son lay tucked up warm in a little basket bedstead, carefully disposed on a low settee immediately in front of the fire and close to it, as if his constitution were analogous to that of a muffin, and it was essential to toast him brown while he was very new. (*DS* 1)

The one-sentence first paragraph of *Dombey and Son* offers an initial indication of some, if not all of the concerns of this essay. It describes the human spatial arrangement of a domestic interior, that is to say, the position that the protagonists occupy in relation to each other. The only one who has any say in the matter is the person whose preeminent power in the novel is signified by the appearance of his name as the very first word of the title and the text. Dombey can choose where to position himself, whereas his wife has just given birth and is at death's door, while his newborn son is, of course, disposed according to Dombey's wishes and preoccupations. We may notice first that Dombey's position is peripheral, that in his delight at the birth of a son, he has allowed him to occupy center stage, placing himself at a distance from the fire, which initially carries its customary domestic connotations as the center of warmth and light. However, the abdication of power is only apparent, and the writing points out the distinction between the patriarch in his "great" armchair and the powerless infant in his "little" basket on a "low" settee. Moreover, there are plentiful signs of something ominous in the relationship between father and son: the placing of the father in a zone of the room that is relatively cold and dark; the distance, the avoidance of close physical proximity, let alone contact; and, above all, the objectification or reification of the child, "new" like a thing rather than "young" like a creature. The grotesque comparison of the child to a muffin operates not only on the level of ironic fairy tale, as a foreshadowing of the theme of the cannibalistic devouring of Paul through the agency of ogresses such as Pipchin or monsters such as Blimber; it also points toward a mythical representation of economic activity, transmuting the child into an item of manufacture for consumption and the fire into an agent of that process.

Whatever disagreements might arise about the details of this interpretation of the opening of *Dombey and Son*, I would hope to be able to claim that it is an appropriately "physiognomical" reading, a necessary response to a central invitation from the novelist and his illustrator to consider the surface of behavior and gesture as critical revelations, to an astute observer, of the "style of life" of Dombey and his kind. I shall argue here in a familiar way that this is a money "style of life," but I hope to add something to our understanding of what this means in the novel through the use of the work of Georg Simmel. In *Dombey and Son*, it seems reasonable to suggest, the money style of life has become dominant among the business classes in metropolitan London as the center of early Victorian capitalism. It is characterized in a critical manner in a number of ways, which could be said to include the confusion of substance and appearance; the neglect or denial of spiritual and moral values, of human emotional bonds, of personality and individuality; and the promotion in their place of abstract intellectualization and calculation and the reification of the self as well as of other human beings. I take both the phrase "style of life" and some aspects of my analysis from Simmel's classic *Philosophie des Geldes* (*The Philosophy of Money*, first published in 1900, but only recently perhaps gaining outside of Germany the reputation it deserves), one of whose aims, as described in the book's preface, to analyze money's "effects upon the inner world—upon the vitality of individuals, upon the linking of their fates, upon culture in general" (54), seems to me to have a bearing on one of those of *Dombey and Son*. That such a broad sociological approach can be combined with "physiognomical" reading is due above all to the work of Walter Benjamin, himself significantly influenced by Simmel; his "secular illuminations" or "dialectical images" of the "style of life" of nineteenth-century Paris offers what is still perhaps a model of close symptomatic reading of the surface minutiae of gesture and behavior, an attempt at a "materialist physiognomics" which we will here try to follow in the case of a literary work.

To provide further illustration of the method, and bring the symptoms of the money "style of life" into greater focus, we must turn, in a development of Raymond Williams's perception that the term *house* is radically confused in *Dombey and Son* (Williams 17), from the domestic hearth of the Dombey home to the fires of Dombey's office. Here it is quite clear that they represent a central territory for the display of power:

> "You respect nobody, Carker, I think," said Mr. Dombey.
> "No?" inquired Carker, with another wide and most feline show of his teeth. "Well! Not many people I believe. I wouldn't answer perhaps," he murmured, as if he were only thinking it, "for more than one."
> A dangerous quality, if real; and perhaps a not less dangerous one, if feigned. But Mr. Dombey hardly seemed to think so, as he still stood with his back to the fire, drawn up to his full height, and looking at his head-clerk with a dignified composure, in which there seemed to lurk a stronger latent sense of power than usual. (*DS* 173–74)

Here Dombey takes over from "Son" in dominating the scene from the vantage point of the fire, apparently taking pleasure (similar to Bagstock with his Native Prince or Bounderby with Mrs. Sparsit) in having a worthy object to subdue. But his subservient here, Carker, is no sooner out of the room than he adopts a copycat (!) posture in front of his own fire next door, confronting Walter Gay and his brother Carker the junior, "standing with his back to the fire, and his hands under his coat-tails, looking over his white cravat, as Mr. Dombey himself could have looked" (*DS* 176). He will take up the same posture in order to intimidate Rob the Grinder as soon as Mr. Perch is out of his office ("while he was gone, Mr. Carker assumed his favourite attitude before the fireplace" [*DS* 296]), and receives Captain Cuttle's inquiry about the fate of Walter "standing astride before the fire as if there were no more spots upon his soul than on his pure white linen, and his smooth sleek skin" (*DS* 452). Bounderby in *Hard Times* will follow suit, making his first appearance in front of the fire: "he thus took up a commanding position, from which to subdue Mrs. Gradgrind" (*HT* 14–15).

Carker thus models himself on Dombey, assimilating his style of dress (the white cravat), appearance, and gesture, in order, of course, ruthlessly to supplant him when the time is ripe. The observation of their patterns of behavior form part of an ironic anthropology of the society of money. In accordance with the imperialist ideology of the time, they are similar to heathen savages in their disregard for any spiritual or moral values that cannot be converted into money terms, or in their "oriental" preoccupation with the nexus of hierarchy and power: "Mr. Carker, as Grand Vizier, inhabited the room that was nearest to the Sultan" (*DS* 171). Anno Dombei, of course, has taken over from Anno Domini, and James Carker is thoroughly contemptuous of his brother's meek acceptance of his menial role in the House of Dombey, founded as it is on an ethic of humility: "But you were going [. . .] to recite some Christian precept, I observed" (*DS* 615). Their world is savagely Darwinian, with dog eating dog, or, in the case of Carker, cat catching mouse. What is once accumulated must be jealously guarded—hence the fireside position, or the stance of Dombey at the party where he receives his adversaries: "the spacious dining room [. . .] might have been taken for a grown-up exposition of Tom Tiddler's ground, where children pick up gold and silver. Mr. Dombey, as Tiddler, looked his character to admiration" (*DS* 491).

But the taken-for-grantedness of these styles of behavior calls for emphasis. In the scene with Carker quoted earlier, Dombey's cool neutrality of tone is striking: there appears to be nothing intrinsically shocking for him in "respecting nobody"; it is even, tacitly, an appropriate attitude for a man of business. Simmel comments on the detached intellectuality of the money lifestyle: "certainly there is something callous about the purely rationalistic treatment of people and things. Yet this is not a positive impulse but simply results from pure logic being unaffected by respect, kindness and delicacies of feeling" (434). Dombey is not able to see through Carker's feigned spontaneity or "charming" display of teeth—obvious enough in its real meaning as a physiognomic sign of rapacity in Phiz's illustration of the scene in which Carker salutes Florence at the Skettleses and all the animals about him are startled and frightened into flight—because he has no sense apparatus adequate to discriminate between substance and appearance. This discrimination, according to Simmel, was characteristic only of human societies prior to the nineteenth century when values were still real and solid rather than monetary and liquid (169). Carker recapitulates him in the most savagely ironic way, spending the time after the death of Paul, when even such a worshipper of Dombey as Mr. Perch is "moved" and expresses his feelings by treating his wife to a veal cutlet and Scotch, in self-satisfied calculation of consequent future moves: "Mr. Carker the Manager treats no one; neither is he treated; but alone in his own room he shows his teeth all day; and it would seem that there is something gone from Mr. Carker's path—some obstacle removed—which clears his way before him" (*DS* 236).

For Simmel, what happens in a money society is that people imitate the colorlessness and neutrality of money as a medium of exchange; losing their feelings, they also lose, or strive to lose, anything that is distinctive and particular—or one might say, in a Dickensian context, "eccentric"—about their personalities. This is, I believe, a potential basis for a rewarding approach to the tragicomedy of *Dombey and Son*, one that answers the criticism not infrequently encountered that Dombey is an unconvincing capitalist because of the absence of entrepreneurial, swashbuckling vividness in his personality. He is rather, to anticipate *Great Expectations*, a "self-swindler." The "new muffin" at the novel's opening, and the assumptions about desirable styles of life that it reveals, can quickly be juxtaposed with the description of Dombey that pointedly contrasts him to Toodles, as "new" and objectified and featureless as possible, in which he is "one of those close-shaved close-cut monied gentlemen who are glossy and crisp like new bank notes, and who seem to be artificially braced and tightened as by the stimulating activity of golden shower-baths" (*DS* 19). Only one of them, mark you; it appears they can be manufactured according to a process like that which prints banknotes: "The statement on bank notes to the effect that their value is paid to the bearer on demand 'without proof of identity' typifies the absolute objectivity with which money transactions operate," observes Simmel (436). Cleanliness is a distinctive part of the get-up; bathing and showering were relatively new at that time and were starting to become part of business culture (Dickens himself had a shower installed in Tavistock House in 1851). Dombey's "golden shower" of money affords the opportunity of ironic reference to Zeus and thus provides a splendid mythological aetiology for his characteristic stiffness and upright rigidity of posture: he is literally "braced" by those daily money showers. No wonder, with such readily imitable and depersonalized formulae as spotlessly clean white cravats, close shaving, and frequent showers, that Carker should be able to ape his master in ways whose ulterior motives escape attention—though he, of course, must add liberal quantities of toothpaste to the budget of his uniform.

This ready duplicability of impersonal forms of behavior—linked by Simmel to the anonymity of money more than (as in Marx and even some of Benjamin's work) to the introduction in modern capitalism after the industrial revolution of ever more sophisticated mechanical means of production—can also be seen in *Dombey and Son* in the dominant style of education. The prevalence of the classical in Blimber's academy and elsewhere in the novel reflects an educational emphasis on intellectuality, abstract rationality, and a "Roman" suppression of emotional self-expression rather than on the development of the particular individual. The content of that education (the classic texts of dead languages and the structure of their grammar) is irrelevant and indifferent to the specificities of modern life, or to any empirical training in their detailed observation. At the physiognomical level, the aim of such an education could be said to be the creation of a certain physical deportment—those "classical and intellectual lineaments" (shared with Oliver Twist) that Mrs. Blimber affects to admire in Paul Dombey's profile (*DS* 146)—and the wifely accomplishments that Dombey wants to take possession of in Edith include the apparent capacity to reproduce these: she appeals to him as a good piece of classical statuary. Only, as with Carker, he takes the essential model to be himself: "Mr. Dombey, being a good deal in the statue way himself, was well enough pleased to see his handsome wife immovable and proud and cold" (*DS* 482). We are told elsewhere that "it flattered him to picture to himself, this proud and stately woman doing the honours of his house, and chilling his guests after his own manner" (*DS* 414). A section of Simmel's book titled "The Typical Relation between Money and Prostitution" enables us to analyze clearly Dombey's purchase of Edith and her embittered acquiescence: "Kant's moral imperative never to use human beings as a mere means but to accept and treat them always, at the same time, as ends in themselves is blatantly disregarded by both parties in the case of prostitution" (Simmel 377).

As with education, so it is with culture. Dombey's inanimate, as opposed to animate, sculptural acquisitions include an undistinguished metallic bust of Pitt, utterly devoid of any "aura" except that, once more, it seems to recapitulate Dombey himself: "Mr. Pitt, in bronze, on the top, with no trace of his celestial origin about him, guarded the unattainable treasure like an enchanted Moor" (*DS* 54). The choice of subject indicates ideological sympathies—the architect of the naval victories over Napoleon, Pitt can be thought of as one of the inaugurators of the "Anno Dombei," the era in which Britannia so rules the waves that mercantile Allahs rewrite time and history. The "treasure" that he guards here, again like Tom Tiddler, is a row of identical books, "precisely matched as to size, and drawn up in line, like soldiers, [who] looked in their cold, hard, slippery uniforms, like they had but one idea between them" (*DS* 54). More fundamentally still, perhaps, the room in which they stand is only superficially a library: it is "in fact, a dressing-room, so that the smell of hot-pressed paper, vellum, morocco, and Russian leather contended in it with the smell of divers pairs of boots" (*DS* 24). From boots to books, the phonemal shift is slight; although Dickens had traversed it in one direction during his lifetime, moving from Warren's of the Strand to Chapman and Hall, Dombey is clearly bent on taking an opposite route, in which things that contain and express personal cultural value are reduced to the anonymity of boots, with their deceptive surfaces (boot polish with Dombey seems to equal toothpaste with Carker). "What is distressing," writes Simmel, "is that we are basically indifferent to those numerous objects that swarm around us, and this is for reasons specific to a money economy: their impersonal origin and easy replaceability" (460). With modernity, it would seem from Puccini's *La Bohème*, in which the philosopher Colline sings a tender aria of farewell ("Vecchia zimarra") to the coat he is about to pawn in the last hours of Mimi's life, only the world of Bohemia with its absence of cash seems to retain a sense of the value and meaning of cultural objects.

Simmel's thinking about the relation between money and time also has relevance for *Dombey and Son*. The importance of money is especially recognized and prized in times of social change, he argues, "because it offers an exact and flexible equivalent for every change of value" (Simmel 126). "We must expect change," Louisa Chick moralizes based on Miss Tox's humanely considerate inquiry about her cough, for she aims to present herself as the official philosopher of Dombeyism with such remarks ("it's a world of change" is another exhibit of her wisdom [*DS* 396]). "The relative speed of circulation of money in relation to all other objects must immediately increase the general pace of life wherever money becomes the general centre of interest," writes Simmel (506), again taking the character of money as the base of a cultural superstructure, arguing even that the rounding of coins is part of a process of making them run faster! At any rate, in *Dombey and Son*, we have numerous instances of an increase in the general speed of life: the railways, the conversion of Staggs's Gardens, the speeding up of the education of Paul and his fellow sufferers at Dr. Blimber's Academy.

It is again in the taking-for-granted of these necessities that Dombey's "self-swindling" is to be observed. Among the many powerful, large structural ironies of the novel, vying with the emergence at the end of the novel of "Dombey and Daughter," in a nonbusiness sense, as a more deeply satisfying alternative to the goal of "Dombey and Son" pursued earlier, is that Dombey's very "Tom Tiddler" method of guarding the most precious "treasure" of all, his son and heir, is the precise means of destroying this cardinal object of his concern. His conversion of all spheres of life into economics—his employing Toodles as wet nurse, for instance, as a mere commercial arrangement, his hostility toward "competitors" for control of his child's development (Florence in particular), his assumption that all expressions of warmth and sympathy toward himself or his son at the time of his bereavement must necessarily be attempts to establish pecuniary obligation—brings as its logical consequence the very disasters he most fears. The obliteration of Staggs's Gardens as a sacrifice to the inexorable march of economic progress makes it almost impossible to find the one person who, in desperate fantasy at least, might reinvigorate his son on his deathbed; the disdainful assumption of power over Carker and Edith means that both will return to destroy him. Even his impersonal sponsorship of Biler, who becomes Boy no. 147 at the Charitable Grinders, turns against him, for the creature is corrupted by his unhappy education and becomes Carker's tool—for money, of course. In Simmel's terms, the confusion of means and ends set in motion by the elevation of money into a power and a means of control to be worshipped as an end in itself rather than to be used as a means to achieving purposeful and/or pleasurable immaterial satisfactions is tellingly illustrated in Dombey. He is a tragicomic Macbeth who has murdered his own son; sitting at table with Edith, he sees, not the ghost of Banquo, but a "little figure in a low arm-chair [. . .] with its bright eyes and its old-young face gleaming as in the flickering of an evening fire" (*DS* 415).

The book is merciless in its comic and ironic ways of underlining the absurdities and disasters of the Dombey style of life, and its duplication throughout the society of the novel, at whatever remote and grotesque distance from its model. The Game Chicken is a splendid example:"Go in and win [. . .] When your man's before you and your work cut out, go in and do it" (*DS* 309) is his humorous pugilistic version of capitalist values, as these are enshrined in Dombey's apparent belief that all personal interactions are competitive. He does not habitually stand in front of the fire, perhaps, but he has a frostiness similar to Dombey's, itself in need of warming up—he wears "a shaggy white great-coat in the warmest weather," we learn (*DS* 305), and when Toots lowers his voice to talk of love, "objected to the softer emotions" (*DS* 449). The sight of Dombey leads him to propose a "friendly" solution to Toots's problems (parodies of friendship—Carker, Bagstock, Feeder, the Game Chicken—being a theme of *Dombey and Son* as well as of *Our Mutual Friend*) in which the cool rational calculation that characterizes the money society is sent up in the Game Chicken's "scientific" assessment of the prospects of knocking out Dombey: "he's as stiff a cove as ever he see, but that it is within the resources of Science to double him up with one blow in the waistcoat" (*DS* 522). His disappointment at Toots's refusal to sanction fisticuffs against the "stiff'un" Dombey (he accuses him of being "mean") leads to an end of the commercial relationship between the pair: "Give me a fi'typunnote to-morrow, and let me go" (*DS* 765). Chicken is comically superior to Dombey and Carker here, perhaps, in that he appears to know when the capitalist venture of knocking "Mr. Toots about the head three times a week, for the small consideration of ten and six per visit" (*DS* 305) is up.

Yet if the novel emphasizes grotesque congruences of money lifestyle, and physiognomy, it also offers grotesque contrasts. Between "stiffness" and "gruffness" a gulf is measured in *Dombey and Son*. On the one hand, the dyed-in-the-wool assimilation of body styles approved in the new money society; on the other, important vestiges of a previous social order in which substance and appearance were still to be clearly distinguished. "The ashes sometimes gets in here," says Toodles to Tox, touching his chest, "and makes a man speak gruff, as at the present time. But it *is* ashes, not crustiness" (*DS* 17), and Paul Dombey, in his loneliness at Blimber's, summons up an image to his mind's eye of "that gruff-voiced Captain with the iron hand" (*DS* 193) and, in doing so, is able to make a clear distinction between contingent disability and a significant physiognomical index of metallic hardness of soul. Cuttle's hook is in fact a brilliant counterimage to the dominant Dombeyan physiognomical language of the novel, which, as we have seen, privileges smooth and bland but deceptive surface over substance. Acquired no doubt like Bunsby's glass eye in consequence of an accident at sea, it has been converted to versatile use serving multiple practical purposes—as toasting fork, as means of blowing kisses to women (*DS* 135), or as something to chew on as an aid to deep thought (*DS* 213). It is not an indifferent, alien, reified object or replaceable commodity or fetish. Nor is it thus surprising that Cuttle's conception of money retains an "old-fashioned" superstition in favor of its substantiality—for him, it includes sugar tongues and silver watches (*DS* 125).

Even more, the hook is an important alternative source of power. Among the uses of Cuttle's "mysterious hook" is that it can serve as a means of keeping order amongst unruly boys during Sunday service (*DS* 206) or of making profound signs in the air like those of Chinese philosophers (*DS* 226). The distance from "hook" to "book" is yet shorter than that from "boot," and the Captain's imperfect nautical literacy (he's a "mighty slow, gruff reader" [*DS* 656]) retains a genuine reverence for the personal spiritual values that books contain. There is a pointed contrast between his view of books and Dombey's—even if he, too, from a quite different angle approaches them as objects (he likes big ones on Sunday, for instance)—because for him the authority of the text clearly transcends that of money. His "commercial" bookkeeping at the Wooden Midshipman (*DS* 522) is carried out not in imitation of professional accountancy ledgers but of the ship's log kept at sea—"the truest book as a man can write" (*DS* 448), which notes winds and calm weather rather than debit and credit or profit and loss.

Indeed, it is important to take proper stock of the fact that "the Captain implicitly believed that all books were true" (*DS* 522). This, we may suppose, includes long novels as well as ship's logs and large Bibles. If, in a mise en abyme perspective that takes off from this belief, *Dombey and Son* itself can be taken as a "true" book, then it seems to throw its authority by and large on the side of money innocents such as Cuttle (though there are some incongruities late in the book—Uncle Sol is to turn out a better capitalist than Dombey, and Walter is to build an even grander business empire, perhaps). At any rate by the novel's end, through the operation of a much deeper logic than that of the power of money, we find another superb structural irony—it is now Dombey, not Son, who asks, "What is money?" (*DS* 818). The father is now himself engaged in a project of recovery of the self, as he begins to understand the "teleological dislocation" of means and ends in a society where money "carries out the function of imposing a distance between ourselves and our purposes in the same manner as other technical mediating elements, but does it more purely and completely" (Simmel 484). For Simmel, "man has thereby become estranged from himself; an insuperable barrier of media, technical inventions, abilities and enjoyments has been erected between him and his most distinctive and essential being" (484), and the crucial agent of this estrangement is, as *Dombey and Son* demonstrates, money.

BIBLIOGRAPHY

Benjamin, Walter. *The Arcades Project*. Cambridge, MA, 1999.
Dickens, Charles. *Dombey and Son*. Ed. Alan Horsman. Oxford, 1974.
———. *Hard Times*. Introd. by Dingle Foot. London, 1955.
Simmel, Georg. *Philosophie des Geldes*. Ed. Jeff Kintzelé and Peter Schneider. Frankfurt am Main, 1993.
———. *The Philosophy of Money*. Ed. David Frisby. London, 1978.
Williams, Raymond. Introduction. *Dombey and Son*. By Charles Dickens. Ed. Peter Fairclough. Harmondsworth, 1970. 11–34.

III. Dickens and Literary Change

The Passing of the *Pickwick* Moment

Malcolm Andrews
University of Kent at Canterbury

> Laughter always implies a kind of secret freemasonry, or even complicity, with other laughers, real or imaginary.
> —Bergson (6)

> Every author, as far as he is great and at the same time *original*, has the task of *creating* the taste by which he is to be enjoyed.
> —Wordsworth (426)

Dickens's comic genius established itself as a result of his skillful and strenuous cultivation of a community of readers who would laugh with him and who would come to relish his particular idiosyncratic humor. He was not just a funny writer waiting for people to discover him. His aim in the mid-1830s was to convert his audience to *Dickensian* comedy. My aim here is to take stock of some of the modes of humorous writing available to Dickens at the start of his career, his selective adaptation of some of them and rejection of others, and his creative recognition of a climate change in popular humor.

As is well known, Dickens inherited, and in *Sketches* and *Pickwick* redeployed, certain routines and techniques in popular comedy—stock characterizations and farcical situations, linguistic tricks, and so on—all associated with writers, performers and caricaturists such as John Poole, Theodore Hook, Pierce Egan, Charles Mathews the Elder, and George Cruikshank. Indeed, according to Arthur Waugh, chairman of Chapman and Hall at the start of the twentieth century, Hook, Thomas Hood, and Poole may all have been suggested for the *Pickwick* project before

William Hall eventually approached Boz on the morning of 10 February 1836 (8). Dickens must have won over thousands of such readers who had been brought up on the comic traditions dominated by these writers and artists, and of course, he was one of those readers. But he had also a shrewd sense of when his readership tired of one comic mode or was stimulated by another. Thanks to serialization, in *Pickwick*, he could seize opportunities to capitalize on accidental comic breakthroughs, the most famous case being that of Sam Weller's promotion from a cameo role to a leading player. In July 1836, *The Literary Gazette* briefly noticed *Pickwick* Number 4, praising "the humour and talent of the clever writer," and instancing, in a long quotation, "the following droll description of Boots, at an ancient inn in the borough" (442). Its editor William Jerdan wrote to Dickens personally, urging him to develop this character "to the utmost" (*Letters* 1: 207). The following month, Mr. Pickwick adopted this entertaining "Boots" as his manservant. In August, the *Gazette* reviewed Number 5 (featuring the Eatanswill elections) and gave a generous sample, again from Sam, now prominent in the story: it was his anecdote about his father's being bribed to cause a road accident to a coach-load of voters, and I come back to that later. In September, the *Gazette* again thanked Dickens for "a monthly laugh, most refreshing to us in dull times" and hoped that "Boz will stick to Mr. Weller, 'Boots', whose facetious character he is working out very humorously" (584). For more than a year and a half, Dickens was improvising before a live audience and was as ravenous for shared laughter as any stand-up comic playing to a new venue. Each monthly part of *Pickwick* was a pilot show, a performance by an apprentice comedian, and Dickens worked his audience every bit as much as he worked his staple material.

* * *

As Queen Victoria came to the throne in June 1837, Mr. Pickwick arrived to take up residence in the Fleet Prison. A cultural climate change was taking place in this decade in comic writing. "A fresh vein of humour had been opened" (Collins 57) according to the *Quarterly Review*, as it looked back over most of *Pickwick* in October 1837. Among all England's comic writers, it declared that "Mr Dickens is not simply the most distinguished, but the first." Six months earlier, the *Court Magazine* had reflected on this new phenomenon, suggesting that Dickens erupted on the scene and single-handedly generated a new vogue for comic writing in mid-1830s England:

> Our readers cannot fail to have observed the sudden turn for the comic, which has recently discovered itself in the literary public. Formerly, the maxim was—"You are nothing if not critical;" now it is "You are nothing if not comical." The appetite for the jocose, the farcical, the extravagant, is immoderate. [. . .] Accordingly, the magazines have become as funny as it was in their power to become [. . .] There is no doubt that this sudden taste for crowding upon the sunny side of the road, was originally generated by a facetious gentleman who, for some months, escaped detection under the name of "Boz." (Collins 33–34)

For some, *Pickwick* was not just the opening of a fresh seam of comedy, but was a mighty transfusion of humor into the anemic body of English culture. Twenty years after its publication, here is how one enthusiast, in a "Remonstrance with Dickens," recalled life before and life after the novel:

> Before *Pickwick* there seems to us to have been but a serious world of it, with plenty of pathos, poetry, romance, and character, but [. . .] a decided drought of this last-mentioned element, till it then burst forth in a genial flood, sweeping down all restraints of primness and puritanism, drowning whole herds of jokers, facetious diners-out and provincial wags, and causing dullards and drivellers, hitherto priding themselves on the thickness of the hide which rendered them impervious to fun, to laugh till their faces, like Prince Hal's, resembled "a wet cloak ill laid-up"—no matter whether they had or had not the ache in their shoulders. (491)

This account of a tsunami of humor sounds hyperbolic, but the writer goes on to tell of his own excruciating experience on one occasion when he was attending a church service. He had been reading *Pickwick* the night before, and suddenly in the middle of the service, he recalled a ludicrous episode involving old Tony Weller; this set him off into fits of smothered laughter, forcing him to hide his head under the pew's prayer-book shelf. His quaking and stifled explosions drew the attention of the authorities, and eventually the verger and two churchwardens marched him away down the aisle, past faces staring in devout horror, with his handkerchief crammed down his throat. The next day, he goes to apologize to the dean, "who, being himself a Pickwickian, gave us absolution in the most kindly way" ("Remonstrance" 491).

So how exactly did Dickens go about drawing his readership into the "secret freemasonry" that would secure shared laughter? What was new about Boz's comedy? I think that four different innovative elements must be mentioned.

(1) *Realism*

The *Court Magazine* writer quoted earlier is investigating the causes of this new vogue for humor and is particularly struck by the "verisimilitude" of Boz's fiction, his "exact representations of trivial things." "His dialogues, without straining for puns or mere surface effects, are excerpts from veritable life [. . .] heightened of course, to make their full impression" (Collins 34). This acclaim for Dickens's realism in *Pickwick* may surprise us, but, for many readers, he did indeed seem to reinforce his comic effects by giving a robust everyday authenticity to action, character, and speech. His comedy thereby becomes an altogether more invasive species in national cultural life. By comparison with him, his humorous precursors were jesters performing on the margins of real everyday life with an array of preposterous farcical situations or shallow caricatures. That is how the *Westminster Review* (July 1837) saw Dickens in relation to Theodore Hook:

> in his [Boz's] writings there is none of that constant straining after the ludicrous, which wearies us in Mr Hook's writings. [. . .] 'Boz' always presents a contrast of remarkable simplicity and truth to nature [. . .] an absence of exaggeration, of coarseness [. . .] and a constant indication of a kindly and refined feeling, which we seek in vain in the writer with whom we are contrasting him. (Buller qtd. in Collins 53)

I will be returning to consider this absence of coarseness and the "kindly and refined feeling." As the originally commissioned Nimrod Club formula faded away once *Pickwick* had really got going, Dickens, helped by the work of Pierce Egan and Charles Mathews, helped also by the encouraging reception of his *Sketches* representing "Every-day Life and Every-day People," increasingly grounded his characterization, dialogue, settings, and the detailed paraphernalia of life in the actual experience of the contemporary world, and the consequence was that the comedy, for all its hyperbole, engaged with a firmer grip. His acute eye for idiosyncrasy raised popular awareness of the comedy inherent in everyday life: it became for readers in the mid-1830s a kind of education in comic sensibility. The reader was invited to see the world through Boz's eyes, and as that habit of perspective became contagious, Dickens soon secured his Bergsonian "secret [or not-so-'secret'] freemasonry of laughers."

(2) *Characterization*
Many contemporary reviewers and modern critics have seen character creation as Dickens's essential trademark comic method. They have also seen the great comic characters as unchanging monoliths of eccentricity, their comic value based in part precisely on their resistance to normal character development. Thus George Orwell famously remarked that the *Pickwick* characters begin as magic-lantern slides and end by getting mixed up in a third-rate movie. V. S. Pritchett said that "Dickens's comedy is the comedy of people who *are* something, rather than the comedy of people who *do* something, [. . .] His comic characters do not ever fit easily into plots" (970). Walter Bagehot had taken the issue a subtle stage further, arguing that the comic effect lay not so much in the caricature per se, funny though that may be, but in the paradoxical

> treating as a moral agent a being who is not a moral agent. We treat a vivified accident as a man, and we are surprised at the absurd results [. . .] we have exaggerations pretending to comport themselves as ordinary beings, caricatures acting as if they were characters. (Hollington 1: 180)

The comedy therefore lies both in the eccentric caricatures and, more interestingly perhaps, in the clash of incompatible modes. But what was also happening in *Pickwick* was that some caricatures were turning themselves into characters. Those obstinately frozen, comically inelastic figures (precisely Bergson's prescription for triggering laughter) begin to thaw as the novel's story warms up, and they become more flexible human beings—most notably Pickwick himself and Sam Weller—and the humor changes accordingly.

(3) *Sex and Violence*
Among much more modern critics, George Ford has suggested that *Pickwick*'s huge success in the 1830s was related to Dickens's skillful acclimatization of Regency humor to early Victorian tastes. I have already suggested that Dickens worked hard to recruit his "secret freemasonry" of laughers, and Ford's point is well taken in this context. He cites a passage from the Eatanswill sequence (chapter 13) that was

"approvingly reprinted in some of the early reviews," concerning old Tony Weller's story, related by Sam, of having been persuaded, with a bribe, to tip some opposition voters off his coach, seemingly by accident:

> "It's a werry bad road between this and London," says the gen'l'm'n. —"Here and there it *is* a heavy road," says my father—"Specially near the canal, I think," says the gen'l'm'n—"Nasty bit that 'ere," says my father—"Well, Mr. Weller," says the gen'l'm'n, "you're a wery good whip, and can do what you like with your horses, we know. We're all wery fond o' you, Mr. Weller, so in case you *should* have an accident when you're a bringing these here woters down, and *should* tip 'em into the canal vithout hurtin' any of 'em, this is for yourself," says he.

Ford concedes that part of the humor comes from the robust cockney speech style, but he argues that the situation itself, as Dickens manages it, contributes in significant ways to the effect:

> The *Situation* here is comparable to endless numbers of situations in Combe, Egan, Hook, and Lever. Thomas Rowlandson could have illustrated it [. . .] by one of his magnificently savage caricatures showing great fat men, with brutal and tremendous faces, tumbling headlong into the canal [. . .] What Dickens has done to this traditional scene by means of his style and tone is to raise it from the level of savage laughter onto a more genial plane [. . .] We do not feel that the canal-water actually penetrated the clothes of Tony Weller's passengers; they must have somehow emerged miraculously dry. (16–17)

So by these means too, Dickens senses changes in the moral climate of the mid-1830s, fashions his comedy accordingly and thereby enlists constituencies of readership that might have been alienated by the older tastes in robust physical comedy. Such tastes were typified in the work of Rowlandson and Gillray. Thackeray reviewed John Leech's *Pictures of Life and Character* in the *Quarterly* in 1854 and compared his work with his cartoon predecessors:

> How savage the satire was—how fierce the assault—what garbage hurled at opponents—what foul blows were hit—what language of Billingsgate flung! Fancy a party in a country-house now looking over [. . .] some of the Gilray comicalities, or the slatternly Saturnalia of Rowlandson! Whilst we live we must laugh, and have folks to make us laugh. We cannot afford to lose Satyr with his pipe and dances and gambols. But

we have washed, combed, clothed, and taught the rogue good manners: or rather, let us say, he has learned them himself [. . .] has become gentle and harmless, smitten into shame by the pure presence of our women and the sweet confiding smiles of our children. (79–80)

Dickens's sensitivity to such changing tastes in graphic satire was explicit when in 1848 he also wrote a review of some drawings by John Leech (*The Examiner*, 30 December 1848):

If we turn back to a collection of the works of Rowlandson or Gillray, we shall find, in spite of the great humour displayed in many of them, that they are rendered wearisome and unpleasant by a vast amount of personal ugliness. Now, besides that it is a poor device to represent what is satirised as being necessarily ugly—which is but the resource of an angry child or a jealous woman—it serves no purpose but to produce a disagreeable result. There is no reason why the farmer's daughter in the old caricature who is squalling at the harpsichord [. . .] should be squab and hideous. The satire on the manner of her education, if there be any in the thing at all, would be just as good if she were pretty. Mr Leech would have made her so. (Slater 2: 144)

Dickens's severity in 1848 about exploiting physical ugliness as a crude index of moral failings is interesting when we think about what he had done a decade earlier with Wackford Squeers.

(4) *Wit and Humor*
Victorians were fond of distinguishing between humor and wit, and generally felt more comfortable with humor. There was a growing unease with the Hobbesian belief that laughter is stimulated by our sudden perception of our superiority to the misfortunes of other people and with forms of satirical comedy or caustic wit that humiliated the infirmities of others. Humor needed to adapt itself to an age that saw a number of humane reforms and a new spirit of inclusiveness (the abolition of the slave trade and Catholic emancipation, for example). The prioritizing of humor over wit may have been the single most significant change in the new climate of comedy. It was a much-contested topic.

R. H. Horne, in his essay on Dickens in *A New Spirit of the Age* (1844), claimed Dickens's works

> furnish a constant commentary on the distinction between wit and humour; for of sheer wit, either in remark or repartee, there is scarcely an instance in any of his volumes, while of humour there is a fullness and gusto in every page, which would be searched for in vain to such an extent, among other authors. (Hollington 1: 98)

However, Horne's famous *Spirit of the Age* precursor, William Hazlitt, had in 1819 defined wit more broadly in terms that could well include Dickens's distinctive comic gifts: "the favourite employment of wit is to add littleness to littleness, and heap contempt on insignificance [. . .] or if it ever affects to aggrandise, and use the language of hyperbole, it is only to betray into derision by a fatal comparison" (n.p.). Hazlitt instances the use of mock heroics as a means of making this "fatal comparison," and of course, Dickens exploits that witty strategy to the full in the early part of Pickwick. So Horne, a quarter of a century later, seems to be narrowing the definition of wit to something similar to a sharp repartee and correspondingly enlarging the definition of humor's scope.

The distinction between wit and humor is elaborated in an 1871 comparison of Dickens and Thackeray:

> He [Dickens] will make a few generations to come laugh. Not as the great and terrible wits make the men and women of the ages which come after them laugh, [. . .] but because his humour is so rich, so thorough, so varied, and so original that it must always appeal to the liking for oddities and eccentricities inherent in human nature, which increases with the pace of life, and is felt more and more as a relief to its growing weariness. There is humour which does not exactly amuse, though it receive the utmost recognition. There is humour which simply amuses, which is merely quite delightful. Mr Dickens had extraordinary humour of the latter sort. He may have intended sometimes to be savagely satirical, but could not keep from caricature, and with exaggeration savageness, even severity, is done away. He was infinitely droll and various in his mirthful moods, and the animal spirits which overflow through all his earlier writings abounded up to the latest of them. (*Dublin Review* qtd. in Collins 552)

The remarks about humor adjusting itself to the changing pace of life are interesting. If I have understood it right, what the writer sees as Dickens's distinctive sense of humor, his eye for human eccentricities, becomes more valuable as the pace of life quickens and pressures increase, and precludes the opportunities for leisurely observation of little oddities of behavior and looks. Boz, in *Sketches* and *Pickwick*, is one of the first to catch on to that—not just nostalgia for a fading culture but also marrying that fading culture with the energies of the modernizing world. That would find an echo in the opening to *Pickwick* chapter 10, where the reader is tempted into a search for the obsolescent coaching inns of old London "in the obscurer quarters of the town" where some have escaped the "rage for public improvement." "Great, rambling, queer old places they are," rich in local color and legends. This corresponds to that "liking for oddities and eccentricities inherent in human nature" that the reviewer identified as so distinctive in Dickens's humor, and so it should be no surprise that the highly idiosyncratic Sam Weller, the source of so much of the human comedy in *Pickwick*, should be first discovered in one of these eccentric, out-of-the-way localities. In a sense, Sam becomes the distillation of Dickens's new humor: genial, sparky, irreverent, imaginative, and playful with bizarre metaphors—a true original. And with Sam nursed into full prominence, Dickens's success is assured.

Horne's point was that just as Dickens's comedy seemed to introduce a new kind of geniality in contrast to older and more savage traditions, so it drew away from abrasive wit. And this shift away from those harsher comic traditions applied also to Dickens's early satire. As T. H. Lister remarked in 1838, "[t]here is no misanthropy in his satire" (Collins 72). It was Carlyle who elevated the status of humor as part of a humane sensibility. "True humour," he wrote in his 1827 essay on Jean Paul Richter, "springs not more from the head than from the heart; it is not contempt, its essence is love; it issues not in laughter, but in still smiles, which lie far deeper" (1:14). He invoked the term "inverse sublimity," used by Richter, to argue that true humor exalts "into our affections what is below us, while sublimity draws down into our affections what is above us" (14). This benign faculty is marked by "warm, tender fellow-feeling with all forms of existence" (14), and for him the "purest of all humorists" was Cervantes, "so gentle and genial, so full, yet so ethereal" (15). Carlyle's notion of humor is yet another kind of disengagement from the savage, masculine humor of Hogarth and the Regency caricaturists: it is gentle, genial, and humane, more fitted to the changing culture and developing domestic ideology of early Victorian England. It corresponds to his drive, endorsed by Dickens, to expel cynical dandyism and its pernicious values from Victorian culture. Again, *Pickwick Papers* arrives as the perfect fictional expression of this transition from Regency to early Victorian laughter; it begins in older traditions of wit, with elaborate and sustained mock heroics, "heaping contempt on insignificance," in Hazlitt's terms. Its humor in the opening, both in its robust ironic manner, its characterizations and its stock comic antics belong to the older traditions that inspired the Chapman, Hall, and Seymour project. But as it develops, it becomes something else: instead of laughing month after month at Pickwick's pompous idiocies, he becomes gradually "exalted into our affections," and Boz's manner of treating him becomes more "gentle and genial," matching the spirit of Carlyle's Cervantes. Indeed, once Sam Weller joined Pickwick, critics acclaimed the partnership as the glorious English version of Quixote and Sancho Panza. The *Metropolitan Magazine* was one of the first (in January 1837) of the journals to make the point:

> The world never saw drollery and wit offered to them before in a form so singular. The renowned Mr Pickwick is, himself, the legitimate successor to Don Quixote; indeed, he is the cockney Quixote of the nineteenth century, and instead of armour of iron, he is encased in a good coating of aldemanic fur, and instead of spear and sword, has his own powers of declamation with which to go forth to do fearful battle upon the swindler, the wrong-doer, and the oppressor of the innocent. (Collins 31)

This was echoed in the following year in T. H. Lister's comments in the *Edinburgh Review*, seeing in Pickwick and Sam "the modern Quixote and Sancho of Cockaigne" (Collins 75). And in 1841, another of Dickens's favorite writers, Washington Irving (whose own writings palpably influenced scenes in *Pickwick*), told Dickens in a letter that he had been rereading *Pickwick* and commented that "Old Pickwick is the Quixote of commonplace life, and as with the Don, we begin by laughing at him and end by loving him" (*Letters* 2: 269n1). Humor, as opposed to wit, encourages affectionate laughter and can teach compassion as much as incite ridicule: "That man [Dickens] is carrying out Carlyle's work more emphatically than any," wrote Caroline Fox in 1841 reflecting on what Dickens had achieved up to and including *The Old Curiosity Shop*. "[H]e forces the sympathies of all into unwonted channels, and teaches us that Punch and Judy men, beggar children, and daft old men are also of our species" (Collins 6).

* * *

Twelve years after completing *Pickwick*, in April 1849, Dickens wrote to a friend "[t]he world would not take another Pickwick from me, now; but we can be cheerful and merry, I hope, notwithstanding, and with a little more purpose in us" (*Letters* 5: 527). In 1836–37, he had acutely recognized what veins of humor to work for a readership used to Regency comedy and yet sensing the change of cultural climate. Three years after completing *Pickwick*, in one odd lapse of judgment, he had tried, rather lamely, to revive Mr. Pickwick and Sam in the pages of *Master Humphrey's Clock*. By this time, they were already heritage waxworks, and Dickens had a hard time reanimating them while at the same time preserving their identities. In 1847, the Cheap Edition of *Pickwick* was published with illustrations by John Gilbert, which are eloquent evidence of the ways in which tastes had changed.

By 1849, even the modified Pickwickian humor, the more genial sympathetic comedy of the latter part of the book, seemed unrevivable. Cheerfulness *with* earnestness was the new taste, a delayed echo from Carlyle's accolade on Richter's characteristic humor—"consistent with utmost earnestness, or rather, inconsistent with the want of it" ("Richter Again" 43). The *Pickwick* moment had well and truly passed. In April 1849, when he wrote that letter, Dickens had just started that captivating and somewhat disappointing novel *David Copperfield*, in which he tries to fuse merriment and purpose in prioritizing that pious construct the disciplined heart. But really, as I have tried to show, the *Pickwick* moment was passing even as he was writing the *Papers* from month to month in the mid-1830s: he relinquished the prototype Nimrod Club hero and the archly ironic, witty narrative manner of the spring and early summer 1836 numbers in favor of exploring a modified comic mode. He steered his vehicle from wit to humor. Dickens's shrewd navigation month after month through this period of cultural transition is somewhat masked nowadays by seeing the project as *Pickwick* the single volume, *Pickwick* "the novel."

We are familiar with that well-marketed product "the book of the film"; the *Pickwick Papers* we know is the book of the serial. The single-entity *Pickwick Papers* never really existed: its materialization as a single block of pages between hard covers in 1837 was a clever illusion by the publishers, bestowing apparent formal coherence on something rather different—a rambling entertainment in installments whose narrative time had shrewdly kept pace with the changing seasons and whose larger agenda had been adjusting to cultural climate change across a year and half—and then stopped. As a long-term experiment in humor, as a means of gauging what ingredients and what narrative manner would make people laugh in 1836 and 1837, it was invaluable. This protracted experiment of monthly one-man shows eventually secured Dickens his audience of fellow laughers and determined the distinctive character of his early comedy.

BIBLIOGRAPHY

Bergson, Henri. *Laughter.* Trans. C. Brereton. London, 1911.
Carlyle, Thomas. "Jean Paul Friedrich Richter." 1827. *Critical and Miscellaneous Essays.* Vol. 1. London, 1872. 1–21.
———. "Jean Paul Friedrich Richter Again." 1830. *Critical and Miscellaneous Essays.* Vol. 3. London, 1872. 1–59.
Collins, Philip. *Charles Dickens: The Critical Heritage.* London, 1971.
Dickens, Charles. *The Letters of Charles Dickens.* Ed. Madeline House, Graham Storey et al. 12 vols. Oxford, 1965–2002. Pilgrim Edition.
———. *Pickwick Papers.* Ed. Malcolm Andrews. London, 1998. Everyman's Library Series.
Ford, George. *Dickens and His Readers.* New York, 1965.
Gazette 10 Sept. 1836: 584.
Hazlitt, William. "On Wit and Humour." *Lectures on the English Comic Writers.* London, 1819. Lecture 1.
Hollington, Michael, ed. *Charles Dickens: Critical Assessments.* 4 vols. Mountfield, 1995.
Literary Gazette 9 July 1836: 442.
Pritchett, V. S. "The Humour of Charles Dickens." *The Listener* 3 June 1954: 970.
"Remonstrance with Dickens." *Blackwood's Magazine* 81 (Jan.–June 1857): 491.
Slater, Michael, ed. *Dickens' Journalism.* 4 vols. London, 1994–2000.
Thackeray, W. M. "John Leech's *Pictures of Life and Character.*" *Quarterly Review* 191 (Dec. 1854): 75–86.
Waugh, Arthur. "The Birth of 'Pickwick.'" *The Dickensian* 32 (Dec. 1935): 8.
Wordsworth, William. "Essay, Supplementary to the Preface." 1815. *The Poetical Works of William Wordsworth.* Ed. Ernest de Selincourt. 2nd ed. Vol. 2. Oxford, 1952. 409–30.

The Chimes and the Rhythm of Life

Matthias Bauer
Eberhard Karls Universität Tübingen

One of the quasi-mythical stories that contributed to Dickens's creative imagination is the account of Dick Whittington, the apprentice boy who became Lord Mayor of London. Based on historical fact,[1] it appears to have been particularly attractive to Dickens not just because it is about the legendary social rise of a boy called "Dick" but also because, according to folklore, the fortune of Dick Whittington was made by his listening to the voice of the bells of St. Mary-le-Bow, which made him return to London after initial disappointment, as they sang out to him, "Turn again, Whittington, / Once Lord Mayor of London!"[2] Dickens, for example, has Dick Swiveller in *The Old Curiosity Shop* hope that "Perhaps the bells might strike up 'Turn again, Swiveller, Lord Mayor of London.' Whittington's name was Dick" (*OCS* 373). In *Barnaby Rudge*, the narrator, on the occasion of Joe Willet's leaving London, points out that

> there were no voices in the bells to bid him turn. Since the time of noble Whittington, fair flower of merchants, bells have come to have less sympathy with humankind. They only ring for money and on state occasions. Wanderers have increased in number; ships leave the Thames for distant regions, carrying from stem to stern no other cargo; the bells are silent; they ring out no entreaties or regrets; they are used to it and have grown worldly. (*BR* 237)

The narrator regrets the disenchantment of the modern world, that is, the disappearance of a kind of providence that magically avails itself of the musical and rhythmical devices provided by the churches in order to convey its message. But in spite of the sense of loss expressed in this comment, the voice of the bells remains central to Dickens's notion of time, change, and life. He turns it from a folk legend to a motif that indicates key qualities of literary art.

Dickens shows us a world in constant metamorphosis, where everything is marked by transformation, including the structures of society, the realm of material things, and the lives of human beings. Because change is inevitable—and whenever someone, such as Miss Havisham in *Great Expectations*, tries to stop its course, it asserts itself all the more forcibly—Dickens repeatedly raises the questions: Can it be influenced for the better? And what such an improvement—or the prevention of a change for the worse—may mean? In this respect, the temporal arts play a decisive role, for their very nature is change. To Dickens, the art of prose is temporal in the sense of being musical and rhythmical; this is why it may serve to represent life and society and why it is suited to influence the nature of their changes. In order to explore this, I focus on a very limited example, which is nevertheless quite instructive, for it presents a poetics of rhythm as one of the foremost instruments at the disposal of a writer seeking to influence change.[3] It does so by connecting rhythm as a subject matter to rhythm as a feature of style.

The story selected, which is to make us see the key function of rhythm as a link between verbal art and the representation of life and society, is Dickens's second Christmas Book, *The Chimes*, published in 1844. It is immediately relevant to the topic of this volume, for the notion of change is central to its idea—an idea which is part and parcel of its verbal realization. *The Chimes* is a story in which, on the one hand, scathing and bitter social satire prevails. There is a set of people apparently in charge of public and private affairs that comprises self-styled Friends and Fathers of the poor (Sir Joseph Bowley, MP), administrators and Justices who wish to show their energy and competence by "Putting Down" whatever is unpleasant (Mr. Alderman Cute) and scientific-minded but inhuman political economists and social reformers (Mr. Filer). These caricatures are contrasted with the protagonist of the story, Toby Veck, called Trotty, a ticket porter standing all day outside a church door waiting for a job, as well as with his daughter Meg, her fiancé Richard, and a poor laborer (Will Fern) and his young niece. The representatives of the ruling classes are shown to intervene, with disastrous results, in the lives of the poor. As Will Fern puts it,

But when work won't maintain me like a human creetur; when my living is so bad, that I am Hungry, out of doors and in; when I see a whole working life begin that way, go on that way, and end that way, without a chance or change; then I say to the gentlefolks "Keep away from me! Let my cottage be." (*TC* 189)[4]

"Chance or change," or rather "without a chance or change" are key words of the story. They indicate, as in a formula, the demand for reform presented in this Christmas Book in a most unconciliatory manner.[5]

But, on the other hand, there is, as Alexander Welsh puts it, "something more profound than the satire" (8). This can be seen in the very speech just quoted, for Will Fern's "Keep away from me! Let my cottage be" is, strangely enough, a rhyming couplet whose lines, by their parallel sound-structure and 5–5 syllable length, evoke the metrical patterns of hymns.[6] The formula "chance or change" itself points to the musicality of poetry, for it is a quotation from James Beattie's *The Minstrel* of 1771 (74), one of the most popular poems of the late eighteenth and early nineteenth centuries.[7] The transcendence of satire is suggested from the beginning by the fact that Trotty Veck is not actually the protagonist of the story but the church bells are—or, rather, the bells in their remarkable affinity with Trotty. The story is named after them. Trotty's life is connected with the ringing of the bells in a variety of interrelated ways from the physiological and psychological to the allegorical as well as supernatural (*The Chimes,* after all, is called "A Goblin Story"): "there were points of resemblance between themselves and him" (*TC* 155). The bells are "invested" by him with "a strange and solemn character" (*TC* 156), with "liking" and "love," and, due to their "deep strong melody," with "a species of awe" (*TC* 156). The bells speak to him, as we see (or rather hear) in the very first of the four sections or "Quarters" into which the story is divided:

"[. . .] Why bless you, my dear," said Toby, [. . .] "how often have I heard them bells say, 'Toby Veck, Toby Veck, keep a good heart, Toby! Toby Veck, Toby Veck, keep a good heart, Toby!' A million times? More!"
"Well, I never!" cried Meg.
She had, though—over and over again. For it was Toby's constant topic.
"When things is very bad," said Trotty; "very bad indeed, I mean; almost at the worst; then it's 'Toby Veck, Toby Veck, job coming soon, Toby! Toby Veck, Toby Veck, job coming soon, Toby!' That way."
(*TC* 161–62)

The sound of the bells is both rhythmically and melodiously translated into human speech[8]:

```
Toby Veck, Toby Veck, keep a good heart, Toby!
 B  o  B [o] B  o  B [o] B    -o=     B [o] B  o

 Toby  Veck, Toby  Veck,  keep a good heart, Toby!
 [əʊ]   [e]  [əʊ]   [e]   [i:] ([ʊ])  [ɑ:]   [əʊ]
 [əʊ][ɪ][e]  [əʊ][ɪ][e]   [i:][ə][ʊ]  [ɑ:]   [əʊ][ɪ]
```

The bell notes appear melodiously as vowel sounds in a change of [əʊ] and [e], as well as [i:] and [ɑ]; the voice of the bells is thus founded on an alteration of back and front vowels (back/front// back/front// front/back// back/front); we note that this is not a monotonous alternation but that it is rhythmically enlivened by the inversion of the back/front sequence in "keep [. . .] heart"; if the offbeat vowels are included, we get additional (short) [ɪ] and [ʊ] (another front/back pair) and perhaps a schwa in "a," that is, a peal of between four and seven bells in all.[9] Dickens, although imitating the different bell notes and their ups and downs, does not represent a systematic, full peal as in the art of change ringing (made popular in English literature by Dorothy Sayers's *The Nine Tailors*), which "is to work out mathematical permutations and combinations" (Sayers 19–20). The attempt at such a representation can be seen in Dante Gabriel Rossetti's poem "Chimes," where by the repetition and permutation of identical words such a mathematical peal is imitated.[10]

Toby Veck's recognition of verbal messages in the melody and rhythm of the bells has its basis in his own existence. And this is not only because his usual place of abode is a niche of an ancient church but because his life is intricately connected with other rhythms, such as the rhythm of the weather. Toby's own rhythm fits in well here, for whenever he has a message to deliver, he moves in his own particular and peculiar trot, from which he derives his nickname:

> Wet weather was the worst: the cold, damp, clammy wet, that wrapped him up like a moist great-coat: the only kind of great-coat Toby owned, or could have added to his comfort by dispensing with. Wet days, when the rain came slowly, thickly, obstinately down; when the street's throat, like his own, was choked with mist; when smoking umbrellas passed and repassed, spinning round and round like so many teetotums, as they knocked against each other on the crowded footway, throwing off a

little whirlpool of uncomfortable sprinklings; when gutters brawled and waterspouts were full and noisy; when the wet from the projecting stones and ledges of the church fell drip, drip, drip, on Toby, making the wisp of straw on which he stood mere mud in no time; those were the days that tried him. [. . .] But coming out, a minute afterwards, to warm himself by exercise: and trotting up and down some dozen times: he would brighten even then, and go back more brightly to his niche.

They called him Trotty from his pace, which meant speed if it didn't make it. He could have walked faster perhaps; most likely; but rob him of his trot, and Toby would have taken to his bed and died. (*TC* 153)

The rhythmical nature of the passage is obvious. It is not only established by the rhetorical figure of anaphora, which is a favorite of Dickens's and, of course, an eminently rhythmical device as it serves to structure a passage through the repetition of an identical unit at the beginning of each clause. We find it in "Wet weather" and "Wet days," as well as in "when the rain," "when the street's throat," "when smoking umbrellas," "when gutters brawled," and "when the wet." Dickens sometimes uses anaphora to point up empty or even threatening rhetoric,[11] but it may also contribute to a specific kind of *energeia* that serves to convey the presence of something alive. This is the case here, for it shows the inclement weather being part of Toby's natural urban world in which his trot signals his particular rhythm of life. The clashing of beats, emphasized by alliteration, "wet weather was the worst; the cold, damp, clammy wet," may almost bring Toby's trot to a stop, but in fact, it never does.

```
wet weather    was the worst;
 B   B  o  [o]  B   o  B
the cold, damp, clammy wet
 o   B [o] B [o]  B   o  B
```

Although marked by repetition, the rhythm is never monotonous; similarly, the alliteration of the consonants [w], [k] is enlivened by the variation of vowel sounds. The hurtful weather will be integrated into the beats of Toby's movement, his rhythm. For to Toby, who stands in the church door most of the day, being is movement, as can also be seen and heard in a leitmotif of his, that is, his favorite phrase, "Here we are and here we go" (first used *TC* 191).

```
Here we are   and here we go!
 B    o B [o]o   B    o  B
```

The rhythm reflects Toby Veck's peculiar trot, which combines a regular alternation of beat and offbeat with variation, as the whole phrase, due to the slight pause after "are," can be grouped into a B–o–B and an o–B–o–B section, the latter being a repetition of the former and marked by an anacrusis supporting the rhythm. This combination of repetition and variation is actually the *Oxford English Dictionary*'s definition of the expression "to ring the changes"[12]—again the topical keyword not just of this volume but also of *The Chimes*. Dickens contrasts a world, a system, and a language "without a chance or change," with a world marked by repetition and variation, that is, by rhythm or "change."

This can be seen more clearly when considering the overall structure of the story, which is marked by the interruption of Toby's rhythm by the three gentlemen mentioned earlier. Toward the end of the first quarter, the door of the house upon whose steps Toby Veck, accompanied by his daughter and her fiancé, has eaten his dinner, opens, and out comes a man (Alderman Cute) who is also, like Trotty, characterized by his pace ("that peculiar compromise between a walk and a jog-trot—with which a gentleman upon the smooth down-hill of life [. . .] *may* come out of his house" [*TC* 165]) and by a rhythm clearly marked by identical repetition: "'What's the matter, what's the matter!' said the gentleman [. . .]. 'What's the matter! What's the matter!'" (*TC* 165). The three gentlemen and this lifeless rhythm literally interrupt the life processes of Toby and his circle: they sacrilegiously prevent Toby from eating his meal, and by facetiously stupid comments make, or try to make, Richard think twice about his proposed marriage. Taking into account that it is the last day of the year, the gentlemen can be seen to interrupt not only the cycle of the day (daily nourishment) and the cycle of life (marriage and getting children) but also the cycle of yearly renewal (there will not be any happy new year for Toby) and the rhythm of a workman's life.[13] One of the gentlemen is expressly shown to lack "proportion"—"This gentleman had a very red face, as if an undue proportion of the blood in his body were squeezed up in his head" (*TC* 166)—a term clearly suggesting that Dickens wished to stress that something is rhythmically wrong.

The locus classicus for this concept is Shakespeare's *Richard II*:

> Ha, ha, keep time! How sour sweet music is
> When time is broke, and no proportion kept!
> So is it in the music of men's lives. (5.5.42–44)

The Chimes *and the Rhythm of Life* 117

The fact that the music of Toby Veck's life is disrupted is further emphasized by the interruption and change in the sound and rhythm of the chimes, which are caused by the gentlemen's intervention:

> "Born bad. No business here!"
> The Chimes came clashing in upon him as he said the words. Full, loud, and sounding—but with no encouragement. No, not a drop.
> "The tune's changed," cried the old man, as he listened. "There's not a word of all that fancy in it. Why should there be? I have no business with the New Year nor with the old one neither. Let me die!"
> Still the Bells, pealing forth their changes, made the very air spin. (*TC* 174)

There is our word again, *change*, but now it does not refer to the "chance or change" lacking because of the failure of those who believe themselves in control. Nor does it primarily refer to the changes of the bells that are in keeping with the natural rhythm of life. To be exact, the bells are still "pealing forth their changes," but the changes are changed for the worse. Thus we immediately recognize the changed rhythmical pattern of the chimes. The clashing beats, enhanced by alliteration, in Toby's self-accusation "Born bad. No business here"—

```
Born bad. No business here.
B    B [o]B  B    o    B
```

—are indeed unheard of up to this point in Dickens's story, especially because the central stress of the line is on the annihilating "No." And when the beats go on, even though they assume a "change" or a "trot," this will be a different, far more repetitive, regular, and monotonous one than before, as we see and hear in the following passage:

```
Put 'em down,  Put 'em down!
B   o    B  [o] B   o    B  [o]
Good old Times,  Good old Times!
B    o   B   [o] B    o   B
Facts and Figures, Facts and Figures!
B    o   B    o    B    o   B    o
Put 'em down,  Put 'em down!
B   o    B  [o] B   o    B
(TC  174)
```

In "Put 'em down," the melody descends from [ʊ] via [ə] to [aʊ]; there is no real progress, but the rhythm, as it were, collapses back on itself. In fact, as we learn a few pages later, now Toby's "trot went to that measure, and would fit itself to nothing else" (*TC* 178). But there is something else. We might be irritated by the words "Good old Times, Good old Times!" heard by Toby in the bells, especially when we remember the narrator's mournful reflection on the disappearance of the bells' sympathy with humankind in *Barnaby Rudge*. The evocation of "Good old Times" in *The Chimes* contributes to the change for the worse, for they take up the exclamations of the red-faced, disproportioned gentleman (the Friend and Father, Sir Joseph Bowley) Toby had heard when his dinner was interrupted. Slater and others have explored the satire of the "Young England" movement with its longing for the restoration of a feudal system; Douglas-Fairhurst, in his edition of *The Chimes* (427–28), quotes lines from Lord John Manners's *England's Trust* about the time when "The greatest owned connexion with the least; / From rank to rank the generous feeling ran, / And linked society as man to man." Why does *The Chimes* not subscribe to this?[14] Is not Toby Veck expressly shown (by another figure of sound) as a *vecchio*, an old man connected to the memories of the past? In *The Chimes*, we are, after all, presented with harmony lost or interrupted, with the link between human beings dissevered and finally reestablished. The answer has to do with what to me seems the central issue in *The Chimes*, namely, movement in time, that is, rhythm.

It is brought home to the reader in what turns out to be Toby's dream; his nightly visit to the church tower and the bells. Toby is magically drawn up to the top of the tower by the sound of the bells, whose "energy was dreadful" (*TC* 196). They mark Toby's despair and subconscious desire to kill himself. Within what—as we are later suggested to believe—is a dream, Toby falls into a swoon when he has reached the bells and wakes up again to see a "Goblin Sight" (*TC* 201), the spirits of the bells:

> He saw them, of all aspects and all shapes. He saw them ugly, handsome, crippled, exquisitely formed. He saw them young, he saw them old, he saw them kind, he saw them cruel, he saw them merry, he saw them grim; he saw them dance, and heard them sing; he saw them tear their hair, and heard them howl. He saw the air thick with them. He saw them come and go, incessantly. He saw them riding downward, soaring upward, sailing off afar, perching near at hand, all restless and all violently active. (*TC* 201–02)

```
He saw them young, he saw them old,
 o  B    o   B      o  B   o  B
he saw them kind, he saw them cruel,
 o  B    o   B     o  B   o  B[o]
```

This is the overly regular alternation of beats and offbeats (enhanced by anaphora and alliteration) which has become the rhythm of the chimes after the change, but in contrast to the earlier groups of three syllables (BoB–BoB), the swarming, the movement, the activity which are the issue now are audibly represented, even made felt, by the group of four syllables (oBoB–oBoB), which are by means of semantic choices (the contrasting pairs young/old, kind/cruel, etc.) further grouped into units of eight syllables or four beats. The spirits of the bells are shown and heard to be the energy of life itself, and what the narrator says a little later about Toby's feeling "cut off from all good people" (*TC* 203) applies to the appearance of the spirits as well: they are perceived as "a bodily sensation" (*TC* 203), that is, similar to and as a rhythm.

In this context, the Goblin of the Bell tells Toby why a longing for the past is wrong: "millions uncountable, have suffered, lived, and died: to point the way Before him" (*TC* 204). This advancement, the "progress onward" to the goal of "greater worth [. . .] greater happiness [. . .] better life" is something envisioned at the transcendent moment "when Time and He [that is, man] began" (*TC* 204). It is thus eschatological or apocalyptic in dimension, and the longing for the past is an interruption that not only must be expiated like a sin (this is what Toby has to do for his doing the bells "wrong in words," a phrase echoing the communion service in the Book of Common Prayer)[15] but will also bring about an even "fiercer and [. . .] wilder" (*TC* 205) movement into the future. It is the negation of past suffering, the loss of a meaningful continuum and rhythmical progress and the lack of trust and hope (*TC* 250). In a vision not unlike Scrooge's in *A Christmas Carol*, Toby Veck is made to see the fatal outcome of that interruption: his own suicide and the misery of his child, who will be desperate enough to kill her baby,[16] a change ("Ah! Changed. Changed. The light of the clear eye, how dimmed. The bloom, how faded from the cheek" [*TC* 208]) that, in an allusion to the book of Job, means death.[17]

The ambivalence of change is thus the ambivalence of death itself. To Dickens, the right kind of living in time will make all the difference. The denial of time will bring about self-annihilation,[18] as can be seen in the last words of the usurer Ralph in *Nicholas Nickleby*:

"At any hour," replied Ralph fiercely. "In the afternoon, tell them. At any hour, at any minute. All times will be alike to me."
[. . .]
The sound of a deep bell came along the wind. One.
"Lie on!" cried the usurer, "with your iron tongue! Ring merrily for births that make expectants writhe, and for marriages that are made in hell, and toll ruefully for the dead whose shoes are worn already! Call men to prayers who are godly because not found out, and ring chimes for the coming in of every year that brings this cursed world nearer to its end. No bell or book for me! Throw me on a dunghill, and let me rot there, to infect the air!" (*NN* 806)

Whereas in *Nickleby*, the attitude that denies time is a source of infection and thus threatens the entire society, in *A Christmas Carol*, the narrator points out that the striking of death will be ineffectual if it has been preceded by actual, pulsating life:

> It is not that the hand is heavy and will fall down when released; it is not that the heart and pulse are still; but that the hand WAS open, generous, and true; the heart brave, warm, and tender; and the pulse a man's. Strike, Shadow, strike! And see his good deeds springing from the wound, to sow the world with life immortal! (*CC* 118)

This is an effect to which the literary artist contributes. By showing the rhythm of the chimes to be closely connected to the rhythm of life itself, Dickens evokes the age-old equation of the human pulse and musical rhythm. Isidore of Seville, for example, in the chapter on music in his seventeenth-century encyclopedic *Etymologies* points out that "however we speak, or however we are moved by the internal pulsing of our veins—these things are demonstrably linked, through their musical rhythms, to the power of harmony."[19] In fact, this observation goes back to the very beginnings of medical research on the human pulse, that is, to the Alexandrian anatomist Herophilos of Chalcedon (fl. ca. 280 BCE), who was also a musical theorist. "The essential phenomenon in the pulse, according to Herophilos, is rhythm, as in music."[20] The history of reflecting on the identity of the pulse and musical rhythm includes the seventeenth-century physician Samuel Hafenreffer, who regarded the pulse as "the sweetest melody of human life" or Johann Joachim Quantz, the flute teacher of Frederick the Great, who advocated the pulse as a natural metronome.[21] Even closer to *The Chimes*, the meaning of *pulsus* as the ringing of bells establishes the close connection of tolling bells, pulsating blood, and musical rhythm. As John Donne puts it in his Meditation 18,

> At inde, Mortuus es, Sonitu celeri, pulsuque agitato. *The bell rings out, and tells me in him, that I am dead.* [. . .] The *Bell* rings out; the *pulse* thereof is changed; the *tolling* was a *faint*, and *intermitting pulse*, upon one side; this *stronger*, and argues *more* and *better life*. (91)

As Alexander Welsh notes, Dickens ironically presents the social reality of his time (e.g., the sad fact of child murder) only as a dream, whereas the reality of the story is a dreamlike happy ending, a reunion of Toby, his family, and his friends (10). Toby has learned to be more mindful of the rhythm of his life, and this is why, in the end, the sad change is changed once more and becomes an ex-change between human beings. This can be seen when the poor man, Will Fern, who has come to town in order to look for the deceased mother of his niece Lilian, finds her in the person of the shopkeeper, Mrs. Chickenstalker:

> The worthy dame, to his surprise, turned very pale and very red.
> "Not Lilian Fern whose mother died in Dorsetshire!" said she.
> Her uncle answered "Yes," and meeting hastily, they exchanged some hurried words together; of which the upshot was, that Mrs. Chickenstalker shook him by both hands; saluted Trotty on his cheek again, of her own free will; and took the child to her capacious breast.
> "Will Fern!" said Trotty, pulling on his right-hand muffler. "Not the friend you was hoping to find?" (*TC* 245)

Thus, finally the New Year is celebrated with a dance, and in order to make every reader notice that it is rhythm that this story is all about, this dance is accompanied not by a fiddler (as in *A Christmas Carol*) but by rhythmical, percussion instruments, by "[t]he Drum (who was a private friend of Toby's)"—the metonymy fits in well with the identification of rhythm and human life—as well as by "the marrow-bones and cleavers, and the bells; not *the* Bells, but a portable collection on a frame" (*TC* 243).

"Trotty [. . .] led off Mrs. Chickenstalker down the dance, and danced it in a step unknown before or since; founded on his own peculiar trot" (*TC* 245). This modulation of the overall rhythm to an individual trot is at the heart of Dickens's story. *The Chimes* is, in keeping with its satirical elements, moralistic, not just in its caricature of the self-righteous but also in its final appeal to its readers, who are told to "endeavour to correct, improve, and soften" (*TC* 245) the stern realities. But its genuine concern is not so much an appeal to do something but rather a peal, a rhythm that must be minded and that makes us part of an unbroken movement. The aim is "growing to time," which is promised to the addressee by the speaker of Shakespeare's Sonnet 18 and which is the transformation into the music of verbal art.

In this respect, the rhythmical patterns and sound patterns in Dickens's story are not just an example of iconicity—signs miming their meaning, in this case providing onomatopoeic correlatives to Toby's perception of the bells, for example—but they are the meaning itself. In the end, they are not signs at all but examples of the very life that the story presents to us as desirable.[22] The music and the dance at the end of the story are not a symbol of a better life but the better life itself, and the rhythm of the story is part of it. This can be seen from the way the rhythm is foregrounded again toward the end of the story:

> You never in all your life saw anything like Trotty after this. I don't care where you have lived or what you have seen; you never in all your life saw anything at all approaching him! He sat down in his chair and beat his knees and cried; he sat down in his chair and beat his knees and laughed; he sat down in his chair and beat his knees and laughed and cried together; he got out of his chair and hugged Meg; he got out of his chair and hugged Richard; he got out of his chair and hugged them both at once; he kept running up to Meg, and squeezing her fresh face between his hands and kissing it, going from her backwards not to lose sight of it, and running up again like a figure in a magic lantern; and whatever he did, he was constantly sitting himself down in his chair, and never stopping in it for one single moment; being— that's the truth—beside himself with joy. (*TC* 241–42)

Rhythmical repetition is enlivened by modulation, as we well notice when considering particular sections of this sequence; for example,

```
He sat down in his chair and beat his knees and cried;
-o-    B    -o-    B    o   B    o   B    o    B
he sat down in his chair and beat his knees and laughed;
-o-    B    -o-    B    o   B    o   B    o    B

he sat down in his chair and beat his knees and laughed
-o-    B    -o-    B    o   B    o   B    o    B
and cried together;
 o    B    oB   o
```

The double offbeat/beat ("anapaestic") is repeated and then followed by an alternating offbeat/beat rhythm; the semantic repetition/modulation (cried/laughed) again pointing to the rhythmical modulation and vice versa; the latter taking place when the asymmetrical two beat–three beat sequence is, after its first repetition, replaced with a two beat–two beat–three beat sequence. Dickens can here quite literally be seen as an agent of change, transformation being brought about by the presence and fascination of what is much more than a stylistic device.[23]

NOTES

1. Sir Richard Whittington, the late medieval Master of the Mercers' company and Lord Mayor of London, famously improved the sanity of the city and founded a charity still extant today. See <http://www.mercers.co.uk/living-tradition> and <http://www.mercers.co.uk/charitable-trusts> (21 Mar. 2012).
2. The traditional verse is reprinted at <http://en.wikipedia.org/wiki/ Richard_Whittington> (21 Mar. 2012).
3. This field has attracted surprisingly little attention in criticism. Perhaps Dickens still suffers from the prejudice expressed by Saintsbury, who, focusing on certain blank-verse elements in Dickens's prose, complains about "a certain poverty in rhythmical resources, a no doubt unconscious conviction that if you want to make prose harmonious you must 'dash and brew' it with the methods of verse itself" (382). Saintsbury seems completely oblivious of the variation of rhythmical structures and the uses to which they are put by Dickens. Baum (75–76) is similarly averse to verse structures obtruding themselves onto prose. Among the few contributions addressing the complex aural dimension of Dickens's prose are Honan and Ho Lai Ming.
4. *The Chimes* and *A Christmas Carol* are quoted from Slater's 1971 Penguin edition. This is to be preferred to other editions because Slater takes prose rhythm into account: "During the early 1840s Dickens was experimenting with a 'rhetorical' style of punctuation, based on speech-rhythms rather than on grammatical sense. This involved especially the lavish use of dashes, colons and semi-colons. [. . .] The present edition, which seeks to convey as fully as possible the distinctive flavour of these little stories as they were first published, reproduces the punctuation used in the original printing of each Book" (xxvii). Slater (*Charles Dickens* 230) points out that the aural dimension of *The Chimes* is evoked by the narrator, at the end, directly addressing the reader as "Listener."
5. On *The Chimes* as a topical satire, see Slater, "Carlyle and Jerrold into Dickens" and "Dickens's Tract for the Times." Kurata tries to find a comprehensive perspective on the exposure of social ills and the fantasy elements of the story.
6. An example is the melody of "Seelenbräutigam" by Adam Drese (1698), which was adapted to a number of English hymns; see www.ehymnbook.org (3 Jan. 2011). I am grateful to Inge Leimberg for this and other suggestions and references.

7   The second book of *The Minstrel* begins "Of chance or change, O, let no man complain, / Else shall he never, never cease to wail; / For from the imperial dome to where the swain / Rears the lone cottage in the silent dale, / All feel the' assault of Fortune's fickle gale; / [. . .]" (41). The combination of "chance or change" with the reference to the "cottage" clearly identifies Fern's speech as an allusion to *The Minstrel*. But whereas Beattie stresses the common subjection to fortune, Fern emphasizes the division of the rich and the poor. Wordsworth in his 1815 preface to *Poems* mentions *The Minstrel* as an example of "The Idyllum" (28).

8   In order to avoid assignations such as "iambic," which are inappropriate to prose rhythm (and, to a large extent, to English prosody in general), I have adopted Carper's and Attridge's system of indicating beats (B) and offbeats (o), with [o] denoting a silent offbeat (pause) and –o= a double offbeat with a slightly more pronounced emphasis on the second part. The system also avoids the problems (discussed, e.g., by Fowler, Hoover, and Pettersson) of relating metrical systems of poetry to prose rhythm.

9   The sounds [ɪ], [ʊ] and [ə] may be said to represent fainter strokes of the [iː], [e] and [əʊ] bells; alternatively [ə] and [əʊ] may represent different bells.

10 Cf. the first section of Rossetti's poem: "Honey-flowers to the honey-comb / And the honey-bee's from home. // A honey-comb and a honey-flower, / And the bee shall have his hour. // A honeyed heart for the honey-comb, / And the humming bee flies home. // A heavy heart in the honey-flower, / And the bee has had his hour" (239).

11 A well-known example is the beginning of *Hard Times* with its imitation of Mr. Gradgrind's manner and nature by means of the anaphoric repetition of "The emphasis was helped by the speaker's [. . .]" (*HT* 1). Another case in point is the "eloquence" of Mr. Chadband in *Bleak House*.

12 "ring" v.¹ 17. trans. "*to ring (the) changes*. a. To go through all the possible variations of a process; to repeat essentially the same word, statement, and so on, in various different ways. Also *to ring (the) chimes*."

13 Thus it is no coincidence that Richard is a blacksmith, a trade that—due to Handel's tune—to Dickens always goes together with the epithet "harmonious"; apart from Pip in *Great Expectations*, there is also, for example, Mr. Morfin's violoncello practice in ch. 58 of *Dombey and Son*.

14 Cf. Mrs. Skewton's ("Cleopatra's") false doting upon the Middle Ages in ch. 27 of *Dombey and Son*.

15 See the 1552 BCP at http://justus.anglican.org/resources/bcp/1552/Communion_1552.htm (21 Mar. 2012): "*And yf any of those be an open and notorious evyll lyver, so that the congregacion by hym is offended, or have done anye wronge to his neyghbours, by woord or deede: The Curate havinge knowledge thereof, shall call hym, and advertyse him, in anye wyse not to presume to the Lordes Table, untyll he have openly declared hymselfe to have truely repented, [. . .].*"

16 On the exchange and interplay of dream vision and reality in this respect and as a structural device in *The Chimes* as a whole, see Frenk (85–119, esp. 90).

17 Job 14:14: "If a man die, shall he live again? all the days of my appointed time will I wait, till my change come."

18 Christina Rossetti, in her poem "Dead Before Death," first published in *Goblin Market and Other Poems* (1862), presents such a death: "So lost till death shut-to the opened door, / So lost from chime to everlasting chime, / So cold and

lost for ever evermore" (ll. 12–14; p. 53). Dickens's Paul Dombey provides an additional perspective on the problem. This "old-fashioned" boy is frequently connected to time, especially by means of Dr. Blimber's clock, which speaks to him in a disturbing fashion: "Grave as an organ was the Doctor's speech; and when he ceased, the great clock in the hall seemed (to Paul at least) to take him up, and to go on saying, 'how, is, my, lit, tle, friend? how, is, my, lit, tle, friend?' over and over and over again." (*DS* 145; see also chapters 12 and 14). It seems as if Paul is overwhelmed by the task of having to live in time, and he dies accordingly.

19 Isidore, *The Etymologies* (III.xvi.3; III.xvii.3) in Lindsay's ed. of the original Latin: "Sed et quidquid loquimur, vel intrinsecus venarum pulsibus commovemur, per musicos rhythmos harmoniae virtutibus esse sociatum." Cf. III.xxii.6: "Strings (chorda) are so called from 'heart' (cor, gen. cordis) because the throbbing [pulsus] of the strings in the cithara is like the throbbing of the heart in the chest." Of course Dickens need not have read Isidore to be familiar with the analogy; Shakespeare's Sonnet 8, where lute-strings and heart-strings "Strike[s] each in each by mutual ordering" takes the link for granted.

20 See Klein, and in the same section "As Galen (K IX 464) reports: 'as the musicians establish their rhythms according to certain definite arrangements of time-periods, comparing arsis and thesis with one another, i.e. the upward and downward beat, so Herophilos supposed that the dilation of the artery corresponds to arsis and its contraction to thesis.'"

21 See Hahn and Kümmel.

22 The fact that the story seems to have been inspired by the bells of Genua (see Slater, *Charles Dickens* 229) gives an added twist to the notion of endowing the bells with a rhythmical voice that points out living (with)in time.

23 I would like to thank the organizers, Lena Steveker and Joachim Frenk, as well as the participants of the Saarbrücken conference on "Dickens as an Agent of Change" for the splendid event and their feedback to my talk, which has also profited from the stimulating discussion at the informal meeting of the *Connotations* Society at Münster in December 2010.

BIBLIOGRAPHY

Baum, Paull Franklin. *The Other Harmony of Prose: An Essay on English Prose Rhythm*. Durham, NC, 1952.

Beattie, James. *The Minstrel; or, The Progress of Genius and Other Poems*. London, 1823.

Carper, Thomas, and Derek Attridge. *Meter and Meaning: An Introduction to Rhythm in Poetry*. New York, 2003.

Dickens, Charles. *Nicholas Nickleby*. Oxford, 1950. The Oxford Illustrated Dickens.

———. *Dombey and Son*. Oxford, 1950. The Oxford Illustrated Dickens.

———. *The Old Curiosity Shop*. Oxford, 1951. The Oxford Illustrated Dickens.

———. *Barnaby Rudge*. Oxford, 1954. The Oxford Illustrated Dickens.
———. *Hard Times*. Oxford, 1955. The Oxford Illustrated Dickens.
———. *The Christmas Books*. Ed. Michael Slater. Vol. 1. *A Christmas Carol/ The Chimes*. Harmondsworth, 1971.
———. *A Christmas Carol and Other Christmas Books*. Ed. Robert Douglas-Fairhurst. Oxford, 2006.
Donne, John. *Devotions upon Emergent Occasions*. Ed. Anthony Raspa. New York, 1987.
Fowler, Roger. "'Prose Rhythm' and Metre." *Essays on Language and Style: Linguistic and Literary Approaches to Literary Style*. Ed. Fowler. London, 1966. 82–99.
Frenk, Joachim. *"Myriads of Fantastic Forms": Formen und Funktionen des Phantastischen in englischen Sozialmärchen des 19. Jahrhunderts*. Frankfurt, 1998.
Hahn, Susanne. "Puls." *Enzyklopädie Medizingeschichte*. Ed. Werner E. Gerabek, Bernhard D. Haage, Gundolf Keil and Wolfgang Wegner. Berlin, 2005. 1202–03.
Ho Lai Ming, Tammy. "Reading Aloud and Charles Dickens's Aural Iconic Prose Style." *Insistent Images*. Ed. Elżbieta Tarakowska, Christina Ljungberg and Olga Fischer. Amsterdam, 2007. 73–89. Iconicity in Language and Literature 5.
Honan, Park. "Metrical Prose in Dickens." *The Victorian Newsletter* 28 (Fall 1965): 1–3.
Hoover, Regina M. "Prose Rhythm: A Theory of Proportional Distribution." *College Composition and Communication* 24.5 (1973): 366–74.
Isidore of Seville. *Etymologiarum sive originum libri XX*. Ed. W. M. Lindsay. 2 vols. Oxford, 1911.
———. *The Etymologies*. Trans., with introd. and notes by Stephen A. Barney, W. J. Lewis, J. A. Beach and Oliver Berghof. Cambridge, 2006.
Klein, Joan Echtenkamp. "Alexandrian Medicine." *Claude Moore Health Sciences Library*. U of Virginia, 2009. Web. 21 Mar. 2012. <http://www.hsl.virginia.edu/historical/artifacts/antiqua/alexandrian.cfm>.
Kümmel, Werner F. "'Die süßeste Melodie des Lebens': Historische Beziehungen von Herzschlag, Puls und Musik." *Herz: Das menschliche Herz—Der herzliche Mensch*. Ed. Susanne Hahn. Dresden, 1995. 11–30.
Kurata, Marilyn J. "Fantasy and Realism: A Defense of *The Chimes*." *Dickens Studies Annual* 13 (1984): 19–34.
Pettersson, Thore. "Prose and Poetry." *Studia Linguistica* 36.1 (1982): 64–87.
"ring." *Oxford English Dictionary*. Web. 10 Feb. 2014. <http://www.oed.com>.
Rossetti, Christina. *The Complete Poems*. Ed. R. W. Crump and Betty S. Flowers. Harmondsworth, 2001.
Rossetti, Dante Gabriel. *Poems*. Ed. Oswald Doughty. London, 1957.

Saintsbury, George. *A History of English Prose Rhythm*. London, 1912.
Sayers, Dorothy L. *The Nine Tailors*. 1934. London, 1959.
Shakespeare, William. *King Richard II*. Ed. Charles R. Forker. London, 2002. The Arden Shakespeare.
— — —. *Shakespeare's Sonnets*. Ed. Katherine Duncan Jones. London, 1997. The Arden Shakespeare.
Slater, Michael. "Carlyle and Jerrold into Dickens: A Study of *The Chimes*." *Nineteenth-Century Fiction* 24.4 (1970): 506–26.
— — —. *Charles Dickens*. New Haven, 2009.
Welsh, Alexander. "Time and the City in *The Chimes*." *Dickensian* 73 (1977): 8–17.

Radical Dickens: Dickens and the Tradition of Romantic Radicalism

Norbert Lennartz
Universität Vechta

There is a long, deeply entrenched tradition in Victorian criticism that sees Dickens as the representative of smug Biedermeier coziness, as the spokesman of the nineteenth-century bourgeoisie that enjoyed rural traditions and cherished its aversion to the metropolis (see Tomalin 232f.). In particular, German-speaking countries were ready to read Dickens as a novelist who seemed to translate Spitzweg's cozy paintings into English topographies and to specialize in a form of humor that was affirmative, but backward and evocative of the good-natured eccentricities to be found in novels by Fielding, Sterne, and Smollett.

The image of Dickens as a shallow humorist was not corrected by Stefan Zweig's seminal and ambivalent study on the three masters of the novel—Balzac, Dostoevsky, and Dickens—which was published in 1923 and which could rely on Chesterton's characterization of Dickens as an "immoderate jester" and "a moderate thinker" (158). According to Zweig, Dickens was not only a writer who refrained from transgressing moral, aesthetic, and artistic boundaries; his art also catered to a Victorian concept of art which was labeled as self-complacently domestic and "digestive" (59). In contrast to Shakespeare and other writers of past "heroic" ages, what Dickens seems to lack for the critics in the 1920s is an artistic greediness, a hungry curiosity to smash the conventions of the Victorian age. Too apathetic like Swift's Gulliver, Dickens was thought to indulge in being tied down by the Lilliputians of Victorian taste. When Zweig eventually credits Dickens with being the discoverer of "the Romanticism of the bourgeoisie" and "the poetry of the prosaic" (65), he uses misleadingly oxymoronic phrases that help neither to define Dickens's romantic inclinations nor to take into account to what extent Dickens was affiliated with radicalism and with a poetry that was not so much prosaic as highly charged with political meaning.[1]

The partial cozification of Dickens (in and outside of Germany) at the beginning of the twentieth century not only worked toward Dickens's marginalization in academic circles and tended to reduce him to being a writer of tear-jerking popular literature and children's stories; it also at times diverted scholars' attention from his radical and subversive side, from his peculiar way of deconstructing the Victorian discourses of his age. In 2007, Sally Ledger focused on Dickens's often neglected "ability to negotiate and even to disregard the gradually encroaching boundaries" that were being established between the popular and the radical, but also between high culture and the emergence of the mass media (3). Ledger convincingly shows Dickens's familiarity with William Hone's pamphlets (*Confession of Thomas Bedworth*) and to what enormous extent he could draw on the crime narratives of street culture and broadside ballads for the composition of *Oliver Twist*. But although popular narratives in the wake of the numerous Newgate novels tended to depict their characters in a glaringly melodramatic light, the subtitle of Dickens's novel, "A Parish Boy's Progress," suggests a more realistic genealogy, "a debt to Hogarth's engravings *The Harlot's Progress* and *The Rake's Progress*" (Ledger 73). What Ledger and other critics, however, fail to see is that both Hogarth and Dickens refer to John Bunyan's allegorical novel *The Pilgrim's Progress* which paved the way for a visionary literature that had nothing in common with the sophisticated religious allegory of Dante, and showed its protagonist Christian, a late-seventeenth-century everyman, striving for salvation in the face of hypocrisy, maliciousness and evil. Dickens's novels, thus, seem to translate Bunyan's allegorical pattern into the nineteenth-century bildungsroman, and in doing so, they transform monsters such as Apollyon and Giant Despair into less fantastic, but vexingly liminal figures of urban evil such as Fagin, Sikes, Uriah Heep, and Quilp. But what is more pertinent to Dickens's romantic radicalism is that his pilgrims more often than not challenge, combat, and (sometimes) triumph over institutions, authorities, and hierarchies in such an anarchic manner that it is even possible to see Dickens in a tradition of literary radicalism that ranges from the dissenting Bunyan to the iconoclastic Blake and Hazlitt.[2]

In his 2008 biography of Hazlitt, Duncan Wu points out not only that both Hazlitt and Dickens worked for the *Morning Chronicle* writing reports from Parliament, but also that in March 1848, Dickens paid homage to Hazlitt by making a pilgrimage to Winterslow Hut, the "birthplace of some of his [Hazlitt's] finest essays," as John Forster (qtd. in Wu 439) puts it.[3] Although Hazlitt and Dickens differ in their choice of genre and technique, it is both their affiliation with Hone and their radical distrust of the nineteenth-century political and cultural climate that unites them. Descended from a Unitarian background in which the French Revolution was welcomed and William Godwin's texts were avidly read, Hazlitt vigorously attacked the pillars of society, the Regency system, and his contemporaries' inclination for utilitarianism and Malthus's subjection of society to the ruthless principles of economy. Unanimous in their rejection of "the check-population philosopher" (Cobbett qtd. in Wu 116) and the "nonsense" (Hazlitt 73) that he writes, Hazlitt and Dickens, both Smelfunguses in terms of aesthetics and politics,[4] had to face different reactions to their radicalism: whereas Hazlitt was vituperated as a hack writer running riot, as a ruffian, and as a filthy sex-obsessed fool, who had disclosed scandalizing details of his private life in a book called *Liber Amoris*,[5] Dickens managed to make his criticism more palatable to a large readership and to establish his reputation as a sentimental writer firmly moored in a middle-class tradition of social critics, as a top earner, and as "a great National Institution" (Quiller-Couch 5).

To what extent Dickens succeeded in sugaring the bitter pill, in concealing the subversive potential of his ideas behind fairytale constructions of good and bad can paradigmatically be shown in the novels *Oliver Twist* (1838) and *David Copperfield* (1850). Considering the fact that young Queen Victoria read and enjoyed *Oliver Twist*,[6] we must assume either that Dickens's radicalism was not taken seriously or that it eluded the notice of the readers whose sympathy was too much absorbed by the sentimental fortunes of the protagonists and their sudden and contrived anagnorisis. Dickens's attacks on Malthusian ideas of the economization of life in the workhouse episode are so patently obvious and have been so extensively dealt with that they now deserve as little reconsideration as Dickens's harsh criticism of the impact of the New Poor Law on children (see Ledger 5).[7] But the fact that, in *Oliver Twist*, Dickens calls the very fundament of

Victorian society and its entire façade of respectability into question in a truly Hazlittian manner has scarcely ever been commented on.

* * *

Sally Ledger is certainly right when she says that the "proliferation of alternative families in *Oliver Twist* draws attention to the absence of conventional parent figures in the novel" (99).[8] It is striking that, in glaring contrast to the Victorians' definition of family life as a haven of (gender-related) harmony,[9] Dickens's fictitious societies seem to be made up of bachelors, spinsters, foster parents, and "perverted" families. In this respect, the Brownlow household is not significantly different from the family of thieves around Fagin: both are almost Shakespearean in their absence of a mother (see Kahn). Whereas the surrogate families of the Victorian authorities—Mrs. Mann's subsidized orphanage most prominent among them[10]—are more in line with Lady Macbeth's fantasies of infanticide, Fagin's gloomy family on the margins of society seems to have quite a lot in common with Brownlow's community of eccentrics: a decent supply of food, fun, and even freedom of movement and speech. Whereas Brownlow's household is an assortment of elderly and barren people whose monotony is occasionally interrupted by Mr. Grimwig's autophagous interjections—"I'll eat my head"—Fagin's little counterworld is not only more vital and remarkably younger; it is also based on abnormal laws of reproduction: although the boys' and girls' family backgrounds remain in the dark, Fagin's existence is compared to that of a reptile that is supposed to have been born in an unnatural and parentless process of abiogenesis, "engendered in the slime and darkness through which he moved" (*OT* 153).

Set against the backdrop of Victorian standards of values, Fagin is thus a monstrosity, a liminal creature precariously wavering between bestiality and humanity, the paterfamilias of a carnivalesque family fathering children according to his own—and some might argue—queer laws of procreation (see Furneaux 46ff.).

But if one applies Victorian moral values to Oliver's existence, one is compelled to regard him also as a liminal figure, whose otherness is defined by the fact that he is a "bastard," a product of "abnormal" procreation violating Victorian moral values. Although in the traditional constellation of characters in early modern drama, the bastard—most noticeably Edmund in *King Lear* or Don John in *Much Ado about Nothing*—is the epitome of malicious anarchy and lasciviousness, Dickens reverses the order of things from the very beginning of the novel. Instead of having Oliver stigmatized with a heraldic bar sinister or other forms of social ostracism, Dickens makes it patently obvious that difference is not indigenous but is arbitrarily imposed by hostile society. Thus it is no longer the concept of God-given degree, but the "power of dress" (*OT* 5), a sartorial chain of being that randomly decides Oliver's position in society: "Wrapped in the blanket which had hitherto formed his only covering, he might have been the child of a nobleman or a beggar" (*OT* 5). But once he is enveloped in the old calico robes "grown yellow" (*OT* 5), he is "ticketed" and made into what society wants him to be: "the humble, half-starved drudge" (*OT* 5), the outcast who has to wear yellow as a sign of his isolation. Recapturing ideas derived from Carlyle's 1834 fictitious autobiography *Sartor Resartus*, Dickens repeatedly shows that the bastard's stigmatization is as coincidental as the clothes that Oliver is alternately given by Brownlow and Fagin. To further underline his radical views and his sympathy with the outsider, Dickens gives the legitimate son the role of the villain, whereas the child born out of wedlock is endowed with unwavering Rousseauistic innocence. When Mr. Brownlow eventually clarifies the ontological obscurity out of which Oliver comes, he can hardly conceal his radical views when he denounces the typical Victorian marriage of convenience as "wretched" and the rightful son, Monks, as a disgrace: "I know that of the wretched marriage, into which family pride, and the most sordid and narrowest of all ambition, forced your unhappy father, when a mere boy, you were the sole and most unnatural issue" (*OT* 409). In order to emphasize the paradox of the unnaturalness of the legitimate child, Dickens via Mr. Brownlow reverts to the concept of kalokagathia and has Monks's face disfigured by syphilitic spots: "a hideous disease which has made your face an index even to your mind" (*OT* 414).

Although approximately ten years, later Charlotte Brontë proves to be staunchly Victorian when, in *Jane Eyre* (1847), she denies Mr. Rochester the freedom to divorce Bertha Mason, the monstrous madwoman in the attic, Dickens proves to be not so much pre-Victorian as radically anti-Victorian when he lets Oliver's father eventually succeed in breaking the "heavy chain" (*OT* 410) of his marriage. Distancing himself spatially from his detestable wife, he even secures the affection of a nineteen-year-old girl, to whom he finds himself "contracted, solemnly contracted" (*OT* 411) by the end of the following year. Because a legal divorce is never mentioned, the reader can only conjecture what that solemn contract was, but considering that it was sealed by the "first, true, ardent, only passion" (*OT* 411) for that girl, we must read this passage as a radical plea for a union of love that challenges moral taboos and leaves us in doubt whether Oliver, as the virtuous offspring of passionate love, is an illegitimate child or the product of a bigamous relationship.

* * *

Although the readers' attention seems to be riveted to the fight between good and evil, between Brownlow's realm of light and Fagin's infernal den of darkness, another rather submerged passage in the novel clearly reveals Dickens's sympathies with the romantic radicals. Because of her questionable family background as Oliver's mother's sister, Rose is not in the position to accept Harry Maylie's proposal of marriage. Assuming the role of a self-effacing Victorian woman, she is ready to forego all chances of happiness and to inflict the pain of renunciation on herself. In this context, Harry's response is of utmost importance, because it shows to what extent he is not only a sentimentalist but also a radical of truly Hazlittian and Blakean dimensions:

> I left you with the firm determination to level all fancied barriers between yourself and me; resolved that if my world could not be yours, I would make yours mine; [. . .] there are smiling fields and waving trees in England's richest country, and by one village church—mine, Rose, my own—there stands a rustic dwelling which you can make me prouder of than all the hopes I have renounced, measured a thousandfold. This is my rank and station now, and here I lay it down. (*OT* 439, 440)

In a few sentences, Harry subjects the foundation of Victorian society to a thorough deconstruction. Calling the barriers on which Victorian ideas of hierarchy rested "fancied," Harry reminds the reader of the "mind-forg'd manacles" which torment people in Blake's poem "London" (l. 8). By making their heterogeneous worlds compatible and leveling all degrees of class difference, Harry makes it patently clear to Rose that he wants Victorian society to be replaced by an egalitarian microcosm of love, by a pastoral idyll which is so remote from the great financial expectations of the Victorians that he denounces their places of social activity as "a world of malice and detraction, where the blood is called into honest cheeks by aught but real disgrace and shame" (OT 439).

What Harry, however, calls for is not so much a romantic revolution, the crushing of "human grapes" in winepresses (Blake, "Vala" 459), but rather a way to withdraw from the bustle of urban society into the quiet of egalitarian country life, a philosophical shift of thought which is clearly distinct from the eruptive outbreaks of blood-eliciting revolutions in history. In this respect, John Lucas's argument that Dickens's novels represent Immanuel Kant's "melancholy man" is intriguing and fits the context. Defining the melancholy man in terms of an individual who, according to Kant, "suffers no abject subservience and breathes the noble air of freedom," who abhors all chains "from the gilded fetters worn at court to the heavy-irons of the galley-slave" (35), Lucas considers *Oliver Twist* to be the first of a long line of novels that translate both the Kantian and Rousseauistic idea of freedom into the Victorian age. But while Lucas comes to see Dickens's melancholy as an expression of growing pessimism and nostalgia for the past, as the feeling that "the noble air of freedom becomes more and more stifled and threatened by the social prison" (xi), it is more apt to say that, in particular in his early novels, Dickens tries to make use of his melancholy and to transform his dismay into radical, but nonrevolutionary steps to reform.

In *Barnaby Rudge* (1840), Dickens shows that riots are more often than not the products of a ruthless and bestial mob that is swayed by evil conspirators. Writing about Dickens's representation of the Gordon Riots in *Barnaby Rudge*, Iain McCalman attributes the novel's "flawed structure" to the author's "political paranoia" (27), to a conservatism that he must have derived from Edmund Burke's scathing criticism of the French Revolution. It is certainly true that Dickens was skeptical about social upheavals and that in this respect, he was not so much in line with Hazlitt as with George Eliot, who, in the parabolic preface to her novel *Felix Holt the Radical* (1866), compares revolutionary changes pejoratively to a "tube-journey," to "a bullet [shot] through a tube by atmospheric pressure" (5). But it would be misleading to attribute Dickens's reservation about revolutions to a conservatism that Wordsworth and the Lakists subscribed to in their later works.

* * *

David Copperfield is a prime example of the extent to which Dickens's novels are indebted to romanticism in their challenge of Victorian ideologies. More than any other of Dickens's novels, it is generically a bildungsroman that derives its tension from the paradox of propagating Victorian values while showing ways of evading them. Flung into the triangular constellation between Steerforth and Traddles, David is at first fascinated by the former's Byronic recklessness, by his unflinching determination to ignore obstacles and to win the race of life: "Roughshod if need be, smooth-shod if that will do, but ride on! Ride over all obstacles, and win the race!" (*DC* 434). In queer readings, David's attraction for Steerforth has been interpreted as a "homoerotic fixation" (Newey 71),[11] but apart from the sexual lure for David, Steerforth seems to embody a romantic radicalism and a disregard for authority that are more spectacular than Traddles's stoic way of drawing skeletons on sheets of paper. Steerforth is elitist, haughty and spellbindingly Byronic and thus represents a position that David has to overcome on his way to becoming a true Victorian writer. But despite Dickens's complying with other Victorian novelists and exorcising the Byronic element by the end of the narrative, it is the beautiful tranquility of Steerforth's body, its "statuesque pose" (Newey 71) that makes it patently obvious that David's farewell to both his Byronic friend and his romantic illusions is dearly bought and irretrievably severs all bonds with his carefree youth: "I saw him lying with his head upon his arm, as I had often seen him lie at school" (*DC* 801).

Even before Steerforth's luridly romantic death, David has gradually developed into a staunch Victorian in the course of his turbulent educational process. When he tries to subject his fragile wife to a strict regimen of mathematical rules, he rigorously subscribes to a Victorian notion of earnestness that Oscar Wilde was to satirize one generation later: "there is no substitute for thorough-going, ardent, and sincere earnestness" (*DC* 613). Having given up on the project of instructing his wife and to familiarize her with Britain's cultural heritage, David is more than eager to fall back on "the habits of punctuality, order and diligence" (*DC* 613), virtues that tally with his later predilection for "robust exercise" (*DC* 823) and that pave the way for his substantial and almost eschatological love for Agnes, the lamb. But David's discovery of his love for Agnes is preceded by a romantic experience that has overtly radical implications: following in the footsteps of Byron's *Childe Harold*, bereft of his love and his friends, David can be seen roaming from place to place, and the more he immerses himself in his "brooding sorrow" (*DC* 820), the less he seems to be able to acknowledge hierarchical structures when he randomly enumerates "the novelties of foreign towns, palaces, cathedrals, temples, pictures, castles, tombs, fantastic streets" (*DC* 820). His erratic pilgrimage, however, comes to an abrupt end, when, surrounded by the romantic sublimity of the Swiss Alps, he suddenly comes across a more subdued pastoral scenery, filled with the "sound of distant singing—shepherd voices" (*DC* 821). Overcome by a fit of sentimental weeping, which redefines Victorian concepts of stern masculinity along romantic lines, he eventually—in Carlylean terms—finds his way from the "Everlasting No" to the "Everlasting Yea" and is ready to accept his love for Agnes, whom Newey (73) intriguingly characterizes in romantic terms as David's Wordsworthian Dorothy.

In spite of its radically romantic leanings, the novel ends on a Victorian note, albeit one that is still interspersed by streaks of romanticism and evocations of radical subversion. The Victorian discourse of optimism and its "gospel of work" (Houghton 250) are counteracted not only by an array of eccentric characters who epitomize blatant inefficiency— Mr. Dick paralyzed by King Charles's fate and Mr. Micawber. It is also juxtaposed with an almost exotic territory that symbolizes a utopian counterworld that is free from the moral exigencies and utilitarian imperatives disseminated in much Victorian writing. Although Dickens was sorely disappointed by America and depicted his encounters with the republicans as a Swiftian confrontation with the Yahoos, his image of Australia is characterized by pantisocratic ideas and thus conspicuously remote from earlier (and later) representations of the terrifying *terra australis*.[12] Taking up Samuel Sidney's cue on Australia as Arcady revisited (see Lansbury 75f.), Dickens seems to take advantage of the remoteness of the country to create an anti-Victorian heterotopia where, on the one hand, radicalism has not turned into the "beastly" behavior of spitting "savages" and where, on the other, people are not affected by the relentless expectations of a society more firmly rooted in Arnold's Hebraism than in the sensuality of Hellenism. Australia, which Dickens never visited, thus becomes the romantic matrix for Dickens's ideas of a budding civilization that is still unencumbered by the clash of ideologies and the supremacy of cant.

The romanticization of Australia becomes even more evident when Dickens imagines the antipodean country as the refuge for fallen women such as Martha and Little Emily. Translating his commitment to the cause of fallen women and to the foundation of the Home with Angela Burdett Coutts into fiction, Dickens always seems to be eager to provide all these women with a past with a propitious future and to seek ways out of their social ostracism. Even Nancy, one of the most depraved female characters in *Oliver Twist*, is offered the chance to be readmitted into Victorian society. But whereas she is too self-destructively attached to her brutish lover Sikes and is finally murdered for her masochistic loyalty, Martha and Emily, in *David Copperfield*, are, by contrast, rewarded by a new life in a remote, heterotopian country, where even Mr. Micawber's Polonius-like verbosity is successfully translated into a career as a magistrate.

What at first looks like a sentimental ending to a variety of turbulent careers turns out to be a radical criticism of the straitlaced and fundamentalist outlook of Victorian society. In a world governed by Murdstonian characters who substitute romantic ideas of individualism for the demand to be obeyed "to the letter,"[13] man is gradually turned into a beast, into a dog in dire need of being caned into submission. In the face of this austere and rigid fundamentalism, Dickens not so much resorts to "a convenient trick by shipping the disorderly elements of fallen women," as Patricia Plummer (275) suggests; he rather endeavors to open up a refuge of individualism and anarchic rebellion that can no longer be reclaimed by Victorian authorities. The various other little spaces of liberty such as Betsy Trotwood's house are constantly in danger of being intruded on by donkeys and other trespassers of similar asinine qualities. Although Betsy's house proves to be a congenial place for the mental extravagances of Mr. Dick, who instead of being confined to the sad existence of a madman in the attic is given scope as an individual and indispensable advisor, the house is only another small (but futile) ark of humanity and tolerance that, within the context of Victorian proprieties and demands for conformity, turns out to be as inadequate as Peggotty's boat in the face of more overwhelming threats.

While these little heterotopias cannot provide lasting protection for the transgressors of Victorian codes of honor, it is Australia, the former destination for convicts, that offers women like Martha, a former prostitute, an opportunity to marry a decent young man, "a farm-labourer" (DC 875), and to live a life of intense seclusion, without molestation and "fower hundred mile away from any voices but their own and the singing birds" (*DC* 874). T. A. Jackson is certainly right when he refers to "the influence of Smollett" in *Oliver Twist*, but to maintain that *David Copperfield* "shows no less clearly the influence of Defoe" (72) is, in this context, slightly misleading, because he fails to appreciate Dickens's invention of Australia as a place of heterotopian radicalism. When Moll Flanders, the ageing thief, prostitute, and bigamist, goes to Virginia (of all places), she is not so much intent on beginning a new life in primordial United States as on grounding her existence in the wealth that she has amassed as a criminal. Presenting her husband with a "scarlet cloak" is no more than an ironical reminder of the fact that Moll Flanders has not discarded the qualities of the Scarlet Whore of Babylon and that she is not reluctant to import her life of dissolution into her new heterotopian existence. What Defoe in a truly Hogarthian manner reveals is that any progress in the depraved world is inevitably based on corruption and on the picaresque individual's willingness to participate in the mechanism of the world's Vanity Fair. What Jackson seems to overlook is the fact that, as a descendant of romantic radicalism, Dickens is averse to the anthropological concept of man as a self-centered *picaro*, tossed about like a tennis ball in Smollett's *Roderick Random*, but eventually seeking satisfaction in revenge or deception. In the Dickensian universe, man is not so much inherently corrupt as the victim of a proliferation of modern "isms," of capitalism, utilitarianism, positivism, Grundyism, Darwinism, Evangelicalism, colonialism and so on.

* * *

In *The Old Curiosity Shop*, the protagonist, little Nell, is eventually victimized and, according to Theodor W. Adorno's groundbreaking 1931 essay, objectified by the world of things as well as by the ruthless 'isms' incorporated by Quilp (see also Hollington). *Oliver Twist* and *David Copperfield*, however, supply their readers with radical trajectories to escape Victorian society's petrified and inhuman structures. In contrast to *Oliver Twist*, which, like a romantic rewriting of Bunyan's narrative, translates the simplified patterns of the medieval morality play into prose and eventually has the good, Rousseauistic man of feeling triumph, *David Copperfield* is more complex, because it is a rare specimen of a Victorian bildungsroman that is—despite its protagonist's acknowledgment of Victorian values—more often than not strikingly uncompromising in terms of romantic radicalism. As in various Victorian novels, most notably in *Jane Eyre*, in which, at the most critical point in her life, the eponymous heroine compares her misery to being drowned in a torrent (Brontë 331), Dickens seems to comply with the Victorian tradition of using the image of the deluge in order to indicate that not only Steerforth's cruel and Byronically tinged Darwinism is about to collapse, but also all ideologies that reduce man to a plaything, hopelessly at the beck and call of manipulators and schemers.

But whereas Victorians such as Charlotte Brontë attribute biblical overtones to the imagery of torrential rain and floods, thus expressing their idea of man's need for purification and the cleansing of his or her soiled self,[14] Dickens subtly appropriates this image for his concept of romantic radicalism. Dickens might "not [have been] given to subtle metaphor," as Jerome H. Buckley (100) points out, but he certainly placed subversive ideas and images into his early novels, and what is more, to put them into a dynamic relationship with representations of Victorian virtues. Hence, it is more than apt to say that Dickens's narratives are neither simply Victorian nor adaptations of romantic novel traditions; rather, they are subversively paradoxical in a sense that critics now only gradually seem to be learning to appreciate. The sentimental and bourgeois worlds that Dickens conjured up (and that, with some, earned him the reputation of being a shallow master of the humorous) are constantly deconstructed by daring depictions of alternative families, redefinitions of social hierarchies and the discovery of topographies in and outside of Victorian Britain that, similar to the heterotopian circus in *Hard Times*, radically turn Victorian values upside down. Dickens's veneration for Hazlitt and the romantic radical tradition thus permeates novels that are not (only) affirmative hallmarks of the Victorian novel.

NOTES

1   For the wider context of Dickens's reception in the early twentieth century, see Lennartz, "The Reception of Dickens in Germany 1900–1945."
2   For the radical tendencies of Dickens's nonfictional texts, see David Paroissien's contribution to this volume.

3   It is quite surprising that Michael Slater does not mention Dickens's veneration for Hazlitt in his recently published biography of Dickens, *Charles Dickens* (2009). In the 1840s, Dickens corresponded with William Hazlitt Jr., the essayist's son, and when in 1868 Alexander Ireland sends him the *List of the Writings of William Hazlitt and Leigh Hunt, Chronologically Arranged* . . . (1868), Dickens expresses his hope that "it will prove a very useful tribute to Hazlitt and Hunt" (Letters 12: 123).
4   For Hazlitt's denigrating views of Italian art, Rome, and the pope, see Wu (370ff.). For Dickens's vituperations of Italy, see Lennartz, "Charles Dickens Abroad — the Victorian Smelfungus and the Genre of the Un-Sentimental Journey."
5   For further details of "Hazlitt-bashing" as "an established subgenre of literary journalism," see Wu (338).
6   See Queen Victoria's diary for December 30, 1838: "Talked of *Oliver Twist*, which I must say is excessively interesting" (Collins 44).
7   Joseph Gold (37) even went so far as to equate the Victorian workhouse with the twentieth-century concentration camp.
8   Holly Furneaux even speaks of the "exuberant diversity of Dickens's fictional families" embracing "such figures as unmarried foster fathers, heterosexually resistant bachelors and spinsters, [and] same-sex couples" and thus contesting the "traditional formulations of the Dickensian domestic that identify a single, statically gendered model" (24). Also cf. chapter 4, "Parenthood: Hermione's Statue," in Belsey's *Shakespeare and the Loss of Eden: Construction of Family Values in Early Modern Culture* (85–128).
9   In *Sesame and Lilies*, John Ruskin famously defines family life and the home in terms of "a sacred place, a vestal temple, a temple of the hearth watched over by Household Gods" (qtd. in Houghton 343).
10 Pinpointing her masculine qualities, Mrs. Mann's name is another indication of the prevalent lack of maternity in *Oliver Twist*.
11 It seems rather contrived to see the relationship between Steerforth, David, and Emily in terms of a "suggestive (homo)erotic triangle of suitor, brother and sister," as Furneaux (125) does, or to read Emily's role only as a means to mediate the boys' homocentric passion, as Léger (304) propounds.
12 See, for the wider context, Lennartz, "Another Heart of Darkness? — Images of Australia in Victorian Fiction."
13 Nineteenth-century literature abounds in fundamentalist approaches that subject individualism to the constraint to obey authorities "to the letter." Cf. Meredith's *Ordeal of Richard Feverel* (1859) and Hardy's 1895 novel *Jude the Obscure* with its epigraph "the letter killeth."
14 The first-person narrator in *Jane Eyre* explicitly refers to Psalm 69,1f, which in the Authorized Version runs as follows: "the waters are come into my soul. I sink in deep mire, where there is no standing: I am come into deep waters, where the floods overflow me."

BIBLIOGRAPHY

Adorno, Theodor W. "Rede über den 'Raritätenladen' von Charles Dickens." *Noten zur Literatur* IV. Frankfurt am Main, 1974. 34–44.
Belsey, Catherine. *Shakespeare and the Loss of Eden: Construction of Family Values in Early Modern Culture*. New Brunswick, 1999.
The Bible. Ed. *Robert Carroll and Stephen Prickett*. Oxford, 1998. Authorized King James Version.
Blake, William. "London." *The Complete Poems*. Ed. W.H. Stevenson. London, 1989. 214.
– – –. "Vala, or the Four Zoas." *The Complete Poems*. Ed. W.H. Stevenson. London, 1989. 293–482.
Brontë, Charlotte. *Jane Eyre*. Ed. Michael Mason. London, 2003.
Buckley, Jerome H. *The Victorian Temper. A Study in Literary Culture*. Cambridge, 1981.
Chesterton, Gilbert Keith. *Charles Dickens*. 1906. London, 1944.
Collins, Philip, ed. *Charles Dickens. The Critical Heritage*. New York, 1971.
Dickens, Charles. *David Copperfield*. Ed. Jeremy Tambling. London, 2004.
– – –. *The Letters of Charles Dickens*. Ed. Madeline House, Graham Storey et al. 12 vols. Oxford, 1965–2002.
– – –. *Oliver Twist*. Ed. Philip Horne. London, 2003.
Eliot, George. *Felix Holt, the Radical*. Ed. Fred C. Thomson. Oxford, 1988.
Furneaux, Holly. *Queer Dickens: Erotics, Families, Masculinities*. Oxford, 2009.
Gold, Joseph. *Charles Dickens: Radical Moralist*. Minneapolis, 1972.
Hazlitt, William. "Malthus." *Selected Writings*. Ed. Jon Cook. Oxford, 2009. 67–83.
Hollington, Michael. "The Voice of Objects in *The Old Curiosity Shop*." *Australasian Journal of Victorian Studies* (2009): 1–8.
Houghton, Walter E. *The Victorian Frame of Mind*, 1830–1870. 1957. New Haven, 1985.
Jackson, T. A. *Charles Dickens. The Progress of a Radical*. New York, 1987.
Kahn, Coppélia. "The Absent Mother in King Lear." *Rewriting the Renaissance. The Discourses of Sexual Difference*. Ed. Margaret Ferguson, Maureen Quilligan and Nancy Vickers. Chicago, 1985. 33–50.
Lansbury, Coral. *Arcady in Australia. The Evocation of Australia in Nineteenth-Century English Literature*. Melbourne, 1970.
Ledger, Sally. *Dickens and the Popular Radical Imagination*. Cambridge, 2007.
Léger, J. Michael. "Triangulation and Homoeroticism in *David Copperfield*." *Victorian Literature and Culture* (1995): 301–25.

Lennartz, Norbert. "Another Heart of Darkness?—Images of Australia in Victorian Fiction." *Anglistentag 2009 Klagenfurt: Proceedings*. Ed. Jörg Helbig and René Schallegger. Trier, 2010. 319–27.

———. "Charles Dickens Abroad—the Victorian Smelfungus and the Genre of the Un-Sentimental Journey." *Dickens Quarterly* (2008): 145–61.

———. "The Reception of Dickens in Germany 1900–1945." *The Reception of Charles Dickens in Europe*. Ed. Michael Hollington. Vol 1. London, 2013.

Lucas, John. *The Melancholy Man. A Study of Dickens's Novels*. London, 1970.

McCalman, Iain. "Controlling the Riots: Dickens, *Barnaby Rudge* and Romantic Revolution." *Radicalism and Revolution in Britain, 1775–1844. Essays in Honour of Malcolm J. Thomis*. Ed. Michael T. Davis. London, 2000. 207–27.

Newey, Vincent. "Rival Cultures: Charles Dickens and the Byronic Legacy." *Romantic Echoes in the Victorian Era*. Ed. Andrew Radford and Mark Sandy. Aldershot, 2008. 67–83.

Plummer, Patricia. "From Agnes Fleming to Helena Landless: Dickens, Women and (Post-)Colonialism." *Dickens, Europe and the New Worlds*. Ed. Anny Sadrin. Basingstoke, 1999. 267–82.

Quiller-Couch, Arthur. *Charles Dickens and Other Victorians*. Cambridge, 1925.

Slater, Michael. *Charles Dickens*. London, 2009.

Tomalin, Claire. *Charles Dickens. A Life*. London, 2011.

Wu, Duncan. *William Hazlitt. The First Modern Man*. Oxford, 2008.

Zweig, Stefan. *Drei Meister. Balzac, Dickens, Dostojewski*. Leipzig, 1923.

Modern Characters in the Late Novels of Charles Dickens

Herbert Foltinek
University of Vienna

Character has been a controversial concept in literary studies for quite a while. The structuralists thought they could abandon what they regarded as an unprofessional notion altogether, replacing it by what was construed as a confluence of different functions. Conversely, this view has never worked with regard to Charles Dickens. Whereas nineteenth-century critics might find fault with Dickens's aesthetics, they invariably thought highly of the characters he had created. All this changed when the modernist reaction to that highly contested term *Victorian realism* set in. Henry James, for one, dismissed *Our Mutual Friend* as the "poorest of Mr Dickens's work," maintaining that the author had fashioned figures not characters (253), an approach which the next generation of critics wholeheartedly denied. In his widely read writings on Dickens, Gilbert K. Chesterton averred that the excellence of this, the greatest of Victorian novelists, lay in his character drawing (*Appreciations* 235). At a later date, the great popularizer J. B. Priestley conceived of Dickens's achievement as founded on the memorable characters he had introduced into English culture. However, as pointed out earlier, such a view became unacceptable to the literary theorists of the late twentieth century, who would restrict the category of character to its function in a literary text. This radical view has recently been watered down again; after all, cognitive analysts suggest the production of character models by the recipient reader. But how might we conceive of a recent theoretical study by Fotis Jannides, *Figur und Person*, which speaks of the employment of "figures" in a text, avoiding the term character altogether? Does this imply a compromise with the late theorists, or has the term been introduced to signify a less material presence (not so different from Henry James's use of the term)?

When we speak of characters in a literary text, we would theoretically have to define whether we use the concept in a mimetic, a textual, a cognitive, or a semantic sense or attempt a combination of these approaches—which is the way we follow in the course of our discussion. Admittedly, it is difficult to forgo a traditional understanding of character in a study of Dickens's creations, because his figures have acquired what might be conceived as an existence of their own. Even an entirely communicative analysis will not be able to abjure the notion of a "Dickensian character"; the collocation is too firmly embedded to be dismissed out of hand.

The figures I wish to examine in the course of my chapter are certainly not "Dickensian characters"; they are anything but traditional and yet, as I hope to show, quite "Dickensian" after all in their striking modernness.

Arthur Clennam, a central presence in the novel *Little Dorrit*, is not characterized in detail; in fact, he might be said to enter the narrative inadvertently. For the reader, he appears first as a voice, an undistinguished partner in a dialogue where he features as "the other," from whom several undistinguished remarks issue. It takes about two pages before "the other" is personalized as a "grave dark man of forty" (*LD* 16) and another two pages before his name is revealed. We next hear that he has "no will" (*LD* 20) of his own and even remains uncertain where he should go—having returned to England after an absence of about twenty years. He is several times referred to as a "nobody," a reticent, indecisive, inactive man, lacking in self-confidence and willpower, a neurotic personality, traumatized by a deprived and severely disciplined upbringing. His warped state of mind is evoked through a telling image: "To review his life, was like descending a green tree in fruit and flower, and seeing all the branches wither and drop off one by one, as he came down towards them" (*LD* 158).

And yet, rather anomalously, he has not become an embittered man; he is still generous and warmhearted. This is revealed by his interest in the impoverished Dorrit family (encountered in the Marshalsea debtors' prison), once he suspects that they have been wronged by his parents. Consequently, he is resolved to engage himself on their behalf. His endeavors are, however, fruitless because any attempt to gain assistance or even information from the infamous Circumlocution Office must inevitably be fruitless. Clennam does not appear especially ineffectual or timid in this respect, because Dickens is mainly concerned with censuring the British administration and the civil service in these encounters. Conversely, the need for some active engagement persists, and this leads to Clennam's association with the engineer Daniel Doyce, a practical, downright man, who accepts Clennam's offer of managing the clerical part of his business activities for him (*LD* I, ch. 23).

In the meantime, Clennam—a nobody (the epithet is emphasized again)—has fallen in love with a young girl who turns out to have fallen for another, a younger man (*LD* I, ch. 28). The disappointment—for Arthur Clennam does not press his suit once he knows of her attachment—has the effect of lowering his spirits once again:

> Why should he be vexed or sore at heart? It was not his weakness that he had imagined. It was nobody's, nobody's within his knowledge, why should it trouble him? And yet it did trouble him. And he thought—who has not thought for a moment, sometimes—that it might be better to flow away monotonously, like the river, and to compound for its insensibility to happiness with its insensibility to pain. (*LD* 196–97)

Clennam remains in close contact with the girl's parents, however—similar to a "widower son-in-law" (*LD* 504). He subsequently gains consolation from working with the so very practical Daniel Doyce, but he becomes dispirited again when the engineer goes abroad to publicize his inventions in foreign countries. In this disconsolate mood, he discovers by chance that his mother has become involved in some business deal with Blandois alias Rigaud, a picaresque French adventurer of shady appearance. Clennam has nothing but a feeling of foreboding to warn his mother against the customer, but drops his usual reserve and quite unaccountably bursts out against him, only to be told off by her, reducing him to feelings of "amazement, suspicion, resentment, and shame" (*LD* 530). Yet he shows no firmness whatsoever on meeting a truculent old lady on a visit to a former lady friend of his. This is the extraordinary figure of "Mr F's Aunt," whom readers of the novel and Dickens himself (*Letters* 75) have at least initially (and perhaps mistakenly) conceived of as a comic character. We are not required to attempt an analysis of this enigmatic character in this connection. What *is* noticeable in the context is that whereas all the other figures seem to be able to get on with the apparently demented old woman, she invariably attacks Clennam, who is visibly frightened and at a complete loss about how to bear her aggressions.

He equally shows little pluck in encountering a proud, emancipated young woman, who bears a deep grudge against his friends and their daughter. On one of their meetings, the embittered Miss Wade hands him an account of her past life, the dispassionately titled "History of a Self-Tormentor" (*LD* II, ch. 21), which Dickens held to be an inherent part of the novel (*Letters* 280). In spite of his misgivings, Clennam dare not refuse the commitment. Why the rebellious Miss Wade should entrust the manuscript to him of all people is never revealed, nor if he makes anything of it. Yet his passive, irresolute reaction to her approach sheds some more light on his character.

His wonted reserve and mistrust would normally keep him from committing himself when advised to invest money in the speculations of a prominent financier in whom everybody puts his or her trust:

> He observed anew that wherever he went, he saw, or heard, or touched, the celebrated name of Merdle; he found it difficult even to remain at his desk a couple of hours, without having it presented to one of his bodily senses through some agency or other. (*LD* 568)

At this point, the notion of proving himself useful to the frustrated inventor Daniel Doyce is persistently on his mind, as are his worries about his mother's imprudent business dealings, until he finally panics and entrusts the entire property to the speculator. When the crash comes, Doyce's firm is ruined, and Clennam finds himself deeply in debt. This induces a complete breakdown in him. Out of a vague urge for self-punishment, Clennam insists on being taken to the same debtors' prison that some time ago held the Dorrits. Refusing all assistance, he also avoids the company of his fellow prisoners. Because he stays completely isolated, his sense of humiliation, self-torment, and despondency increases day by day. The chapter notes (Charles Dickens's jottings for the novel) indicate the progress of his depression through the entries "drooping downward" and again "always downward." When he is in this state, the villainous Blandois/Rigaud seeks him out to abuse him, but Clennam, by now marked a loser, fails to stand up to him.

His depression, despair, and privation eventually bear down on him, and he contracts jail fever. Yet, at this point, Dickens brings about a complete turn of events. Little Dorrit, who has always loved him, comes to his rescue. Daniel Doyce, having gained a fortune abroad, returns with happy tidings, and so the story comes to a happy ending, leaving the lovers to a "modest life of usefulness and happiness" (*LD* 801). It is noticeable, however, how the quiet little wedding is carried out, Clennam characteristically remaining completely inactive about it (*LD* II, ch. 34). Has he really changed into a settled, "normal" personality?

Little Dorrit, and in particular the character of Arthur Clennam, found little favor with Dickens's early-twentieth-century critics. In his magisterial *History of the English Novel*, Ernest Baker includes the character among what he sees as the hollow "stage figures begotten of the plot, who are unfortunately always too near the footlights to escape notice" (300). Sylvère Monod likewise dismisses him as an entirely un-Dickensian figure: "He has an imperturbable seriousness and dignity. The reader never laughs or smiles at him or because of him" (417). We might read this observation as confirming the characterization of a depressed personality.

Little Dorrit contains a line ever so engrossing to narratologists as to at least one film producer: "This history must sometimes see with Little Dorrit's eyes" (*LD* 159). Charles Dickens was not a literary theorist, but he was absolutely aware of the potential of perspective. The scenes that follow are, in fact, conveyed as Little Dorrit might have witnessed them. The novel embraces different narrative situations; much of the text, however, is communicated, filtered as it were, through the mind of Arthur Clennam—the prime "focalizer." Passages rendered in psycho-narration lead to monologues preceded by an introductory phrase and even more intimate monologues in direct speech. But we also come across passages in which Clennam's thoughts are rendered in narrated monologue (free indirect style)—a stylistic form that is rarely found in other works by Dickens. One of Clennam's musings at the fireside ends as follows:

> He looked at the fire from which the blaze departed, from which the afterglow subsided, in which the ashes turned grey, from which they turned to dust, and thought "How soon I too shall pass through such changes and be gone!" (*LD* 158)

Or, conversely, Clennam reflects on his relationship to Little Dorrit: "Had he ever whispered to himself that he must not think of such a thing as her loving him, that he must not take advantage of her gratitude, that he must keep his experience in remembrance as a warning and reproof; that he must regard such youthful hopes as having passed away" (*LD* 712). Clennam's doubts and hesitations come to the fore in these lines.

Yet another passage may be rendered in psycho-narration. Clennam's state of mind after the departure of a visitor to his room in the prison is expressed as follows: "[Clennam,] with the feeling that he was more despised, more scorned and repudiated, more helpless, altogether more miserable and fallen, than before, was left alone again" (*LD* 733). This quote, as well as other representations of Clennam's state of mind, outlines something akin to what a modern therapist might well call a mental disorder.

Let us now turn to another, in our view, modern character—Eugene Wrayburn, a major figure in *Our Mutual Friend* whom Henry James dismissed entirely in his previously mentioned review of the novel: "Wrayburn lounges about with his hands in his pockets, smoking a cigar, and talking nonsense" (258). Once again, Chesterton voices a different assessment of the character, whom he does not hesitate to classify as a well-bred gentleman while at the same time drawing our attention to the inner weakness that may beset a representative of the upper class:

> In Eugene's purposeless pursuit of Lizzie Hexam, in his yet more purposeless torturing of Bradley Headstone the author has marvellously realised that singular empty obstinacy that drives the whims and pleasures of a leisured class. (*Charles Dickens* 176)

Eugene Wrayburn is introduced together with his friend Mortimer Lightwood; both correspond to the schema of upper-middle-class young men: graduates from public school, lawyers but hardly engaged in professional activities, and indolent because they can rely on parental support, socialites of sorts. At this point, however, their characterizations begin to differ. Lightwood is the straighter, more conventional one of the two, whereas Wrayburn is anything but common, a figure that has the potential to confuse or even surprise. As Bert Hornback has pointed out, Wrayburn's friend Lightwood serves to initiate the plot of the novel, which he finally winds up. It is he who narrates the story of John Harmon (the titular figure of *Our Mutual Friend*) and of the estate he is supposed to claim. Otherwise, he functions as a companion and confidant of Wrayburn, who primarily acts as a marginal figure. Yet the roles soon change. When Lightwood is called to identify a dead body, believed to be that of John Harmon, Wrayburn joins him on his errand, moved by a whim to relieve his boredom. Contrary to

Lightwood, he appears not only languid but also moody, irresponsible, and reckless even; liable to fits of depression; and a gloomy person (as he is frequently called) given to bizarre, "singular" notions. He is, in fact, a fragmented self. His intrusion in the Harmon affair is repeatedly challenged, but he counters all specific inquiries or mere approaches through dismissive or even sardonic remarks. He quickly gets impatient with people whom he perceives as common and whom he clearly despises. Above all, he shows only contempt for work (which the Victorians after all venerated as a virtue). When questioned about his own occupation, he answers evasively, at times cynically. And yet his interest is roused on encountering Lizzie Hexam, the illiterate daughter of a waterside man or scavenger, supporting herself through manual labor. His indolence vanishes immediately, and he is out to pursue her. But the girl may be a match for him. She is strong-minded and quite determined to move to another place if he persists in following her against her will.

In any case, "it passed into Mortimer Lightwood's mind that a change of some sort, best expressed perhaps as an intensification of all that was wildest and most negligent and reckless in his friend, had come upon him" (*OMF* 166), which Lightwood, who has known Wrayburn since boyhood, finds most perplexing. In a long talk, Wrayburn still gives vent to an inability to decide on anything, emphasizing his uncertainty, shiftlessness, and carelessness even. He is not even sure that his mind is set on anything that might really interest him: "At times I have thought yes; at other times I have thought no. Now, I have been inclined to pursue such a subject; now, I have felt that it was absurd, and that it tired and embarrassed me. Absolutely, I can't say" (*OMF* 286). But there is more to come. In his meetings with Lizzie, Wrayburn appears less self-centered, more earnest, and even more generous; however, his disagreeable, arrogant behavior toward whoever comes his way has certainly not changed. He can be fierce when he senses censure or mere disapproval of his indolent ways. This shows, for example, during his encounter with the Jewish tradesman Riah, whom he deliberately addresses as Mr. Aaron and frivolously relegates to the synagogue (*OMF* 405). Here we have to bear in mind that Dickens specifically introduced the figure of Riah to expose the vice of anti-Semitism (Slater 517, 527). The saintly Riah is constantly derided for his Jewishness by his master, the moneylender Fledgeby, one of the most unsympathetic characters Dickens created, a nasty piece of work. And yet, by uttering unprovoked insult, Wrayburn behaves no better than does Fledgeby, acting out one of the many parallel structures of the novel. Similar to the latter, he will have his comeuppance, a near-tragic one against Fledgeby's comic castigation.

Wrayburn's careless disregard for the less privileged may have its consequences, however, as is shown by his disdainful treatment of Bradley Headstone and its aftermath. Headstone, a schoolteacher, professes an interest in Lizzie Hexam and has become Wrayburn's rival, who refuses to take him seriously. In fact, Wrayburn cruelly taunts him, mocking his lack of refinement, his social inferiority, and his physical awkwardness. When Headstone begins to stalk him, Wrayburn responds by leading him ever so often on a wild chase through the nightly streets of London. This reaches a stage at which the two contenders find themselves unable to leave off, having become obsessed, as it were, with each other. But whereas Eugene Wrayburn seems to draw some sadistic pleasure from their pairing and recklessly incites his opponent to the utmost limit, Bradley Headstone is reduced to a murderous hatred for the other.

Wrayburn's careless ways appear even more noticeably in his unkind behavior toward Lizzie's friend, the crippled Jenny Wren—"Eugene Wrayburn saw the tears exude from between the little creature's fingers as she kept her hand before her eyes. He was sorry, but his sympathy did not move his carelessness to do anything but feel sorry" (*OMF* 533). However, his worst offense is that he should brutally ply Jenny Wren's father with drink to find out where Lizzie has gone, knowing that this will probably kill him—as, in fact, it does. Once he has the information of her whereabouts, he has no further use of the alcoholic. He finds Lizzie in the country where she has gone to escape his persistent, reckless suit and the threatening approaches by Bradley Headstone, against whom she feels a deep-seated aversion. As the earlier chapters of the novel show, Dickens was at pains to draw a psychologically convincing, independent-minded personality in Lizzie Hexam.[1]

Having found Lizzie, Wrayburn insists on a heart-to-heart talk, which takes place in pleasant surroundings on the river, evocatively called the "silver river"—ironically, as it turns out, because the meeting ends in disaster. She admits indirectly to loving him, yet implores him once again to leave her alone, because the difference in their statuses is too wide: "If you do truly feel at heart that you have indeed been towards me what you have called yourself to-night, and that there is nothing for us in this life but separation; then Heaven help you, and Heaven bless you!" (*OMF* 695). Wrayburn, for his part, cannot resolve to stop seeing her but is equally certain that he will never marry her: "She must go through with her nature, as I must go through with mine" (*OMF* 696). A large part of his thought process, by way of contrast, is rendered in quoted monologue, but often not in coherent sentences. Without reaching a conclusion, his divided mind, running around in self-reflective circles, expresses itself in repetitions—"Out of the question to marry her [. . .] and out of the question to leave her" (*OMF* 698)—and again, "this is a bad business" (*OMF* 697).

In his careless ways, Eugene Wrayburn little foresees that his enemy Headstone should have followed him on his walk along the river. Wrayburn is savagely attacked, seriously injured, and pushed into the water by Headstone. He is rescued from drowning by Lizzie (a waterman's daughter who drags dead bodies from the river after all), but he is so seriously wounded that the surgeons think him beyond help.

Lizzie Hexam and, ironically, Jenny Wren, whom Wrayburn has treated arrogantly, care for the invalid, who lingers on, failing to make an actual recovery but urging Lightwood not to charge the perpetrator to protect Lizzie's reputation. He eventually gains the strength to express his wish to be married to her, but when she has become his wife, his health deteriorates again because he feels that he will die, unable to start a new life. How could he think of reforming while "looking back on such a trifling, wasted youth as [his]" (*OMF* 754).

Against all odds, and against his inventor's first intention,[2] however, Eugene Wrayburn makes a slow, but complete recovery. But how will he change? The notion that he is redeemed by a passage through purgatory or even reborn by a symbolic baptism in the river seems too fanciful. His "wickedness," as he calls his irresponsible conduct, is surely not gone. He shows no regret at having contributed to the death of the drunkard (Jenny Wren's father) or at having incited Bradley Headstone to such an extent that the schoolmaster turned into a murderous aggressor. The reader merely learns that Wrayburn's debts have been settled and that his marriage is accepted by his class-conscious father after all. In the meantime, his friend and partner Mortimer Lightwood has apparently gained a few clients to his practice. Would Wrayburn be able to assist him, thus making a living? In the penultimate chapter, the two friends are said to have "discoursed of the future" (*OMF* 813)—but this is all we ever hear.

How could Eugene Wrayburn change? How could such a complex personality turn into an ordinary man, shedding his diverse and contradictory traits? Conversely, how could the other, how could Arthur Clennam turn to a "modest life of usefulness and happiness" (*LD* 801), as we are told? Would this ever so reflective, brooding, inactive person be invigorated as it were by his Little Dorrit? For the endings of the two novels, Dickens recurred the formula "They lived happily ever after," but does it really work in the case of these two so very unconventional characters?

For a Dickensian hero, Arthur Clennam is singularly lacking in self-assurance, always given to pondering, culminating in self-doubt, indecisive, timid, questioning his goal in life, disembodied as it were, moved by "inconsistencies, anxieties, and contradictions" (*LD* 393). His only merit, it would seem, is his ethical will, an active altruism that comes to the fore in various encounters. Admittedly, he is not censorious; the criticism of the Circumlocution Office, which is so eloquently expressed, is voiced by the narrator. But then, there is the unlikeable character of Eugene Wrayburn, so very self-assured and yet despondent, self-centered, unapproachable, indifferent to the needs of others, critical of the society he finds it convenient to sponge on. And yet he is very much aware of his lack of directions and his own hollowness, alienated, a "man without qualities," quite oblivious to the moral dimension of his daily doings. He insidiously seeks to ingratiate himself with Lizzie Hexam, whom he loves but for whom he shows little respect. Could such a person ever change, even though the change was brought about by an almost successful attack on his life? In other words, is Eugene Wrayburn curable? Is he capable of leading a stable, active, practical life? And can Arthur Clennam be built up into a firm, settled man? The novels provide no answers to these questions. As Arthur Clennam and Eugene Wrayburn finally retreat into traditional roles, they cease to be modern characters. Dickens's endings take both characters—and both novels—back to Victorian modes of writing and thinking.

NOTES

1   Orwell's class-conscious censure that the author should have "given her" to Bradley Headstone like a mindless plaything is surely wide off the mark (Orwell 61).

2   Dickens seems to have wavered whether Wrayburn should expire or survive. From an entry in his *Book of Memoranda* (Kaplan) and the working notes ("Eugene dying"), we may gather that the author was in fact resolved to let him die. Markus Stone, the illustrator of the novel, remembered that Dickens had in fact reached this decision. And, after all, Eugene himself states that he "ought to die." All things considered, the ultimate decision to let the character survive may have been a concession to the popular reader.

BIBLIOGRAPHY

Baker, Ernest A. *The History of the English Novel*. Vol. 7. London, 1936.
Cheadle, Brian. "Improvising Character in *Our Mutual Friend*." *Essays in Criticism* 59 (2009): 211–33.
Chesterton, Gilbert Keith. *Appreciations and Criticisms of the Works of Charles Dickens*. 1911. London, 1970.
— — —. *Charles Dickens*. London, 1914.
Dickens, Charles. *Little Dorrit*. Ed. Harvey Peter Sucksmith. Oxford, 1979.
— — —. *Our Mutual Friend*. Ed. Michael Cotsell. Oxford, 1989.
— — —. *The Letters of Charles Dickens*. Vol. 8, 1856–1858. Ed. Graham Storey and Kathleen Tillotson. Oxford, 1995.
Hornback, Bert. "Mortimer Lightwood." *Dickens Studies Annual* 39 (2008): 249–60.
James, Henry. "Review of Our Mutual Friend." *The House of Fiction*. Ed. Leon Edel. London, 1957. 253–58.
Jannides, Fotis. *Figur und Person. Beitrag zu einer historischen Narratologie*. Berlin, 2004.
Kaplan, Frank, ed. *Charles Dickens's Book of Memoranda*. New York, 1981.
Monod, Sylvère. *Dickens the Novelist*. Norman, 1968.
Orwell, George. *Collected Essays*. London, 1961.
Priestley, John Boynton. *Charles Dickens. A Pictorial Biography*. London, 1961.
— — —. *Literature and Western Man*. London, 1960.
Slater, Michael. *Charles Dickens*. New Haven, 2009.

IV. Dickens and Changes in Popular Culture and in the Theater

The Cultural Politics of Charles Dickens's *Hard Times*

Doris Feldmann
Friedrich-Alexander-Universität Erlangen-Nürnberg

Hard Times, Dickens's most self-consciously "political" novel, first published in *Household Words* in 1854 with the aim of making the journal successful in commercial terms, has always been considered different from his other novels because of its presumed "artlessness." This has sometimes been explained away by the serial publication in weekly installments and the concomitant constraints such as lack of time and space. Some attempts have been made to "rescue" *Hard Times* artistically by exploring the intricate patterns of imagery that underpin the novel's alleged thematic concerns (see Harrison, esp. 115–16; Johnson), in particular the conceptual opposition between "fact" and "fancy," which I think is misleading.[1] Much of the critical discourse on *Hard Times* regards the circus, Sleary's fanciful horse riding, as the chief alternative to the factual forces of utilitarianism—an alternative that is, however, considered to be deplorably inadequate because it lies in the tawdry arena of popular entertainment. Another counterpart is, of course, the figurative language of the narrator, his metaphoric playfulness, which, for some critics, appears to be opposed to the literal-mindedness of the utilitarians (see, e.g., Dahmane 139). This debate about the "politics" of *Hard Times* is in fact an old one. It can be situated in larger tendencies in Dickens criticism that fashion Dickens into either a radical or a reactionary (see also Coles). Some critics have found his attacks on Utilitarianism and political economy in *Hard Times* crude, unjustified, and faulted;

others have argued that in "reality," that is, in his journalism, Dickens's views on educational reform and trade unions were much more "advanced," that is, "modern."[2]

My own reading of *Hard Times*, and especially of the circus and the narrative voice, centers on what I would like to call its cultural politics — a politics with a complicated and ambivalent dynamics that makes it difficult to identify a single, clear political agenda. As I argue, the novel is preoccupied with various forms and meanings of culture: from different forms of popular entertainments to the epistemological question of how people attach meaning to themselves and to their world.[3] In the Victorian period, the term *culture* underwent significant semantic shifts,[4] and *Hard Times* comprises its diverse and shifting meanings.

In the eighteenth century, culture had stood for the cultivation of plants as well as for a process of human training. Both these meanings are implied in the allegorical titles of the three books into which the novel is divided: the organic metaphors of "Sowing," "Reaping," and "Garnering" refer to the prototypical education of the Gradgrind children and, by analogy, of the workers. In the first half of the nineteenth century, "culture" turned into a more abstract category that came to mean a general habit of the mind and the general state of intellectual development in a society. Again, both aspects are relevant to *Hard Times* — with its metonymic presentation of fathers, schoolmasters, political economists, and other (patriarchal) representatives of intellectual formation. Yet another meaning of culture was refinement and artistic achievement, associated with a cultural elite and social distinction. Matthew Arnold's notion of culture as a study of perfection, as "the best which has been thought and said in the world" (190), already points to the growing separation of "high" culture from popular culture that the Victorians witnessed and that included negotiations about boundaries, functions and property rights. In the late nineteenth century and in the twentieth century, culture took on another new meaning, developed by anthropologists, now referring to (the life of a community) what Raymond Williams has called "a whole way of life" (*Culture* xviii),[5] including its material, intellectual, and spiritual dimensions. This organic and inclusive notion of culture fits the famous presentation of Coketown, the metaphorical "KEY-NOTE" (*HT* 20) in *Hard Times*: the abstract image of everyday life in a city that materially and visibly represents the more hidden, psychic, spiritual, and intellectual structures intertwined with industrial capitalism.[6]

A close look at nineteenth-century reviews of Dickens's work shows that Dickens has always forced his middle-class critics to address the balance between "high art" and "popular entertainment," between "timeless" literary fame or "intrinsic" literary value and market-driven popularity.[7] Dickens himself was astutely aware of literature as a business and of himself as an entrepreneur and as a brand (John, "The Novels" 154). Modern critics even regard Dickens as the first global media star and, in doing so, make him a contemporary of our age. But regardless of such anachronisms (which happen to make Dickens grow younger every year), his texts are of interest in the process of an evolving cultural modernity. From a historical perspective, the novel was the premier form of the emergent literary mass market, and *Hard Times* can be seen as a "commodity text"—a term associated with serial publication and a highly competitive weekly periodical market.[8] It is a critical common place that Dickens loved and used or even appropriated[9] nineteenth-century forms of popular entertainment that he "borrowed" from many different media. This includes "spectacular theatre," a predecessor of film (see Glavin 196), and also extends to a melodramatic aesthetics complete with formulaic structures, emotional semiotics and transparent character types.[10] Some of the characters in *Hard Times* act out roles that derive from another theatrical genre, the pantomime—the popular form of stage entertainment that draws on fairy tales and nursery rhymes (see Lodge 406–8). *Hard Times* also features sensational plot developments concerned with sex and crime (Louisa's almost adultery and Tom's bank robbery) that are reminiscent of the Newgate novel[11] or of the Penny Dreadful. These cross-generic and cross-media influences make inquiries into Victorian popular culture imperative.[12] The term *popular*, however, is as problematic as the term *culture*. On the one hand, it is associated with consumer culture, an emergent mass market and, since the 1950s, with a manipulative "culture industry";[13] on the other hand, it can refer to an aesthetics of pleasure, to aisthetics,[14] which emphasizes the body and sensuality, and to (nostalgic) notions of a socially inclusive culture of the populace that seems to be able to transcend class boundaries.

For some critics, Dickens's belief in the socially cohesive potential, the communal, healing function of popular culture is his "most firmly held political view" (John, "The Novels" 143). Such assessments resemble Victorian analyses of popular culture: they restrict the topic to those practices that the middle classes advocated as tools for instructing the masses.[15] In his essay "The Amusements of the People" (1850),

Dickens himself recommends taking advantage of the popular appeal of "the lower class of dramatic entertainments," converting entertainment into "a means of public instruction" (13)—an idea which he seems to have 'dramatized' in *Hard Times* a few years later. Sleary, whom most critics see as the spokesman for the novel's avowed message (see also Schlicke 143; John, "The Novels" 142), formulates the famous doctrine or "mantra": "People mutht be amuthed, Thquire [. . .] they can't be alwayth a working, nor yet they can't be alwayth a learning. Make the betht of uth; not the wurtht" (*HT* 35).[16] This message is repeated by the narrator: "I entertain a weak idea that the English people are as hard-worked as any people upon whom the sun shines. I acknowledge to this ridiculous idiosyncrasy, as a reason why I would give them a little more play" (*HT* 51). Thus popular entertainment can paradoxically complement hard work and utilitarian programs: by providing the working people with "some physical relief—some relaxation," by "giving them a vent—some recognized holiday" (*HT* 23), it can ameliorate the intolerable working and living conditions and, in doing so, can serve as a mechanism of middle-class social control or "discipline."[17] The narrator explicitly registers the politically regulating function of recreation for the "common people" (*HT* 124) when he addresses utilitarian economists and schoolmasters:

> Cultivate in them, while there is yet time, the utmost graces of the fancies and affections, to adorn their lives so much in need of ornament; or, in the day of your triumph, when romance is utterly driven out of their souls, and they and a bare existence stand face to face, Reality will take a wolfish turn, and make an end of you! (*HT* 124–25)

The popular cultural forms that the novel foregrounds do not belong to the culture of the street, to the emerging mass culture of the new urban industrial working class.

Instead, "fancy," the term around which the possibilities of popular entertainment cluster in *Hard Times*, is primarily a "fanciful" mode of presentation through a narrative voice that is saturated with the imaginative aesthetics of fairy tales and their antirationalistic resonance.[18] Gradgrind is presented as an ogre (cf. *HT* 11), Sissy becomes "a good fairy in his house" (*HT* 206).[19] Mrs. Sparsit considers herself the bank fairy, whereas the townspeople regard her as the bank dragon "keeping watch over the treasures of the mine" (*HT* 87). Faced with a proliferating modern "fact-ology" in the form of empirical or mathematical ideals of "exactness" and technological or commercial notions of "progress," the narrator takes recourse to forms of popular culture that are located in a lost, prelapsarian past, in

> the best influences of old home [. . .]. The dreams of childhood—its airy fables; its graceful, beautiful, humane, impossible adornments of the world beyond: so good to be believed in once, so good to be remembered when outgrown, for then the least among them rises to the stature of a great Charity in the heart, suffering little children to come into the midst of it, and to keep with their pure hands a garden in the stony ways of this world [. . .]. (*HT* 149)[20]

On the level of individual identity, fairy tales and nursery rhymes can be seen as expressions of a desire to maintain a bond with childhood; they serve as Romantic symbols of transcendence, here typically presented in a secularized as well as a domesticated form. On a broader level of cultural memory,[21] folk tales or fairy tales were coming into fashion in the context of the "discovery" of folk culture, a culture that suggested the possibility of a return to a premodern, "purer," "more grounded" culture of "the people." Folk culture, the first concept of popular culture, was invented by middle-class intellectuals in late eighteenth and early nineteenth centuries, at the (precise) moment when traditional cultural relations began to collapse through the impact of industrialization.[22] In using classical mythology and biblical imagery as further and equally valid sources of fancy in *Hard Times*, Dickens not only tries to establish a common ground of a "shared" cultural heritage; he also blurs the boundaries between "high" and "low" culture.[23]

Within a dominant social setting that values progress, the nostalgic (re)construction of premodern, quasi-mythical cultural traditions is not merely a reactionary movement: it is an aspect of modernization—not its counterpart. The presentation of such a "past" in the form of fairy tales, theatrical spectacle, and poetic language exhibits the curious character of nostalgia as a condition of any present that longs for a past that has never existed except as a fiction.[24]

The central image of popular entertainment in *Hard Times* is Sleary's horse riding. Many critics have remarked that Sleary's company, which is portrayed as an exotic, alien culture complete with its own language, exemplifies an alternative model of society in the sense of a community:

> There were two or three handsome young women [. . .], with their two or three husbands, [. . .] and their eight or nine little children, who did the

> fairy business when required. The father of one of the families was in the habit of balancing the father of another of the families on the top of a great pole; the father of a third family often made a pyramid of both those fathers [. . .]. All the mothers could (and did) dance upon the slack wire and the tight rope [. . .]; none of them were at all particular in respect of showing their legs [. . .]. (*HT* 30–31)

Because this acrobatic performance is primarily based on cooperative interaction, it indicates the opposite of social alienation. Likewise, the women's sensuality shows them to be in harmony with their bodies and therefore speaks against self-alienation. On the one hand, such an indeterminate sensuous plenitude stands in stark contrast to the abstractedness of the utilitarian world of fact. On the other hand, the show could also be interpreted in terms of a very modern concept of culture: the semiotic sense of a dynamic web of significance,[25] in which relationships become ethically relevant as imaginatively or metaphorically understood relations of affinity.

In the narrator's description of the circus, Dickens is drawing on his memories of Astley's Amphitheatre on the south bank of the Thames, which was famous for its equestrian shows (see Cunningham 21).[26] It is important to note, however, that Dickens is not only a nostalgic apologist for an "escapist" culture of entertainment, but he is also a keen observer of popular culture and a cultural critic: he both deploys and analyses popular cultural modes. Instead of evoking the illusionary restoration of a pure and authentic form of cultural entertainment, which is cleansed of historical accretions and has not yet been touched (i.e., defiled) by modernity, the narrator emphasizes the modern, commercial side of Sleary's circus with its "fairy business" (*HT* 30) or "comic infant bithnith" (*HT* 210)[27]:

> He had reached the neutral ground upon the outskirts of the town, which was neither town nor country, and yet was either spoiled [. . .]. A flag, floating from the summit of the temple, proclaimed to mankind that it was "Sleary's Horse-riding" which claimed their suffrages. Sleary himself, a stout modern statue with a money-box at its elbow, in an ecclesiastical niche of early Gothic architecture, took the money. (*HT* 12–13)

All allusions to a respectable and dignified past, to the pastoral and the sacred are relativized in a satirical manner and exposed as anachronisms by the narrator. In contrast to the description of Coketown, the textual representation is more realistic here, because the illusionary character of the circus is a priori openly acknowledged. Because illusion is part of their business, the circus people live—so to speak naturally—in a hybrid culture with a fuzzy logic. This becomes apparent in the characterization of Sleary: he constantly drinks brandy and water, is "never sober and never drunk" (*HT* 31), and looks "with one fixed eye and one loose eye" (*HT* 31), with "the fixed eye of Philosophy—and [its] rolling eye, too" (*HT* 35).

The circus provides the horizon for deciphering other significant functions of culture in the sense of a habit of the mind. From a modern critical perspective, Sleary's horse riding could be seen to illuminate notions of an embodied mind, grounding knowledge in (human)[28] bodily experience. Similarly, the narrator's creative construction of meaning through analogy and metaphor could be interpreted in terms of cognitive theory, in which metaphors are regarded as basic patterns equivalent to the way in which the human mind works, creating understanding and allowing for dynamic cross-space mappings.[29] By contrast, on the level of characters, Gradgrind's rationalistic model of cognition reduces knowledge to language in terms of literal speech, claiming to represent accurately something that is already there and fully knowable. This is what the school lesson at the beginning of the novel exemplifies: when Gradgrind asks for a definition of a horse ("Quadruped. Graminivorous. Forty teeth [. . .]" [*HT* 7]), he cuts off concrete life experiences by forbidding Sissy—"Girl number twenty" (*HT* 7), in his diction—to talk about the circus. His mechanistic world view not only leads to social and psychic forms of repression and alienation; it also opens up ways to use language as a manipulative tool,[30] as exemplified by Bounderby, the factory owner and banker, who calls himself "a man who, when he sees a Post, says 'that's a Post,' and when he sees a Pump, says 'that's a Pump,' and is not to be got to call a Post a Pump, or a Pump a Post or either of them a Toothpick" (*HT* 84).

In feigning a mimetic representation of reality, he can easily pass off his lies, his fictions about himself as a self-made man, as plain truth. Moreover, Bounderby constructs and upholds the various "popular fictions" of Coketown, for instance that the workers want to be fed with gold spoons (cf. *HT* 57, 86). In doing so, he puts fiction in the service of rational calculation and utilitarian interests.

But why should the narrator, another image maker (and, by analogy, Dickens himself), who insists on the usefulness of fancy in the context of a life which is determined by "machinery and reality" (*HT* 222), be considered more reliable than Bounderby? "[A]llegorical fancy"

(*HT* 153) can, after all, also be used for destructive purposes, which is implied for instance in Bounderby's "wicked imaginations" (*HT* 195), Mrs. Sparsit's (mis)use of figurative language,[31] and in her melodramatic construction of a "mighty Staircase with a dark pit of shame and ruin at the bottom" (*HT* 153) for Louisa. At various points in the novel, the narrator openly concedes the subjective-fictional character of his perspective. His awareness of the problematic relationship between language and knowledge manifests itself in the frequent use of verbs such as *seemed* or *appeared* and of conjunctions such as *as though* or *as if*. The "as-if" attitude in aesthetics corresponds to an "as-if" approach in ethics.[32] In the case of the metaphoric presentation of factories as fairy palaces, the narrator explicitly distances himself from those who invented the image: "the great factories [. . .] looked, when they were illuminated, like Fairy palaces—or the travellers by express-train said so" (*HT* 52).

Instead of a realistic description of a factory, readers are offered a provocative simile that allows them to recognize its artificiality and to consider its ideological implications (see Lodge 409). The point of view from the train is determined by a new space-time continuum that also produces a new kind of perception: like magic, technology transforms reality in fantastic ways. The railway may have turned the world into "moving pictures" (see Marsh 204),[33] the cultural "ancestors" of cinema, but they are only "moving" in the sense that tourist's pleasures are, for they turn a blind eye to the agony and suffering of the workers: "The atmosphere of those Fairy palaces was like the breath of the simoom: and their inhabitants, wasting with heat, toiled languidly in the desert" (*HT* 86). Instead of polarizing "the Romantic" and "the Utilitarian"[34] by constructing an imagined alternative culture, the narrator turns to discourses of fancy, to forms of magic and wonder that simulate the uncanny return of seemingly uncontrollable forces into a realm associated with enlightened rationality: modern capitalist mass production.[35]

The aesthetic and ideological discontinuities[36] inherent in this kind of cultural politics are precisely what *Hard Times* has to offer: it is because of Dickens's sense of the dialectic of progress and regress, of enlightenment and mythology[37]; it is because of the openly acknowledged complicity between resistance and containment—the two poles between which the study of popular culture has tended to oscillate (see Hall 228)—that a reading of *Hard Times* as a symptom of cultural complexity and cultural change becomes possible.

NOTES

1 I agree with Malone (14) here, who maintains that such pairs of opposing terms mask the complexity of the text.
2 The relationship between *Hard Times* and Dickens's journalistic project *Household Words* is a very close one, materially as well as thematically. See Ledger (210–12).
3 According to Lupton, *Hard Times* deals with fundamental epistemological problems, highlighting the possibilities and limits of aesthetic experience and judgment.
4 The following brief outline of the term's semantic history in the nineteenth century is based on John and Jenkins (1–6), and the *Oxford English Dictionary* entries on *culture*.
5 Williams calls this new understanding "the 'social' definition of culture, in which culture is a description of a particular way of life, which expresses certain meanings and values not only in art and learning but also in institutions and ordinary behavior" (*The Long Revolution* 41).
6 Dickens's abstract, unifying style resembles the formative principle of Coketown, which is the need to create uniformity—a totalizing principle which is also characteristic of Gradgrind's educational system. For a more detailed discussion, see Johnson (409–13).
7 Rodensky's informative article registers inherent tensions as well as changes in the use of the term *popular* in Dickens reviews from the late 1830s onward.
8 On Victorian novels as commodity texts, see Miller (8); on the periodical market, see Ledger (209). The charges made by contemporaries against Dickens as a writer of popular fiction resemble those made against successful nineteenth-century women writers who are seen to challenge the cultural hegemony of upper-class men of letters. According to Carr (161), Dickens's periodical *Household Words* involves his making use of a feminine disguise.
9 Appropriation here implies the exploitation and silencing of "other" cultural forces than those of the middle classes. See John, "The Novels" (147).
10 John, *Dickens's Villains*, analyzes the complexities of the cultural politics that attend the history of melodrama.
11 Ledger (213–14) analyzes another melodramatic tableau that draws on Newgate fiction: Stephen Blackpool's nightmarish vision of a Newgate hanging (see *HT* 122–23).
12 See also John, *Dickens's Villains* (24). The shift of emphasis from questions of aesthetics to those of ideology, which John (25) diagnoses, however, tends to create a new reductive binary opposition. In the last years, enquiries into Dickens and popular or even mass culture have proliferated and continue to do so. See, for example, John, *Dickens and Mass Culture*.
13 The term was coined by Horkheimer and Adorno, who argued in the final chapter of their book *Dialectic of Enlightenment* that mass-produced culture (re)enforces the capitalist ethos and is a danger to "high art."

14 Aisthetics (or aisthesis) can roughly be understood as a kind of sensual epistemology. With the heightened emphasis on the body and on the affective dimension of perception, aisthetics has gained interest today and is often discussed in the context of a rediscovery of eighteen-century aesthetics, especially of Baumgarten's theory of "sensate cognition"; see, for example, Adler.

15 On the edifying discourse that dominated Victorian discussions of popular culture, see Denisoff (136–38).

16 See also *HT* (218), where Sleary himself repeats his message: "Don't be croth with uth poor vagabondth. People mutht be amuthed. They can't be alwayth a learning, nor yet they can't be alwayth a working, thy an't made for it. You *mutht* have uth, Thquire."

17 For Malone (see 24n8), the circus is a model of industrial organization in its highly developed system of disciplinary surveillance.

18 Critics have related Dickens's concept of fancy to Shelley's and Coleridge's discussions of fancy and imagination, in which only imagination is granted the status of a vital and creative form of human perception; see Barnes (241). Barnes (over) interprets fancy—in the sense of imagination—as a form of resistance against hegemonic forces.

19 Bounderby is compared to a conqueror; Mrs. Sparsit, to a captive princess (see *HT* 36).

20 For the functions of "childish lore," see also *HT* (222). It is important to note that it is not childhood as such, a symbol of transcendence during the Romantic age, that should be remembered but the fictions of a domestic-familial childhood.

21 According to Assmann (128–133), one of the leading theoreticians in the field, cultural memory is defined through its (temporal) distance to the everyday and as long-term memory. It is constructed and maintained through "figures of memory" such as, for instance, ritual or ceremonial interactions (celebrations, festivities), cultural formations (texts, pictures, rites), or institutional communication (practice, recitation).

22 See Storey (1–3). Dickens's defense of fairy tales in his article "Fraud on the Fairies" (1853) is actually an attempt to prove their "usefulness" (97) in a utilitarian age.

23 A similar strategy of "elevating" popular culture can be found in the analogies Dickens draws between the circus on the one hand and Shakespeare and the reading of poetry on the other. See *HT* (13 and 17).

24 Stewart (23) uses the term *narrative* instead of fiction. This "narrative" ensures that nostalgic desire is never satisfied—a process which is not simply experienced as a loss but also as a surplus of signification.

25 In the interpretative (anthropological) theory of culture (in the wake of Clifford Geertz), culture is understood as "a web of significance" that man himself has spun, as a historically transmitted pattern of meanings expressed in symbolic form by means of which people communicate, perpetuate, and develop their knowledge about and attitude toward life.

26 Sleary refers to "Athley'th" in *HT* (209).

27 I disagree with Schlicke (153), who maintains that Dickens omits or at least minimizes the circus's commercial side.

28 Sleary also includes animal perception (exemplified by the behavior of a well-trained dog that belonged to Sissy's father), rejecting purely biological notions such as "instinct." See *HT* (217f).

29 The seminal book by Lakoff and Johnson, *Metaphors We Live By* (1980), has inaugurated a field of research that combines cultural and cognitive analyses. For a brief outline of this field of research, see Richardson.

30 For a more detailed discussion, see Feldmann.

31 For example, Mrs. Sparsit names her wages "annual compliment" (*HT* 83).

32 This is also exemplified by Rachel, who remains faithful to her "idea" of Stephen (cf. *HT* 187), and by Sissy, who upholds an image of her father in which rational knowledge is suspended and which allows her to believe in his return (cf. *HT* 218).

33 Another aspect of modern visual culture is exemplified by Mrs. Gradgrind, whose repeated presentation as a faint "transparency" (e.g., *HT* 16, 152) makes the corporeal-mental alienation process, which is also characteristic of Coketown, obvious. For the "transparency" as an art form popularized by the dioramas, see Carr 165.

34 According to Malone (22), this rhetorical opposition is just another "popular fiction."

35 Many critics have noted that *Hard Times* (and Dickens's writing in general) cannot escape the mechanism of materialist ideology to which it objects. Some critics even maintain that the very form of Dickens's writing draws deeply on the energies of modern capitalist production (accumulation, investment, circulation, exchange). For a short summary of such approaches, see Connor (3, 28).

36 One of the more problematic inconsistencies in *Hard Times* can be located in Sissy's depiction as a house fairy, which devalues her status as an oppositional figure. Her power as a "child-woman" depends on her selflessness, on her entire forgetfulness of the self; see Carr (170). Moreover, as a child of the lower classes, Sissy is appropriated by the middle class (she rehabilitates Louisa) and becomes "the watchdog of bourgeois morality" (Malone 22).

37 The destructive, totalitarian aspects of "progress" have been analyzed by Horkheimer and Adorno (28): "In the enlightened world, mythology has entered into the profane. In its blank purity, the reality which has been cleansed of demons [...] assumes the numinous character which the ancient world attributed to demons [...] It is not merely that domination is paid for by the alienation of men from the objects dominated: with the objectification of spirit, the very relations of men—even those of the individual himself—were bewitched."

BIBLIOGRAPHY

Adler, Hans, ed. *Aesthetics and Aisthesis: New Perspectives and (Re) Discoveries*. Bern, 2002.

Arnold, Matthew. *Culture and Anarchy and Other Writings*. Ed. Stefan Collini. Cambridge, 1993.

Assmann, Jan. "Collective Memory and Cultural Identity." *New German Critique* 65 (1995): 125–33.

Barnes, Christopher. "*Hard Times*: Fancy as Practice." *Dickens Studies Annual: Essays on Victorian Fiction* 34 (2004): 233–58.

Carr, Jean Ferguson. "Writing as a Woman: Dickens, *Hard Times* and Feminine Discourses." *Charles Dickens*. Ed. Steven Connor. London, 1996. 159–77.

Coles, Nicholas. "The Politics of *Hard Times*: Dickens the Novelist versus Dickens the Reformer." *Dickens Studies Annual: Essays on Victorian Fiction* 15 (1986): 145–79.

Connor, Steven. Introduction. *Charles Dickens*. Ed. Steven Connor. London, 1996. 1–33.

Cunningham, Hugh. "Amusements and Recreation." *Oxford Reader's Companion to Dickens*. Ed. Paul Schlicke. Oxford, 1999. 18–23.

Dahmane, Razak. "'A Mere Question of Figures': Measures, Mystery, and Metaphor in *Hard Times*." *Dickens Studies Annual: Essays on Victorian Fiction* 23 (1994): 137–62.

Denisoff, Dennis. "Popular Culture." *The Cambridge Companion to Victorian Culture*. Ed. Francis O'Gorman. Cambridge, 2010. 135–55.

Dickens, Charles. "Frauds on the Fairies." *Household Words* 8.184 (1 Oct 1853): 97–100.

———. *Hard Times*. 1854. Ed. Fred Kaplan and Sylvère Monod. 3rd ed. New York, 2001. Norton Critical Edition.

———. "The Amusements of the People." Part I. *Household Words* 1.1 (30 Mar 1850): 13–15. Part II. *Household Words* 1.3 (13 Apr 1850): 57–60.

Feldmann, Doris. "Erkenntnis und Sprache in Charles Dickens' *Hard Times*." *Literatur in Wissenschaft und Unterricht* 19 (1986): 195–214.

Glavin, John. "Dickens and Theatre." *The Cambridge Companion to Charles Dickens*. Ed. John Jordan. Cambridge, 2001. 189–203.

Hall, Stuart. "Notes on Deconstructing the Popular." *People's History and Socialist Theory*. Ed. Raphael Samuel. London, 1981. 227–40.

Harrison, John R. "Dickens's Literary Architecture: Patterns of Ideas and Imagery in *Hard Times*." *Papers on Language and Literature: A Journal for Scholars and Critics of Language and Literature* 36.2 (2000): 115–38.

Horkheimer, Max, and Theodor W. Adorno. *Dialectic of Enlightenment*. Trans. John Cumming. New York, 1975.

John, Juliet. *Dickens and Mass Culture*. Oxford, 2010.

———. *Dickens's Villains: Melodrama, Character, Popular Culture*. Oxford, 2001.

———. "The Novels and Popular Culture." *A Companion to Charles Dickens*. Ed. David Paroissien. Malden, 2008. 142–56.

———, and Alice Jenkins. Introduction. *Rethinking Victorian Culture*. Ed. Juliet John and Alice Jenkins. Basingstoke, 2000. 1–12.

Johnson, Patricia E. "*Hard Times* and the Structure of Industrialism: The Novel as Factory." *Studies in the Novel* 21.2 (1989): 128–37. Repr. in Charles Dickens. *Hard Times*. Ed. Fred Kaplan and Sylvère Monod. 3rd ed. New York, 2001. 409–18.

Lakoff, George, and Mark Johnson. *Metaphors We Live By*. Chicago, 1980.

Ledger, Sally. *Dickens and the Popular Radical Imagination*. Cambridge, 2007.

Lodge, David. "How Successful Is *Hard Times*?" *Working with Structuralism*. Boston, 1981. 37–45. Repr. in Charles Dickens. *Hard Times*. Ed. Fred Kaplan and Sylvère Monod. 3rd ed. New York, 2001. 400–409.

Lupton, Christina. "Walking on Flowers: The Kantian Aesthetics of *Hard Times*." *ELH: English Literary History* 70.1 (2003): 151–69.

Malone, Cynthia Northcutt. "The Fixed Eye and the Rolling Eye: Surveillance and Discipline in *Hard Times*." *Studies in the Novel* 21.1 (1989): 14–26.

Marsh, Joss. "Dickens and Film." *The Cambridge Companion to Charles Dickens*. Ed. John Jordan. Cambridge, 2001. 203–23.

Miller, Andrew. *Novels behind Glass: Commodity Culture and Victorian Narrative*. Cambridge, 1995.

Richardson, Alan. "Studies in Literature and Cognition: A Field Map." *The Work of Fiction: Cognition, Culture and Complexity*. Ed. Alan Richardson and Ellen Spolsky. Aldershot, 2004. 1–29.

Rodensky, Lisa. "Popular Dickens." *Victorian Literature and Culture* 37.2 (2009): 583–607.

Schlicke, Paul. *Dickens and Popular Entertainment*. London, 1984.

Stewart, Susan. *On Longing: Narratives of the Miniature, the Gigantic, the Souvenir, the Collection*. Baltimore, 1984.

Storey, John. *Inventing Popular Culture: From Folklore to Globalization*. Oxford, 2003.

Williams, Raymond. *Culture and Society: 1780–1950*. London, 1958.

— — —. *The Long Revolution*. London, 1961.

Conjuring Dickens: Magic, Intellectual Property, and *The Old Curiosity Shop*

Christopher Pittard
University of Portsmouth

In a letter from 31 December 1842, Charles Dickens describes rehearsals for a *Twelfth Night* performance:

> [John] Forster and I have purchased between us the entire stock in trade of a conjurer, the practice and display whereof is entrusted to me. [. . .] if you could see me conjuring the company's watches into impossible tea caddies, and causing pieces of money to fly, and burning pocket handkerchiefs without hurting 'em—and practising in my own room, without anybody to admire—you would never forget it as long as you live. (*Letters* 3: 416)

Dickens and Forster would again perform magic at a Christmas party in 1843:

> a hot plum pudding was produced from an empty saucepan, held over a blazing fire, kindled in Stanfield's hat, without damage to the lining [. . .] three half crowns being taken from Major Burns and put into a tumbler-glass before his eyes did then and there give jingling answers unto questions asked of them by me [. . .]. (*Letters* 4: 10)

Dickens would perform magic throughout the 1840s, culminating in performances given in summer 1849 at Bonchurch as "The Unparalleled Necromancer Rhia Rhama Rhoos" (Forster 2: 192).

In this chapter, however, I wish to consider how conjuring is represented in an earlier novel, *The Old Curiosity Shop*. Paul Schlicke, whose analysis of Dickens's fascination with popular entertainments has provided the foundation for subsequent studies of the relationship of such entertainments to Dickens's novels, touches only briefly on the subject, despite magic acts being one of the few popular entertainments of which Dickens had direct experience as both performer and spectator. Conjuring does not quite fit into Schlicke's wider argument that Dickens's presentation of popular entertainment (especially in *The Old Curiosity Shop*) is essentially nostalgic, for rather than being in decline in the 1840s, magic was gaining in popularity, crossing the boundaries of both theatrical space and the private parlor. It acquired a new cultural resonance from the mid-nineteenth century, theorized (like so many aspects of Victorian culture) in Darwinian terms, as resting

> upon a universal instinct to deception—a biological tendency appearing throughout the animal world from simple forms to the highest orders, which acts as a constant force in the process of natural selection. [. . .] In the struggle of primitive man to increase his personality, conjuring came into existence. (Triplett 431)

I am more interested, however, in the implications of the importance of secrecy and originality in conjuring. In the following discussion of the resonances of conjuring in *The Old Curiosity Shop*, I propose that Dickens's representations of magicians are a self-reflexive comment on his own conditions of creativity, and, furthermore, that reading the novel as a narrative of what Simon During calls "secular magic" (1) (that is, magic that makes no claim to supernatural or religious agency) allows us to situate the novel within an important historical context: the mid-nineteenth century debate about intellectual property and copyright.

I take my cue from James Buzard's insight that *The Old Curiosity Shop* provides "a metafictional reflection on the conditions of [Dickens's] own creativity" (17). Whereas Buzard locates such self-reflexivity in the Punch and Judy man Mr. Codlin as an analogue for Dickens (20), I argue that there is a yet more suggestive candidate available. The beginning of chapter 19 sees Nell and her grandfather having supper at the Jolly Sandboys Inn in the company of Codlin, Short, and other representatives of popular entertainment. The company is joined by further entertainers, one of whom is

> a silent gentleman who earned his living by showing tricks upon the cards, and who had rather deranged the natural expression of his countenance by

putting small leaden lozenges into his eyes and bringing them out at his mouth, which was one of his professional accomplishments. (*OCS* 150)

This conjuror is Sweet William, a nickname "probably intended as a pleasant satire upon his ugliness" (*OCS* 150). Although his appearance is brief, it is nonetheless telling, inasmuch as William represents the artist physically deformed by the marketplace. Dickens is careful to present Sweet William's routine of inserting lozenges almost as an afterthought; he is a performer of legerdemain first, a physical contortionist second. Reading this hierarchy of entertainments in this way requires us to read his description with a certain amount of irony; William has, in fact, very clearly failed to make his living with card tricks and has resorted to more sensationalist routines. Dickens inserts a further irony in describing such acts, those that have "deranged" William's appearance, as "professional accomplishments." Skill and dexterity in card manipulation might conceivably be seen as a profession; inserting lozenges into one's eyes is certainly not. It is not, I believe, going too far to see Sweet William as a personification of characteristically Dickensian concerns over the dignity of the artist and the threat of the literary marketplace to such dignity.

Dickens's specification of William as a card conjuror makes him the model for a number of similar magicians throughout the novel. First, there is Quilp himself, who we are told "[a]mong his various eccentric habits he had a humorous one of always cheating at cards, which rendered necessary on his part [. . .] a close observance of the game, and sleight of hand in counting and scoring" (*OCS* 184). Quilp even comments, "You think I'm a conjuror, sir [. . .]. If I was, I should tell my own fortune—and make it" (*OCS* 364). He performs his own linguistic sleight of hand by punning on "fortune." There is also Quilp's opponent on this occasion, Dick Swiveller. Baffled by Quilp's sleight of hand, Swiveller uses his own magical skills (we later see him entertaining Sally Brass by "conjuring with ink-stands and boxes of wafers" [*OCS* 275]) when he exacts a conjuror's revenge on Quilp:

> "Will you be kind enough to add to it, sir," said Dick, producing a very small limp card, "that that is my address, and that I am to be found at home every morning. Two distinct knocks, sir, will produce the slavey at any time. My particular friends, sir, are accustomed to sneeze when the door is opened, to give her to understand that they are my friends and have no interested motives in asking if I'm at home.—I

beg your pardon; will you allow me to look at that card again?" "Oh! by all means," rejoined Quilp.

"By a slight and not unnatural mistake, sir," said Dick, substituting another in its stead, "I had handed you the pass-ticket of a select convivial circle called the Glorious Apollers, of which I have the honour to be Perpetual Grand." (*OCS* 110–11)

Garrett Stewart reads this incident as an index of the contrast between Dick and Quilp: "We are to recognise the mistake, in its widest implications, as being quite unnatural and by no means slight, for Quilp should under no condition gain admittance to this society of poetry lovers. He is excluded by his very nature" (102). This slight error becomes another kind of slight, a calculated but subtle insult. But there is a third meaning in *slight*, a homophonic pun on *sleight*; Dick's insult is delivered through a magic trick, a substitution of one card for another. The rhythms of conjuring are evident in the way Dickens paces this scene, delaying the revelation of the substitution through the use of a patter (that is, a prepared linguistic routine) that bears little resemblance to what the conjuror is actually doing and serves to confuse the spectator's recollection of the sequence of events (a dynamic evident in Dick's attempt, later in the novel, to describe the conjuring routine performed by the Single Gentleman and his "temple" [*OCS* 273]). Dick's lengthy description of the conditions of entry to his lodgings only makes sense in terms of patter, a verbal disorientation, which proves to be startlingly successful. Quilp, otherwise so vigilant where cards are concerned (as in the game with Mrs. Quilp), does not even notice that the card has been exchanged; his exclamation here seems to be one of the few places in the novel where he is genuinely surprised.

But it is not only the written text of the novel that alludes to conjuring. Hablot Browne's illustration for chapter 12, showing the grandfather playing cards with List and Grove, carries suggestive visual echoes of Hieronymous Bosch's *The Conjurer* (c. 1490) in its moral lesson of the trickster and the gullible member of the public accompanied by a child. I do not wish to place too much emphasis on this comparison; there is, after all, little historical evidence to suggest that Browne had seen Bosch's painting, although he may have been aware of its various reinterpretations and copies. But the coincidence of composition suggests that Browne draws on a wider popular trope, the triad of the trickster, the gullible fool, and the child—as Elina Gertsman notes, *The*

Conjurer illustrates a Flemish proverb pertinent to *The Old Curiosity Shop*: "He who lets himself be fooled by conjuring tricks loses his money and becomes the laughing stock of children" (32). The dupe in Bosch's image is accompanied by a child who looks up at him with an expression that mingles amusement with concern. Browne restages the image as a separation of child and parent. Nell's pose is not one of concern but of resentment; she is excluded from the scene, and indeed, Browne's composition invites us to only see her as an afterthought, a distraction, or even a conjuror's misdirection. As Buzard notes, "To look at Nell is to miss everything else" (23).

Conjuring, therefore, is the paradigmatic state of *The Old Curiosity Shop*, especially so if we accept Mark M. Hennelly's argument that "curiosity is analogous if not synonymous with Freud's notion of the *uncanny*" (87). In his analysis of the novel's succession of doubles and its obsession with death, Hennelly notes that for Freud, "nostalgic curiosity or *heimlich* desires for the paradisal beginnings of life and a curious dread of the infernal end of life subliminally overlap" (87). Likewise, Jehangir Bhownagary emphasizes the uncanniness of conjuring in his discussion of the tripartite structure of performing secular magic. The magic performance, Bhownagary argues, has three stages: mimesis, in which the conjuror must present a recognizable world (in order to then subvert it); struggle, in which the magician attempts to trick an audience that will not willingly allow itself to be misled; and vertigo, where the uneven struggle between conjuror and audience is overcome and the observers of magic find themselves in an uncanny world where their perceptions are disoriented (32). Such a structure might also be usefully applied to *The Old Curiosity Shop* itself, in the way it moves from mimetic narrative to uncanny representation. The novel itself is framed by secular magic, being originally published within Dickens's abortive periodical *Master Humphrey's Clock*. Humphrey himself is yet another of the narrative's conjurors; in the frame text, he tells how he has become alienated from society: "Various rumours were circulated to my prejudice. I was a spy, an infidel, a conjurer [. . .]" (*Humphrey's* 6). Humphrey creates his own community from the circle of friends, the "alchemists" (*Humphrey's* 11) who meet to tell stories (of which *The Old Curiosity Shop* is one), and who find an endless supply of manuscripts in the casing of the titular clock. But the epistemology that connects *Master Humphrey's Clock*, *The Old Curiosity Shop*, and conjuring is that of the secret. The magician is one who holds something back, who derives his effects from keeping his techniques hidden. *The Old Curiosity Shop* is far from being (in Barthesian terms) the most hermeneutic of Dickens's novels; the only real mystery of the novel is unraveled well before the halfway point. But nor is *The Old Curiosity Shop* dominated by the proairetism of the picaresque; it thematizes mystery and secrecy, not least through its succession of conjurors. One of Nell's first sentences is "That, I must not tell" (*OCS* 12). Even Quilp, supposedly obvious in his drives and desires, has a "secret heart" (*OCS* 110). Likewise, *Master Humphrey's Clock* revels in secrecy; it begins with the tantalizing statement "The reader must not expect to know where I live" (*Humphrey's* 5). Humphrey's circle of alchemist-narrators are similarly guarded in their dealing with each other. Humphrey's first recruit is a deaf man, about whom he comments,

> To this hour, I am ignorant of his name. It is his humour to conceal it, or he has a reason and purpose for so doing. In either case, I feel that he has a right to require a return of the trust he has reposed; and as he has never sought to discover my secret, I have never sought to penetrate his. (*Humphrey's* 10)

In a context where the intellectual property debate theorized information as a commodity, however, Dickens is at pains to distinguish secrecy from selfishness: Humphrey says of his clock cornucopia that "mine is not a selfish love; I would not keep your merits to myself, but disperse something of pleasant association with your image through the whole wide world" (*Humphrey's* 12). Secrecy is not simply the miserly holding back of riches in information; rather, it adds to the value of the narrative being told. Humphrey's deaf associate is, one feels, the more interesting for being mysterious.

This discursive formation recalls D. A. Miller's influential discussion of the "open secret." Miller argues that the power of the secret lies not in the content of the withheld information, but rather in the open knowledge that such information exists to be hidden; in Miller's words, "the social function of secrecy—isomorphic with its novelistic function—is not to conceal knowledge, so much as to conceal the knowledge of the knowledge" (206). Conjuring, as a discourse of secrecy, takes advantage of this formation in fetishizing the power of hidden knowledge wielded by the magician. Likewise, just as Miller notes that the secrets of our subjectivity are often "no more esoteric, perhaps, than Oedipus and his commonplace complex" (194), so too are the secrets of conjuring often banal deceptions given disproportionate substance by their status as "secrets." Thus Jim Steinmeyer refers to conjurors as, epistemologically speaking, "guarding an empty safe" (16). Francesca Coppa has recently read conjuring through Miller's theory, but she does so to question the discursive centrality of the "secret" in conjuring. Coppa argues that the valuation of secrets and hidden knowledge obscures the role of the body in producing conjuring effects, a relationship she reads in gendered terms, as opposing the male magician (representing knowledge and secrecy) to the obviously bodily figure of the female assistant, whose objectification on stage reflects the lack of status afforded to physicality in magic performance (86–87). Coppa points out, for instance, that secrets in magic are not really that secret; they are shared among a wide range of backstage staff and inventors (89). Whether or not the 'secret' is more important to the practice of magic than the body is open to debate; the crucial point here is that, for Victorian conjurors and writers, knowledge is not only power but also money. Coppa is right to challenge the way in which intellectual commodities—that is, secrets—are fetishized in conjuring, but she misses the point that these "secrets" are not simply given away; they are earned, or more accurately sold, in texts such as magicians' biographies and conjuring manuals.

Returning to Sweet William, his appearance also draws on this idea of open secrecy. The next we see of him, after his entrance, he is perfecting his routines:

> [T]he silent gentleman sat in a warm corner, swallowing, or seeming to swallow, sixpennyworth of halfpence for practice, balancing a feather upon his nose, and rehearsing other feats of dexterity of that kind, without paying any regard whatever to the company, who in their turn left him utterly unnoticed. (*OCS* 151)

In a novel where virtually every character is at some point or other caught up in webs of surveillance and careful observation (and even Nell is not so innocent; consider, for instance, her surveillance of the sisters at Monflathers' school [*OCS* 246–47, 316–17]), Sweet William represents a striking exception, left "utterly unnoticed." Even critics of *The Old Curiosity Shop* follow this lead; he is rarely noted in critical discussion of the novel, despite the potential for parallels with Dickens himself, a fellow conjuror. William himself dramatizes conjuring here as the open secret; his routines are hidden in plain sight.

And yet he is noticed by at least one figure: the narrating voice of *The Old Curiosity Shop* itself, whose lack of certainty over what is being seen represents a vertiginous surrender to the pleasures of conjuring. Is Sweet William really swallowing coins, or does he just seem to be? What exactly are those feats of dexterity "of that kind"? Is his hand too fast for the narrator's eye? Are William's actions here performance, or merely practice? Here, the otherwise omniscient narrator finds himself—and himself alone—in the uncanny position of the spectator of magic and finds the experience uncomfortable. Little wonder, then, that the narrator quickly passes over Sweet William, as a character with disturbing magical powers of narrative self-reflexivity.

What, however, is the wider significance of these references to conjuring? Understanding the importance of Sweet William and other "amateur" conjurors (of which *The Old Curiosity Shop* abounds) requires us to consider a debate contemporary with the appearance of the novel, the mid-nineteenth century debate over intellectual property and copyright. Dickens's own concerns with these questions, aligned along the axes of financial security for authors and the dignity of the literary profession, are already well documented and only require a brief rehearsal here.[1] From an early stage of his career, Dickens's fiction was especially prone to unsolicited appropriation both on page and on stage, leading to his firm support for the campaign in the late 1830s to reform copyright law, spearheaded by Thomas Noon Talfourd (the dedicatee of *The Pickwick Papers*). Talfourd's bill, first proposed in 1837, sought to build on the Copyright Act of 1814, which had extended the term of protection to twenty-eight years or the lifetime of the author, whichever was longer. Talfourd's first bill proposed to protect literary works for the lifetime of the author plus sixty years, and to reassert the copyright of authors for existing texts once the 28-year period had expired. Despite vocal support from William Wordsworth and the backing of Dickens, the bill was unsuccessful, and subjected to various amendments in future bills (the 60-year postmortem term was ultimately deemed inessential). The Copyright Act was finally passed in 1842, proposed by Lord Mahon (after Talfourd had lost his seat in 1841), and secured copyright for 42 years from the date of publication (Feather 146). Such was the British debate occurring during Dickens's writing and publication of *The Old Curiosity Shop*. His most notorious engagement with questions of copyright, however, occurred during his American tour in 1842, and his famous speech to a dinner held in Boston regarding international copyright: "I hope the time is not far distant when (your writers), in America, will receive of right some substantial profit and return to England from their labours; and when we, in England, shall receive some substantial profit and return for ours" (qtd. in Welsh 31). Here, the twin motives of economics and authorial dignity coincide.

The Copyright Act of 1814, and Talfourd's proposed reforms, effectively placed the author (as opposed to the patron or publisher/ bookseller) at the center of the debate over literary ownership (Feather 124). Thus, in theorizing copyright, cultural historians have privileged categories of originality, individuality, and property. Mark Rose comments: "Copyright is founded on the concept of the unique individual who creates something original and is entitled to reap a profit from those labours" (2). Similarly, far from being a natural right, the very concept of intellectual property is a historically determined one that comes into being with the individualization of the author in the Middle Ages and the creation of a literary marketplace in the seventeenth century (Rose 3). The importance of originality and individuality to copyright was a development of the Lockean discourse whereby property was created by an individual removing materials from nature and transforming them into something new through labor. In this argument, Rose notes that

> A work of literature belonged to an individual because it was, finally, an embodiment of that individual. And the product of this imprinting of the author's personality on the common stock of the world was a "work of original authorship." The basis of literary property, in other words, was not just labor but "personality," and this revealed itself in "originality." (114)

It is through these concepts that *The Old Curiosity Shop* obliquely addresses contemporary debates about intellectual property. The novel is full of facsimiles and copies, characterized according to the accuracy of their imitation. Mrs. Jarley's waxworks, for instance, are presented positively, because they represent a general exchange of ideas rather than a detailed copying of features (the models are vague enough to represent any number of celebrities); in other words, they conform to the legal distinction between *idea* and *expression*. By contrast, Sampson Brass's precise copying of texts is represented as an act of violence: "Mr Sampson Brass sat upon his stool copying some legal process, and viciously digging his pen deeper into the paper, as if he were writing upon the very heart of the party against whom it was directed" (*OCS* 252). It is not too much of a shift to imagine Brass here as the adaptor/plagiarist, "writing upon the very heart" of the "original" author.

These scenes hover around the two key categories of intellectual property that Rose identifies, personality and originality. But both clash noisily in the character of Quilp, who has been variously interpreted as a pleasure principle, demonic force, and sexual energy. A reading of *The Old Curiosity Shop* in the context of magic and copyright reveals Quilp as a deranged conjuror of originality. John Bowen is only partially right to comment that "*The Old Curiosity Shop* is a deeply repetitive novel [. . .] many of the characters feel compelled to repeat themselves in words or action" (151), for Quilp strenuously resists such a compulsion whenever he can. His key weapon is to be unexpected, both in the numerous occasions in the novel where he appears out of nowhere, but also in the bullying of his wife: "by an unexpected skip or leap, he made his wife start backward with an irrepressible shriek" (*OCS* 43). Thus one of the adjectives most frequently used to describe Quilp is "uncommon"; he scratches his head in an "uncommonly vicious manner" (*OCS* 51) and has "uncommon agility" (*OCS* 80), which he uses in the service of his "taste for doing something fantastic" (*OCS* 80). Similar to a conjuror, he makes unpredictable use of objects in ways other than their intended function; the minute hand of a clock (Master Humphrey's?) serves as a toothpick (*OCS* 49). Yet, whereas the conjuror must make his performance intelligible before subverting his audience's expectations, Quilp moves directly to uncanny disorientation. Such extreme originality, inevitably, leads to incomprehension on the part of his observers, as, for instance, when he entertains himself "with a melodious howl, intended for a song, but bearing not the faintest resemblance to any scrap of any piece of music, vocal or instrumental, ever invented by man" (*OCS* 380).

Quilp's relations with others are similarly based around the Romanticist dyad of author/plagiarist. Quilp simultaneously despises and expects unoriginality in others, because it ensures his own striking originality. His initial approach to Nell intends to reduce her to facsimile: "My number two, Nelly, my second, my Mrs Quilp" (*OCS* 53). He despises Brass as a mere copyist: "Some people would have spared themselves the jabbering of such a parrot as you" (*OCS* 94). In describing Mrs. Quilp, he notes that "she never has a will of her own" (*OCS* 42); her replies are "customary" (*OCS* 43), rehearsed and repeated, as compared to the originality of her husband: "the small *lord of the creation* took his *first* cigar and mixed his *first* glass of grog" (*OCS* 43, emphasis added). No wonder, then, that his bitterest household enemy—his mother-in-law—should bear a name challenging Quilp's monopoly on artistic originality and authenticity; Mrs. Jiniwin is too *genuine* for Quilp's comfort. Tom Scott, too, threatens Quilp's status as the only one to defy convention. How else to interpret his seemingly disproportionate rage at Scott's standing on his head? In Quilp's world, the only person who is allowed to turn the world upside down is Quilp; such is Scott's trespass on his originality that Quilp is stung into repetition, continually referring to Scott as "You dog!" (*OCS* 48). Even on the rare occasions when Quilp does slip into repetition, Dickens is careful to undermine such moments by calling attention to the inadequacies of representation or by taking the narrative in a surreally unexpected direction. The most striking example of this occurs when Brass visits Quilp following his own sleight of hand in disposing of Kit. The "chant" Quilp sings, "being a monotonous repetition of one sentence in a very rapid manner" (*OCS* 461), is indeed a repetition, but an incomprehensible one; the scene violently regains a Quilpian sense of originality when Brass enters to find Quilp surrealistically attacking the ship's figurehead that represents Kit.

Browne's illustration, an image in which all three bodies are distorted out of recognizable scale, emphasizes the reader's sense of disorientation. In this sense, those who consider Quilp's presentation throughout the novel to be inconsistent miss the point; inconsistency represents the rejection of imitation (to act consistently is, after all, to imitate one's own earlier actions). Dickens famously called himself the Inimitable; Quilp represents the one who will not imitate. But ultimately, of course, Quilp's attempts to be utterly original are doomed to failure, primarily because the wider structure of the novel makes clear the irony of Quilp's situation. The one character who strives to embody originality is, in fact, the least original personality of the novel, and Dickens labors Quilp's parallels with Punch. If Dick Swiveller represents (as Stewart suggests) the literary world in which texts are to be exchanged, quoted, and played with in a creative commons, then Quilp is a satire of the opposite: the artist who too zealously insists on the autonomy of his own creative processes and who lacks the perspective to see that his own creativity is itself informed by an intertextual reinvention and borrowing.

It may seem that I have wandered some way from conjuring. How, then, do ideas of intellectual property relate to magic? One way of making this connection might be to consider copyright as a kind of spiritualism, both being discourses that seek to maintain the presence and rights of the self after death; as Pettitt notes, Dickens's speculations "on the future life of his own intellectual property brought with it uncomfortable intimations of mortality" (200). Those campaigning for copyright reform were also fighting for a professional and economic future (Pettitt 4), and the extension of the term of copyright following the 1842 act moved this horizon beyond the death of the author. Postmortem protection had been, after all, the raison d'être of Talfourd's proposals (Feather 142). But if concepts of intellectual property were important to novelists and mechanical inventors, they were absolutely crucial to conjurors, as their art is entirely dependent on the ownership of secrets (or, at least, the appearance of secrecy) and the originality of effects. Early Victorian literary representations of conjurors insist on their placement in an economy; the conjuror is always a figure with something to sell rather than the disinterested artist who must reluctantly enter the marketplace. The *escamoteur* thus becomes an exemplary critical figure for Marx and Engels, who frequently deploy secular magic as a metaphor for intellectual and rhetorical dishonesty.[2] Likewise, in Henry Cockton's *The Life and Adventures of Valentine Vox, the Ventriloquist* (1839), a novel heavily inspired by Dickensian picaresque, the conjuror Signor Antonio Hesperio de Bellamoniac (in reality, the more prosaically named John Tod) colludes with a newspaper editor to publish a false review to promote ticket sales (Cockton 6). In 1859, an English translation appeared of the *Memoirs* of the French conjuror Eugène Robert-Houdin, a key point in the Victorian conception of the conjuror, and was reviewed by Edmund Saul Dixon in *Household Words* in 1859. Robert-Houdin was largely responsible for the creation of the modern idea of the magician, of the gentleman artist in evening dress. But the *Memoirs* also consolidated the figure of the conjuror as a stakeholder in the intellectual property debate. Thus Robert-Houdin makes some impressive promises to his readers:

> [W]hat you seek in my book will be displayed before your eager gaze. You will know how a magician is produced, and you will learn that the tree whence my magic staff was cut was only that of persevering labor, often bedewed by the sweat of my brow; soon, too, when you come to witness my labors and my anxious hours of expectation, you will be able to appreciate the cost of a reputation in my mysterious art. (26)

Reputation becomes a commodity with a "cost" paid for by "the sweat of my brow." Such intangibles are not to be relinquished easily. Elsewhere, Robert-Houdin describes reading an advertisement for a conjuror called Olivier: "His programme contained the whole of Pinetti's tricks, which was almost my own. Which of the two was the plagiarist?" (126). Robert-Houdin's immediate response is not a consideration of recurrent tropes or themes in conjuring, or even the acknowledgement of a creative community of magicians, but the enclosure of a cultural commons into private competition (and for all the bonhomie of Dickens's Jolly Sandboys, Short nevertheless warns Nell that "we must be off early to-morrow morning, my dear, because unless we get the start of the dogs and the conjuror, the villages won't be worth a penny" [*OCS* 153]). Graham Jones notes that Robert-Houdin is obsessed with originality, and it is on this that he bases his claim to artistry (37); Jones develops this point not so much in the direction of intellectual property as towards a reading of Robert-Houdin as a victim of a Bloomian anxiety of influence. It would, perhaps, be more historically accurate to describe Houdin's self-image in the terms Thomas Carlyle uses to describe the heroic man of letters: "[a]n original man;—not a secondhand, borrowing or begging man" (qtd. in Pettitt 7). But Robert-Houdin's claim to originality is, as Jones notes, misleading. The price of the text's credo of intellectual originality is historical accuracy. Thus Robert-Houdin implies the invention of a routine, Second Sight (in which his blindfolded son can describe objects given to his father), yet this routine was already being performed regularly in Europe by Pinetti in the late eighteenth century, and in the United States and the United Kingdom throughout the 1830s and 1840s (Jones 47). Regarding Robert-Houdin's unanswered question, "Who was the plagiarist?" the history of conjuring makes the answer uncomfortably clear.

The point I wish to make here is that conjurors not only had a stake in the early Victorian intellectual property debate but that they also challenge the ways in which cultural historians have theorized that debate. The historiography of Victorian intellectual property can be mapped according to two sets of oppositions. The first is the distinction between mechanical and literary modes of production, and the question of how the writer is represented, as either artist or inventor. Thus Claire Pettitt reads *Little Dorrit* as an appropriation of the mechanical model of creation in which intellectual property is patented rather than copyrighted. In presenting the inventor Daniel Doyce as the heroic but embattled creator, Pettitt contends, Dickens draws a complex analogy between the literary creation of the author and the mechanical creation of the engineer, presenting a "representation of the inventor [that] also reflects Dickens's model of his own creativity" (193). Trey Philpotts disagrees, pointing to Henry Morley's 1853 article in *Household Words*, "Patent Wrongs," as suggestive of Dickens's reluctance to draw parallels between the artist and inventor, insisting on *copyright* as opposed to *patent* (20). Yet, whereas such debates have tended toward an either/or mode of thinking about patents and copyrights, early Victorian conjuring existed squarely in the middle of such debates. Even if much of the energy of Robert-Houdin's *Memoirs* is spent in an attempt to renounce his background and upbringing as watch repairer and mechanical engineer ("Real sleight of hand must not be the tinman's work but the artist's, and people do not visit the latter to see instruments perform" [235]), the biography never escapes from the fact that Robert-Houdin's reputation as artist was built on his skill as an inventor.

Such slippage is also linguistic; no less a Victorian authority than Samuel Smiles notes that the term *conjurer* was used in the eighteenth century to denote a machine inventor (33). *The Old Curiosity Shop*, likewise, presents a conjuror whose wonders are based in mechanical invention. The final magician I wish to identify is, in many ways, the most crucial to the novel's resolution, the Single Gentleman. Dick Swiveller, a man with an eye for such things, assumes that the Brass's lodger is "some great conjuror or chemist" (*OCS* 271). Yet the reputation of the Single Gentleman's creativity is based entirely on mechanical invention, as represented by his strange metal temple:

> Greatly interested in his proceedings, Mr Swiveller observed him closely. Into one chamber of this temple he dropped an egg, into another some coffee, into a third a compact piece of raw steak from a neat tin case, into a fourth he poured some water. Then, with the aid of a phosphorus-box and some matches, he procured a light and applied it to a spirit lamp which had a place of its own below the temple; then he shut down the lids of all the little chambers, then he opened them; and then, by some wonderful and unseen agency, the steak was done, the egg was boiled, the coffee was accurately prepared, and his breakfast was ready. (*OCS* 271–72)

The Victorian conjuror was neither literary artist nor mechanical inventor and yet was both simultaneously, showing off mechanical tricks dressed in linguistic patter.

The second opposition is between public and private, between "a culture belonging to the people, and that of knowledge as privately owned" (Pettitt 153). Pettitt phrases this second opposition in terms of a dilemma:

> the privacy afforded by copyright law is always partial—the right to own one's ideas for a limited period before they become public property. And for those ideas to achieve a market value, they must be published and on display, thus always running the risk of piracy and copying. Display, therefore, both creates and threatens the value of intellectual property. (180)

Much discussion of Dickens and intellectual property has seen him as shuttling back and forth between the poles of these oppositions, balancing a concern for private literary creation and ownership with his relations with a wider community of readers. Dickens restlessly policed the ownership of his creations, yet he also needed to put them at risk of imitation and piracy by making them public. The need to find a resolution to such a dilemma, I suggest, explains Dickens's fascination with conjuring in the 1840s, because magicians seem to have the best of both worlds; they make their performances public but keep their methods private. Such secrets may be, as Miller suggests, open secrets, but even an open secret is marked as the property of its holder (indeed, Miller suggests, it constitutes the very subjectivity of its holder). Ultimately, although Sweet William's body is distorted by the demands of the marketplace, he represents the best available compromise between the artist and his public: a self-reflexive artistry that invokes wonder in its spectators but that keeps enough back as the artist's own property.

In conclusion, my ultimate claim is that it should be clear that the coincidence of the period of Dickens's greatest engagement with conjuring with agitation over issues of copyright is not accidental. Both discourses mediate between the public and the private, between public display and private secret, and the transformation of ideas and techniques into tangible properties. Recent critical readings of Dickens's ideas of authorship have tended to move between the poles of the mechanical intellectual property enshrined in the patent and the artistic property of copyright; conjuring reconciles and combines these opposites. But there is another political aspect to secular magic, which would have appealed to Dickens as an agent of cultural change. Recent theorizations of conjuring have seen it as offering insights into how we conceive "alternatives to seemingly settled realities" (Coppa, Hass, and Peck 10). Such a reading stresses the potential of conjuring as hegemonic critique, each miracle effectively a way of saying that the world does not have to be the way it appears. *The Old Curiosity Shop* presents a multitude of conjurors: Master Humphrey, Quilp, Dick Swiveller, the Single Gentleman, and, most explicitly, Sweet William himself. Each of their conjuring routines has a transformative effect (on others' lives, their narratives, and their own bodies). Dickens, however, shows us the real potential of conjuring: to show us things not as they are, but as they could be.

NOTES

1 In addition to the standard biographical accounts of Dickens's intervention in the intellectual property debate, see also the accounts given by Alexander Welsh, Andrew Burke, Amanda Clayburgh, Gerhard Joseph, Claire Pettitt, and Trey Philpotts, among others.

2 For instance, in the first volume of *Capital*, Marx accuses the American H. Carey of performing a "conjuring trick" in reconfiguring slavery as developed capitalist free association, rather than bare commodity relations (543); such rhetoric occurs throughout Marx's and Engels's writings, particularly in *The German Ideology* and Engels's *Anti-Dühring*. Jacques Derrida also considers Marx's use of conjuring as metaphor in *Specters of Marx* (1994; first published in French in 1993).

BIBLIOGRAPHY

Bhownagary, Jehangir. "Creativity of the Magician." *Leonardo* 5.1 (1972): 31–35.

Bowen, John. *Other Dickens: Pickwick to Chuzzlewit*. Oxford, 2000.

Burke, Andrew. "Purloined Pleasures: Dickens, Currency, and Copyright." *Dickens Studies Annual* 41 (2010): 61–79.

Buzard, James. "Enumeration and Exhaustion: Taking Inventory in *The Old Curiosity Shop*." *Dickens Studies Annual* 39 (2008): 17–41.

Clayburgh, Amanda. "Towards a New Transatlanticism: Dickens in the United States." *Victorian Studies* 48.3 (2006): 439–59.

Cockton, Henry. *The Life and Adventures of Valentine Vox, the Ventriloquist*. 1839. London, [c. 1880].

Coppa, Francesca. "The Body Immaterial: Magicians' Assistants and the

Performance of Labor." Coppa, Hass and Peck 85–106.

———, Lawrence Hass, and James Peck, eds. *Performing Magic on the Western Stage from the Eighteenth Century to the Present.* Basingstoke, 2008.

Derrida, Jacques. *Spectres of Marx: The State of the Debt, the Work of Mourning, and the New International.* Trans. Peggy Kamuf. New York, 1994.

Dickens, Charles. *The Letters of Charles Dickens.* Ed. Madeline House, Graham Storey et al. 12 vols. Oxford, 1965–2002.

———. *Master Humphrey's Clock and A Child's History of England.* 1841; 1853. Oxford, 1958.

———. *The Old Curiosity Shop.* 1841. London, 2000.

Dixon, Edmund Saul. "Out-Conjuring Conjurors." *Household Words* 9 April 1859: 433–56.

During, Simon. *Modern Enchantments: The Cultural Power of Secular Magic.* Cambridge, MA, 2002.

Feather, John. *Publishing, Piracy and Politics: A Historical Study of Copyright in Britain.* London, 1994.

Forster, John. *The Life of Charles Dickens.* 2 vols. New York, 1876.

Gertsman, Elina. "Illusion and Deception: Construction of a Proverb in Hieronymus Bosch's *The Conjurer*." *Athanor* 22 (2004): 31–37.

Hennelly, Mark M. "Carnivalesque 'Unlawful Games' in *The Old Curiosity Shop*." *Dickens Studies Annual* 22 (1993): 67–120.

Jones, Graham M. "The Family Romance of Modern Magic: Contesting Robert-Houdin's Cultural Legacy in Contemporary France." Coppa, Hass and Peck 33–60.

Joseph, Gerhard. "Construing the Inimitable's Silence: Pecksniff's Grammar School and International Copyright." *Dickens Studies Annual* 22 (1993): 121–36.

Marx, Karl. *Capital: A Critical Analysis of Capitalist Production.* Vol. 1. 1867. London, 1971.

Miller, D. A. *The Novel and the Police.* Berkeley, 1988.

Pettitt, Claire. *Patent Inventions: Intellectual Property and the Victorian Novel.* Oxford, 2004.

Philpotts, Trey. "Dickens, Invention, and Literary Property in the 1850s." *Dickens Quarterly* 24.1 (2007): 18–26.

Robert-Houdin, Jean Eugène. *Memoirs of Robert-Houdin: Ambassador, Author and Conjurer.* Philadelphia, 1859.

Rose, Mark. *Authors and Owners: The Invention of Copyright.* Cambridge, MA, 1993.

Schlicke, Paul. *Dickens and Popular Entertainment.* London, 1985.

Smiles, Samuel. *Self Help: With Illustrations of Character, Conduct and Perseverance.* 2nd ed. London, 1866.

Steinmeyer, Jim. *Hiding the Elephant: How Magicians Invented the Impossible.*

London, 2004.
Stewart, Garrett. *Dickens and the Trials of Imagination*. Cambridge, MA, 1974.
Triplett, Norman. "The Psychology of Conjuring Deceptions." *American Journal of Psychology* 11.4 (1900): 439–510.
Welsh, Alexander. *From Copyright to Copperfield: The Identity of Dickens*. Cambridge, MA, 1987.

POPULAR DICKENS: CHANGING *BLEAK HOUSE* FOR THE EAST END STAGE

Chris Louttit
Radboud Universiteit Nijmegen

From the very beginning of his career until after its end, Dickens's contemporary critics often remarked on the ability of his fiction to cross class boundaries. In an 1837 review, for example, George Henry Lewes mentions that "'Boz' has perhaps a wider popularity than any man has enjoyed for many years," appealing to both "intellectual" and "common people." Lewes continues engagingly in this vein, noting that "[f]requently we have seen the butcher-boy, with his tray on his shoulder, reading with the greatest avidity the last 'Pickwick;' the footman [. . .], the maid-servant, the chimney-sweep, all classes, in fact, read 'Boz'" (qtd. in Rodensky 590). Looking back over Dickens's career in 1877, Edmund Whipple claimed that Dickens's "popularity [. . .] was confined to no class, but extended to all classes, rich and poor, noble and plebeian. The Queen on the throne read him, and so did Hodge at the plow" (qtd. in Collins 333). Critical remarks such as these provide eloquent, if rather impressionistic, evidence of Dickens's broad appeal. But how, more specifically, might we begin to work out what ordinary readers, what Jonathan Rose calls "the general reading public" (195) and Richard Altick calls "the English common reader,"[1] thought of Dickens? How exactly did they receive, understand, and respond to Dickens's work?

As Jonathan Rose has argued, "if you are tracking the reactions of London reviewers to Charles Dickens, source material is hardly a problem" (195). Discovering the "opinion" of the common reader is, however, more difficult. In making a start on this act of recovery, Rose has suggested archival sources such as social surveys, library registers and, perhaps most importantly, working-class autobiographies and memoirs. Rose's own research on the working-class reception of Dickens demonstrates interestingly how Dickens "spoke directly to the workers" and was "repeatedly" invoked by them "to describe their own life experiences" (207). Yet, largely because he focuses on working-class readers across a number of decades, Rose's discussion of the reception of Dickens, while enlightening, remains quite broad. In what follows I approach the issue of Dickens's popular audience from another, more specific, angle by offering an account of two East End dramatizations of his novel *Bleak House*, which appeared in June 1853 before the novel had even finished its serial run.

It should be admitted that examining theatrical adaptations of Dickens does not provide direct evidence of the reception of his fiction among working-class readers. Indeed, it runs the risk of what Rose calls "the receptive fallacy": the act of trying "to discern the influence of a text on an audience simply by examining the text," even if that text is created for a popular audience (209). Narrowly conceived, then, this essay does not explore the reception of Dickens's texts themselves. It argues nonetheless that plays such as those about to be discussed provide invaluable evidence of the popular response to Dickens and shed light on him as a cultural phenomenon. Here I agree with Sally Ledger's response to Ian Haywood's claim that Dickens was "not truly popular in the sense that he was available directly to working-class readers" (qtd. in Ledger 5). She suggests convincingly that, to understand the true extent of Dickens's "quite staggering" "popular 'reach,'" we need to consider the cultural life of the novels beyond the monthly installments (5).[2]

Analysis of the texts and production histories of these neglected adaptations of *Bleak House* allows us, in other words, to consider what it was about Dickens that appealed to this East End audience. It also offers us the chance of reflecting further on the popular politics or popular radicalism of Dickens that has begun to be the focus of critics in recent years. This realigning of our understanding of Dickens from middle-class moralist to popular radical is best expressed in Sally Ledger's important study *Dickens and the Popular Radical Imagination*, where she claims that the fact "[t]hat Dickens was a radical political writer on the side of the poor and the dispossessed was blazingly clear

Popular Dickens 193

to his contemporaries and to many critics in the first half of the twentieth century" (2).³ The consideration of two East End versions of *Bleak House* that follows keeps these broad questions about Dickens in mind and ask if these plays radicalize his work, or if they conceive of it as effective popular entertainment, or, indeed, if it is possible to disentangle these two categories of "radicalism" and "popular entertainment" from each other.

Theater historians have attempted, especially in the past few years, to rescue and to reinterpret the critically maligned genre of Victorian melodrama. As Caroline Radcliffe and Kate Mattacks point out,

> Victorian drama has long been dogged by value judgements over the lack of literary merit, and critical methodology is emerging in favour of [. . .] an "intertheatrical" approach whereby the textual evidence is read alongside the complex relationships between theatres, players and audiences [. . .]. (1)

Criticism that engages with the popular Victorian theater must therefore, in some sense, be an act of the imagination as well as one of critical recuperation. It is not possible, of course, to go back to June 1853 to experience the stagings of *Bleak House* themselves. We must instead reconstruct an impression of them, as Radcliffe and Mattacks suggest, from the play manuscripts and from what we know about the performance history and reception of these works. Such critically imaginative reconstruction can only benefit our understanding of Dickens as a cultural phenomenon.

It should be noted, however, that this act of recuperation is particularly difficult for the East End theater. There is, first of all, a relative paucity of available evidence about the production and reception of plays in the Victorian East End. The Royal Pavilion Theatre in Whitechapel and the City of London Theatre on Norton Folgate, where the adaptations of *Bleak House* were performed, were not legitimate but rather neighborhood theaters, known particularly for nautical and domestic melodrama. As such, they were largely ignored by both the general and theatrical metropolitan press, and at this point in the century, the local East End papers had yet to be founded.⁴ Thanks to the scholarship of Jim Davis and Victor Emeljanow, though, we do have a general sense of the kind of audience that attended East End theaters. As they explain in their study *Reflecting the Audience*, it was surprisingly diverse:

> [T]he East End community, and consequently the Pavilion's potential audience, was a mixed one, in which the more debauched and more respectable inhabitants lived in close proximity[. . . . This] is implied by the *East London Observer* in an [1857] account of the Ratcliffe Highway [. . .] A community "connected with pitch, tar, marine stores and the Thames Tunnel" might be thought to exist there, yet, "strange though the fact may appear in this long street of crimp slopsellers, flaring gin palaces, sailors' Boarding Houses, equivocal coffee shops, and flash Dancing saloons there are steady, hard working, respectable [. . .] and *wealthy* tradesmen with staid matrons." (57)

According to Davis and Emeljanow, then, the inhabitants of Whitechapel who might have sat in the stalls at the Pavilion were quite a humble group. Many, indeed, were connected with riverside industries. Yet it is also dangerous to generalize too much about their "low character," as many were well-off residents of the neighborhood with an interest in popular entertainment.

It is not entirely impossible, moreover, to build up some sense of a play's popularity and success with this audience. More specifically, playbills and advertisements in *The Era* newspaper tell us that an adaptation of *Bleak House* ran in June and July of 1853 for five weeks at the Pavilion Theatre and three weeks at the City of London Theatre. This information is significant because it revises Philip Bolton's estimate of the popularity of *Bleak House* on the stage. In his detailed bibliographical study *Dickens Dramatized*, Bolton argues that "[t]he initial theatrical responses to the novel indicate a continuing decline in the growth rate for the Dickens dramatizing industry" (349). It is indeed true that there was not the sheer number and range of adaptations as there had been of great favorites like *The Pickwick Papers*, *Oliver Twist*, and *Nicholas Nickleby*. I would suggest, however, that Bolton's research slightly underestimates the popularity of these very early adaptations of *Bleak House* with the predominantly, though not exclusively, working-class East End audience. What this tells us more generally is that Dickens was beginning to disappear from the West End theaters during the 1850s but remained a lively staple of East End repertoires.[5] This pattern also interestingly confirms the more general trend in Dickens's critical reception from the mid-1850s to the early twentieth century, with the maintenance of a popular interest but an increasingly negative response from professional critics.[6]

Other fragments of evidence suggest that those involved with the *Bleak House* productions had a sense that they were working on a distinctive version of the inimitable, what we might call for the purposes of this essay "Popular Dickens" or "East End Dickens." George Dibdin Pitt, the coauthor of the Pavilion production, was a prolific playwright for the non-legitimate stage who wrote, according to the data collected by Philip Bolton, five adaptations of Dickens's works including *Bleak House*.[7] Bolton usefully provides transcriptions of notes from the manuscripts of other Dickens plays that give us an indication of Pitt's broad strategies in approaching the adaptation of Dickens's fiction. On the manuscript of *The Battle of Life*, staged at the Britannia Theatre, Pitt criticizes the Lyceum play of this Christmas story, written by Albert Smith and starring the famous theatrical couple Mr. and Mrs. Keeley, for "being too Quiet." He explains that his piece, "tho' taken from the work varies in many respects both form that and the Albert Smith Drama [. . .] that it may suit the taste of the Audience. It is in many instances higher coloured and more melodramatic" (*Dickens Dramatized* 298).[8] A note on the manuscript of Pitt's adaptation of *The Seven Poor Travellers*, staged at the Pavilion Theatre in 1855, provides further evidence that he knew what had to be done to please his popular audience; the "little sketch" had been "dramatized by the Veteran Author to embrace the main incidents of the tale without any superfluous matter" (*Dickens Dramatized* 374).[9]

A fascinating 1854 letter to the editor of *The Era* by the lessee and stage manager of the Pavilion Theatre, Frederick Neale, gives us a slightly different sense of what it was about Dickens that appealed to this audience. In the letter, Neale energetically rebukes *The Era* (the main source of London theater news and reviews) for not including his *Bleak House* in that year's dramatic chronology. He writes,

> Allow me to correct an error in the Dramatic Chronology for 1853, published in your last Sunday's Paper. It is there stated (under the date of June 14), "*The only dramatized version of Bleak House, by Dickens, playing at the City of London Theatre.*" Now in the very same month, and, if I mistake not, on the *same night*, we produced a version of the "Great Master's" work at the Pavilion [. . .] which version had a *successful run of five weeks* to most excellent houses. I have written this to prove that *Mr. Charles Dickens's* works are appreciated at the *eastern part of the metropolis*, and that its inhabitants can enjoy the beautiful creation of life-like characters with the same *gusto* as *the denizens of Belgravia*. As a *proof*, every work of the renowned author of "Pickwick" has not only been *read with avidity*, but all his Christmas (and other) works have been

presented in *a dramatic form at the Pavilion* and the other theatres. (12, emphasis in the original)

We might read this letter as a predictable—and flamboyant—grab for publicity by an ambitious theater manager. Even if this is so, what is striking is the seeming earnestness to prove—a word notably repeated here—that Dickens was an important and well-loved part of the East End theatrical scene. The aspect of Dickens's work that Neale picks up on, "his beautiful creation of life-like characters," might not seem a particularly profound response. It is significant, however, in helping us understand one quite basic way in which Dickens's work appealed to this audience. They felt able to identify with his life-like, "real" characters who represented the kind of person, perhaps, that they might encounter in their day-to-day lives.

It is the texts of the plays themselves, of course, which provide the most detailed evidence of the strategies that were adopted in changing Dickens, and Dickens's *Bleak House*, for the East End stage. In her useful study *Dickens, Novel Reading, and the Victorian Popular Theatre*, Deborah Vlock reminds us that stage dramatizations of Dickens's work were as much involved in dialogue with each other as with the original serials. As she eloquently puts it, "they existed independently of the novels, whispering amongst themselves, jockeying for position on the boards" (35). This is also true, to an extent, of the East End adaptations of *Bleak House*. The rivalry between the two productions is, in fact, well demonstrated by another of Pitt's manuscript notes, where he promises, rather sensationally, that his will be the "only Version in which Captn Hawdon is Resuscitated and is the Ghost of himself." What is still striking, nonetheless, are the emphases that they share as interpretations of this great novel.

Both of them, for instance, spend a great deal of stage time around the novel's scenes of "low" or even "vagabond" life at Krook's rag and bottle shop, at George's Shooting Gallery, and the brickmaker's cottage. We can surmise that these locations and the characters who inhabit them would appear as heightened versions of ordinary, everyday life for East End audiences. It might seem strange to us now to consider what seem exaggerated or grotesque characters such as Miss Flite, Krook and Phil Squod as "realistic" characters. Yet, as Frederick Neale, the manager of the Pavilion Theatre pointed out, what appealed to the East End audience was Dickens's "life-like characters." This point is, moreover, not an isolated one.

As William Macready put it forcefully in 1839, "Dickens seizes the eager attention of his readers by the strong power of reality. [. . .] In everything of that kind that he presents to us, there is, in his manner of doing it [. . .] the truth of life as it is" (qtd. in Vlock 32). What was considered "realistic" or "truthful" was dependent in part, it seems, upon shared notions of social life as a theatrical and performative act. One benefit of studying almost forgotten plays such as these is to remind us once more of this aspect of Victorian culture, which enables us to put our own conceptions of what is "realistic" into perspective.

The attention both plays give to the novel's scenes of ordinary life also needs to be considered in the context of the types of plays that were a part of the repertoire of East End theaters. As Heidi J. Holder has recently shown, "the audiences of the east apparently could not tire of seeing the problems of the London poor resolved on the stage" in examples of "[t]he subgenre of urban melodrama" (263). Plays focusing on the working poor such as James Elphinstone's *London Labour and the London Poor*, staged at the Pavilion in 1854, became particularly popular in the 1850s and 1860s at the time of the "heyday of the 'social explorer'" and the success of Henry Mayhew's first-hand accounts of street life (Holder 263). It is perhaps unsurprising that, staged and received in this context, these East End adaptations of *Bleak House* emphasize the scenes that deal directly with the urban poor. They might be understood, indeed, as Dickens viewed through the lens of urban melodrama and social explorers such as Mayhew. Dickens's text is certainly given a more hard-hitting and realistic edge at certain points in these adaptations. The sixth scene in the Pavilion play, for instance, adapts the episode from chapter eight of *Bleak House* in which Esther and Ada join Mrs. Pardiggle on one of her missions to improve the poor. In Dickens's novel, the brick maker, "looking very dissipated" lying on the floor, is an angrily (and in a sense justifiably) recalcitrant figure who admits to drunkenness and beating his wife (*BH* 99). In the version staged at the Pavilion, his character is made even more stubborn and violent. A stage direction in the manuscript describes the brick maker "laid" on the stage as in Dickens's text and Phiz's illustration, but significantly adds that he is "smacking his Short Wife" rather than merely admitting to it after the event (Pitt).

Both plays also have much less to say about the aristocratic elements of *Bleak House*. Much like Andrew Davies's 2005 BBC television version, they leave out Dickens's withering anti-aristocratic political satire, focused on the abuses and idleness of Boodle, Coodle, Doodle, Foodle, and the rest of the Chesney Wold set. Given that much of Dickens's social satire in the novel is delivered rather indirectly by its ironic omniscient narrator, it is perhaps unsurprising that this does not translate well to the (popular) stage. The plays focus instead on the more melodramatic or theatrical aspects of Dickens's intriguingly divided text. Tulkinghorn and Smallweed function as the bad characters who must be controlled, and the action of both plots is resolved in part through marriage and domestic harmony. In this way these stage versions of *Bleak House* function in narratological terms more like Dickens's early fiction in which "the main source of evil" is "a 'bad' individual character" rather than "a government institution" (Ledger 201). They therefore lack the "shift from a focus on individuals to a more structural social and political critique" (Ledger 199) that occurs in the development from Dickens's early, rather haphazard novels to the mature and well-planned ones.

This last point suggests that these stage versions of the novel rather blunt the satirical potential of Dickens's text. Yet this is not quite true. Certainly the one staged at the Pavilion Theatre ends with marriage and domestic harmony but still offers a rather subversive conclusion to the (in June 1853) as-yet-unfinished events of the novel. The impoverished law writer Nemo (otherwise Captain Hawdon) comes back from the dead to inherit from the Chancery suit and reclaim his wife and illegitimate child, and the crippled Phil Squod becomes a rather unlikely hero by shooting Tulkinghorn dead. In many other different ways, moreover, the plays offer up a more "popular" brand of radicalism, one that is focused largely on the struggles of the working poor and their resourcefulness in confronting these struggles. With this shift of emphasis, satiric energy is directed not so much toward the abuses of Chancery or the cronyism of Parliament but rather toward the misuse of the "comic coroner's inquest," or Jo's "inkwhich" from chapter 11 of the novel. It is true that in the plays the broad humor of the scene is stressed at the expense of Dickens's more darkly ironic and indirect account in the novel. Another striking piece of external evidence suggests, however, that the radical potential of such scenes was clear to Dickens's popular audience at the time. In a note in the manuscript for the Pavilion Theatre version of *Bleak House*, Pitt makes the following remarks. He seems to be directing them at the Lord Chamberlain's Chief Licenser of plays. He writes,

Note
having recieved Information, that an offence has been given by Mr Dickens, in the Description of the Inquest, as making it too ludicrous—I have left that Scene out in this Version and interwoven the Witnesses in the Death Scene—this is also will be the only Version in which Captn Hawdon is Resuscitated and is the Ghost of himself—the Lord Chamberlain has, I understand, recieved Instructions to suppress any Comic Coroner's Inquest, as in the Work—GDP

However much we might disagree with Pitt's judgments about the virtues of the fictional scene, what is interesting here is his nervousness about the potential of Dickens's scene to offend the authorities. Some of this twitchiness may be put down to Pitt's own experience with the censor as the author of rather lurid crime melodramas such as *Sweeney Todd* and, according to one critic, "the most censored playwright of the nineteenth century" (Stephens 46). Dickens could also obviously get away with more subversion than could Pitt, owing both to his status and to the genre in which he wrote. It seems sensible finally to attribute it to Pitt's awareness of the radical tradition of the comic set-piece trial sequence in which Dickens writes and that has been analyzed in detail by Ledger in *Dickens and the Popular Radical Imagination* (39–105).

Both plays, more generally, present Dickens as a voice sympathetic to the concerns of the poor. There is no omniscient narrator to comment on the action or to tease out the injustices of this world. Individual characters, including Esther, Allan Woodcourt, and Jo, are used nonetheless to comment indirectly and abstractly on the plight of marginal figures such as Nemo, or to rather more bluntly point up the moral of a scene. Such statements can tend toward the sentimental, as in the following impromptu soliloquy in the City of London play prompted by the unhappy suffering and death of Nemo:

Wood
And this is the state of man. Already the breath is out of his body, all desert him—Alas! poor remains of mortality farewell—thou once had a mother to whose ear the first accents of thy infant voice were Seraphic—[. . .] The rich and poor must alike come to this—alike must die, and alike be forgotten in the Tide of Time. (Lee)

Yet they can also effectively (and rather more subtly) draw attention to a social issue of pressing concern to the London poor. In the Pavilion staging, for example, Jo is given lines that attack Mrs. Jellyby's "telescopic philanthropy." He points out that

> [i]f there be black slaves a sufferin in forin Parts, there be plenty of White Slaves a suffrin here, and why send a shillin so far off—when theres a hand stops your'n and a leetle thin small voice within as says, it be your duty to look at yr own brothers and sisters here, afore you send to the stranger & the savage. (Pitt)

The outrage of Dickens's narrator at the folly of "telescopic philanthropy" and foreign missions is put into the mouth of one of the chief victims of the policy.

This example suggests a very different Jo on the stage from the one that appears in the novel. In his article "*Bleak House* and the Playhouse," Philip Bolton convincingly argues that adapters of the novel throughout the nineteenth century saw "theatrical gold" in the "life and death of Jo the orphan" (84). Alert to the pathos and theatricality of Jo's story, dramatists made it central to the action: Jo became the plum part, and his death scene, the dramatic curtain call of the play. Bolton suggests that the appeal of Jo can be related to the interest and sympathy for "suffering children" evident in Dickensian figures such as Oliver Twist and Smike from *Nicholas Nickleby*, also both great successes on the stage. This is certainly partly true. What these very early plays add to Bolton's account is a striking re-interpretation of Dickens's street urchin. In the novel, Jo gradually becomes a sickly and pathetic figure, continually described as weak and "ragged" and in fear of being moved on. In the plays, however, Jo is a much feistier fellow, imbued with the spirit of Sam Weller and the Artful Dodger as much as with the fictional original. In a fascinating scene in the City of London play, Jo is introduced as one of the bearers of Smallweed's chair. Jo complains about the miserly payment he has just received with the remark that "I'm poor in pocket, but I scorns to take nothing from the poor in Spirit." Smallweed continues:

Old S
Impudent rascal—Ah, the pitch of insolence the London poor have come to—I should like to send 'em all to the treadmill

Joe
I dare say you would—but poor as they is, they gets their bread in the same old way or another by hard working and making themselves useful,

and that's more than many can say, and drives over 'em in their carriages and looks upon as dogs and dirt under their feet. (Lee)

In this scene Jo, much as he was in the Pavilion play with Mrs. Jellyby, is not only a "tough subject," but also an impassioned social critic. We might even imagine the audience enthusiastically cheering or applauding his comments about the "hard-working" poor. Indeed, the Jo who appears on the East End stage is not just "tough" but also quite moralistic. At one point in the Pavilion version, he observes "[w]hat fools & beasts Menfolks & Womenfolks they makes o' themselves When they is drunk" (Pitt). Later, in response to the brick maker's violence against his wife, he opines that "a man as would hit a woman, don't deserve to have a woman to hit at" (Pitt).

By the very end of both plays, however, we return to the sentiment and pathos more often associated with the character. Jo remains center stage as he expires and utters his famous line, repeated at many points during the action: "He wos wery good to me, he wos." Given the tougher, if not exactly incendiary, portrayal of Jo that we have seen, especially in the City of London version, this might not only seem rather sudden and unconvincing in dramatic terms but might also be viewed as a diminution of the radical potential of these adaptations. That both versions close with Jo's emphatic delivery of "He wos wery good to me, he wos" can also be interpreted in a different way. It suggests that the audience expected to see certain scenes and hear certain lines when they went to the theater. It is noticeable, for example, that characters such as Krook, Snagsby, and Miss Flite are given their most memorable lines of dialogue from the novel. In the case of one of the manuscripts, there is even a note prescribing how Snagsby's line "not to make too great a point of it" should be delivered (Pitt). We might speculate not only that the audience enjoyed the toughness of the stage Jo but also that much of the pleasure of going to see Dickens on the stage was concerned with moments, such as Jo's death scene, that would be recognized from the serial parts and from discussions about them. Indeed, in the Pavilion staging, Jo's memorable line is curiously memorialized. Captain Hawdon suggests "a stone" should be "raised to [Jo's] memory," "for few in thy simple state have exceeded thy worth." With his dying words Jo selflessly tells the audience what should be put on it: "Raised by the friend of poor Jo, who was allus werry good to him, he was" (Pitt). It is difficult for the modern reader not to detect a parodic note in such a conclusion. Yet it is entirely possible that the Pavilion Theatre audience enjoyed this final chance to hear Jo's well-known catchphrase before the curtain fell.

Much criticism of Dickens is now concerned, to borrow the title from a recent essay collection, with "Contemporary Dickens" and with what his work means for the present day. Such a focus is of course interesting and valuable. This essay has demonstrated, on the other hand, that it is worthwhile reengaging once more, as far as we can, with the popular reception of Dickens in his own time to try to reconstruct how his work and characters such as Jo were understood then. In reading these manuscripts and trying to understand the context of the popular stage, it becomes clear how fluid the boundaries were between supposedly high and low culture. The Pavilion Theatre version of *Bleak House*, for instance, includes multiple playful references to Shakespeare. Heidi J. Holder confirms that "Shakespeare's plays were performed with considerable regularity at East End venues" (268), and the Pavilion was no exception.[10] It seems likely, as a result, that those involved with the Pavilion *Bleak House* would have expected at least some of the audience to understand the allusions. At one point, Jo also makes a reference to "Pop Goes the Weasel," a popular song from the time that had also been turned into a short play on the bill of the Pavilion and theaters like it. *Bleak House*, then, was a part of a dynamic stage culture, with no rigid boundaries between different kinds of plays and their wider contexts. There is certainly more work to be done on what might be called the "popular" or "unauthorized" reception of Dickens's fiction on the Victorian stage. It may be the case that Dickens's satirical novelistic attacks on parliamentary cronyism, aristocratic "dandyism," and the abuses of Chancery are largely absent in the stage adaptations. Yet Dickens's attentiveness to the sufferings of the honest poor, and their neglect by those more interested in poverty abroad, is made directly and urgently apparent. This, however, is only part of the story. Both plays certainly conceive of Dickens as a radical voice sensitive to the concerns of his audience. But they also emphasize—and give new theatrical life to—his great talents in evoking pathos and in creating intensely popular and "life-like" characters. They help us, moreover, to begin to understand better what Dickens meant to this popular audience and work out, to adapt Jonathan Rose, what someone such as Jo would have thought of *Bleak House*.

NOTES

1 The phrase "the English common reader" is taken from Altick's seminal study of the same name.
2 Lisa Rodensky offers an analysis of Dickens's popularity, but her study is based on a reading of Dickens's critics' engagement with his "popularity" in more abstract terms in periodicals that positioned themselves as "serious and selective" (586).
3 Further discussion of Dickens's radicalism is provided in Sen.
4 As Michael Booth puts it, "Although East End drama was reviewed in the local press and in the *Era*—especially during the pantomime season—it was the exceptional critic or writer of repute who made the journey East" (58).
5 There were exceptions to this pattern, such as Tom Taylor's official adaptation of *A Tale of Two Cities* staged at the Lyceum Theatre in 1860 and Dion Boucicault's version of *The Cricket on the Hearth*, titled *Dot*, at the Adelphi Theatre in 1862.
6 For a recent succinct account of Dickens's shifting critical fortunes, see Mazzeno.
7 As well as *Bleak House*, the works he adapted were *Nicholas Nickleby* (City of London Theatre, 1838), *The Battle of Life* (Britannia Theatre, 1847), *Hard Times* (Pavilion Theatre, 1854), *The Seven Poor Travellers* (Pavilion Theatre, 1855). He also appeared as Wardle in *Pickwickians!!!* at the Surrey Theatre in 1837.
8 Any idiosyncrasies in the spelling and syntax of quoted manuscript sources remain unchanged.
9 Such statements demonstrate that Pitt was experienced in catering for the demands of his audience. John Russell Stephens has movingly shown that, after a long but not entirely successful career, Pitt finished his life not only writing for the working poor but also living in close proximity to them in the very neighborhoods where his plays were staged.
10 Playbills in the British Library show, in fact, that *The Merchant of Venice* and *Othello* were part of the Pavilion's repertoire in the first week of April in 1853, just before *Bleak House* was staged.

BIBLIOGRAPHY

Altick, Richard D. *The English Common Reader: A Social History of the Mass Reading Public 1800–1900*. Chicago, 1957.
Bolton, H. Philip. "*Bleak House* and the Playhouse." *Dickens Studies Annual* 12 (1983): 81–116.
— — —. *Dickens Dramatized*. London, 1987.
Booth, Michael. "East End Melodrama." *Theatre Survey* 22 (1976): 57–67.
Collins, Philip, ed. *Dickens: The Critical Heritage*. London, 1971.
Davis, Jim, and Victor Emeljanow. *Reflecting the Audience: London Theatregoing, 1840–1880*. Hatfield, 2001.
Dickens, Charles. *Bleak House*. Ed. Andrew Sanders. London, 1994.

Holder, Heidi J. "The East-End Theatre." *The Cambridge Companion to Victorian and Edwardian Theatre*. Ed. Kerry Powell. Cambridge, 2004. 257–76.
Ledger, Sally. *Dickens and the Popular Radical Imagination*. Cambridge, 2007.
Lee, Austin. *Bleak House*. City of London Theatre, 1853. MS 52940 K. British Lib., London.
Mazzeno, Laurence W. *The Dickens Industry: Critical Perspectives, 1836–2005*. Rochester, NY, 2008.
Neale, Frederick. "The Pavilion Theatre and the Dramatic Chronology." *Era* 8 Jan. 1854: 12.
Pavilion Theatre Playbill. 4 April 1853. MS Playbills 168. British Lib., London.
Pitt, George Dibdin. *Bleak House, or The Spectre of the Ghost Walk*. Pavilion Theatre, 1853. MS 52940 M. British Lib., London.
Radcliffe, Caroline, and Kate Mattacks. "From Analogues to Digital: New Resources in Nineteenth-Century Theatre." *19: Interdisciplinary Studies in the Long Nineteenth Century* 8 (2009): 1–18. Web. 20 May 2010. <http://www.19.bbk.ac.uk/index.php/19/article/viewFile/499/359>.
Rodensky, Lisa. "Popular Dickens." *Victorian Literature and Culture* 37 (2009): 583–607.
Rose, Jonathan. "How Historians Study Reader Response: Or, What Did Jo Think of *Bleak House*?" *Literature in the Marketplace: Nineteenth-Century British Publishing and Reading Practices*. Ed. John O. Jordan and Robert L. Patten. Cambridge, 1995. 195–212.
Sen, Sambudha. "*Bleak House* and *Little Dorrit*: The Radical Heritage." *English Literary History* 65 (1998): 945–70.
Stephens, John Russell. "Playwright *In Extremis*: George Dibdin Pitt Revisited." *Theatre Notebook* 53 (1999): 41–47.
Vlock, Deborah. *Dickens, Novel Reading, and the Victorian Popular Theatre*. Cambridge, 1998.

The Frozen Deep: Gad's Hill, June–July 1857

Robert Tracy
University of California, Berkeley

> 'Tis bitter cold,
> And I am sick at heart.
> —*Hamlet* I.1

In *Andersen's English* (2010), Irish playwright Sebastian Barry has turned Hans Christian Andersen's 1857 visit to Charles Dickens into a drama that examines dichotomies between Dickens's public and private personae, the authorial control he exercised over his wife and family, and the fictions he told himself about his own life. Barry himself has often written about members of his own family, shaping their lives to fit his theme in plays—*The Steward of Christendom* (1995) and *Our Lady of Sligo* (1998)—and in novels—*The Whereabouts of Eneas McNulty* (1998) and *The Secret Scripture* (2008).

Barry is fascinated by people caught on the wrong side of Irish history: Catholic loyalists who hoped for a peaceful transition to Home Rule under the British Crown after the First World War but who were thrust aside after the Easter Rising of 1916 and the War for Independence (1918–21). Thomas Dunne, the protagonist of *The Steward of Christendom*, is based on his great-grandfather, superintendent of the Dublin Municipal Police in the last years of British rule. In the play, Dunne lives on into bitter old age, remembering how he had to hand over Dublin Castle to the new Irish Free State and resign his post on January 16, 1922. Eneas McNulty fought in the British Army during the war but was unwelcome in Ireland after 1922.

Andersen's English, which toured in the United Kingdom from February through May 2010, places Charles Dickens and Hans Christian Andersen at the center of another play about misreading the direction that history is taking, in this case the direction of the domestic history of Dickens and his family, and Andersen's failure to read the signs and to understand the hints. It is also a skeptical look at the images of contented family life that Dickens projected in some of his novels and that made him the laureate of middle-class domesticity. Barry is interested in the dichotomy between Dickens as celebrator of family life and his decision to separate from his wife Catherine at the end of the 1850s. Barry's Dickens is a complex and unlikable character, welcoming Andersen to Gad's Hill but privately resenting and ridiculing him, creating an image of a happy family life in which he no longer believes, and being jingoistic in his enthusiasm for British imperialism.

Andersen's English is about Andersen's visit to Dickens at Gad's Hill in June and July 1857. The visit, as recorded in Dickens's letters and in the recollections of his children, was a disaster, largely due to Andersen's poor English and to his failure to understand that he had been invited for two weeks but stayed for five. Kate Dickens later recalled "a bony bore who stayed on and on" (Slater, *Charles Dickens* 429). Dickens's letters during and just after the visit turn Andersen into a Dickensian grotesque. When Andersen finally left on July 15, Dickens placed a card in his room: "Hans Christian Andersen slept in this room for five weeks—which seemed to the family AGES" (*Letters* 8: 372). He replied cordially to Andersen's letter of thanks, written on August 1, assuring him that he was much missed by the friends he had made during his visit but did not answer any later letters from Andersen.

Dickens seems to have enjoyed Andersen's company in 1847 (Johnson 2: 619), when the Danish writer was lionized by London society. He perhaps pretended not to notice that Andersen had serious difficulties with the English language. "We knew one another so well, although we were meeting for the first time," Andersen told a Danish friend; "We stood there and talked for a long time—talked English, but he understood me, I him" (Bredsdorff 189). Dickens brought him a twelve-volume edition of his own works, each one inscribed "For Hans Christian Andersen. From his Friend and Admirer, Charles Dickens." "I must see you, and thank you," Andersen wrote in a letter that a facsimile shows as misspelled and heavily crossed out but nevertheless in English, "that is one last flower for me in the dear England!" Dickens replied with an invitation to dinner at Broadstairs on Andersen's last night in England and early next morning walked over to Ramsgate to see him off. "As the ship glided out of the harbour, I could see Charles Dickens on the furthermost point. I thought he had left long ago. He raised his hat and finally raised one hand to heaven" (189–97). Over the next decade, Andersen dedicated two books to Dickens, and the two corresponded occasionally, Dickens with invitations to visit: "We should receive you most heartily" (4 July 1849; Bredsdorff 199).

> You ought to come to me [. . .] and stay in my house. We would all do our best to make you happy [. . .] You now write English most admirably, [. . .] this letter of yours now lying on my desk is a perfect Englishman's. [. . .] I love and esteem you more than I could tell you on as much paper as would pave the whole road from here to Copenhagen. (*Letters* 8: 144–45, 5 July 1856)

Not surprisingly, Andersen believed he would be a welcome guest and looked forward to long talks with a fellow writer he greatly admired. When Andersen wrote in early April 1857 to say he was coming to England, Dickens responded enthusiastically, inviting him to Gad's Hill, promising "a pleasant room [. . .] with a charming view," emphasizing how easy it was to get to London and even offering Tavistock House if the visitor needed a room in London. "Little Dorrit at present engages me closely," he added.

> I hope to finish her story by about the end of this month [April], and that you will find me in the summer quite a free man, playing at cricket and all manner of English open-air games [. . .] You will find yourself in a house full of admiring and affectionate friends, varying from three feet high to five feet nine. Mind! You must not think any more of going to Switzerland. You must come to us. (*Letters* 8: 307)

In accepting Dickens's invitation, Andersen asked him not to "lose patience that in English I shall express myself so heavily and awkwardly" (Bredsdorff 209–10). Dickens had gently satirized the Englishman's insular scorn of foreign languages and those who spoke them in Mr. Meagles, laughed at Mrs. Plornish's belief that she was intelligible to Cavaletto, and would do so more savagely in Mr. Veneering's dismissive phrase "Not English!" But even before Andersen arrived, Dickens, inviting Miss Coutts to visit for a day, told her that "Hans Christian Andersen may perhaps be with us, but you won't mind *him*—especially as he speaks no language but his own Danish, and is suspected of not even knowing that" (*Letters* 8: 340). An insincere delight in anticipating guests is not uncommon, but Dickens seems to have decided before Andersen arrived that he would be a nuisance, using his narrative abilities to turn him into an unintelligible clown in letters, as Dickens had turned Leigh Hunt into a sponger and a sneak in *Bleak House*, and Harriet Martineau into a paradigm of domestic disorder and "telescopic philanthropy."

Andersen arrived on 11 June, and host and household quickly lost patience with his efforts to communicate. "We are suffering a good deal from Andersen," Dickens wrote Miss Coutts, after a month of the Dane's presence. "I have arrived at the conviction that he cannot speak Danish." Dickens made a comic story out of Andersen's fear that a cabman meant to drive "him into remote fastnesses, to rob and murder him. He consequently arrived here with all his money, his watch, his pocket book, and documents, *in his boots*—and it was a tremendous business to unpack him and get them off" (372–73).

As Andersen's stay lengthened, the story became more extravagant:

> whenever he got to London, he got into wild entanglements of Cabs and Sherry, and never seemed to get out of them again until he came back here. [. . .] One day he came home to Tavistock House, apparently suffering from corns that had ripened in two hours. [. . .] Satisfied that the Cabman was bent on robbery and murder, he had put his watch and money into his boots—together with a Bradshaw, a pocket book, a pair of scissors, a penknife, a book or two, a few letters of introduction, and some other miscellaneous property. (*Letters* 8: 383)

"His unintelligible vocabulary was marvelous," Dickens later told William Jerdan.

> In French or Italian, he was Peter the Wild Boy; in English, the Deaf and Dumb Asylum. My eldest boy swears that the ear of man cannot recognize his German; and his translatress declares [. . .] that he can't speak Danish. (382–83)

Andersen, meanwhile, believed that his English was adequate. In a letter of 18 June he declared that he understood Dickens the best as far as speaking goes, and now—exactly a week since I came—he says that I am making surprising progress in speaking English; every hour it is better, but then I speak without fear, and even the little ones begin to understand me. (Bredsdorff 212–13)

His "Et Besøg hos Charles Dickens i Sommeren 1857" ("A Visit to Charles Dickens in the Summer of 1857") appeared in a Copenhagen newspaper, *Berlingske Tidende* (24 January–2 February 1860), describing the visit as idyllic, a happy rural interlude with a happy family. Dickens "came out to meet me, with bright looks and a hearty greeting," he later recalled, "and such as in the first hour he stood before me, the very same he remained all the time of my visit, ever genuine, and cheerful, and sympathetic"(Andersen 185). "Though I had not much previous practice in speaking English, or hearing it spoken, yet from the very first I could understand nearly all that Dickens said to me," Andersen later remembered.

> In France, Italy, and Spain the Dane feels himself among foreign races: such is not the case in England; here one feels that the blood is of our blood, and the language of the same root as our own. [. . .] I soon understood any single speaker who addressed me, but when the whole circle kept up a lively talk, the words ran too fast into each other, and I sat like a deaf man among the talkers [. . .] after a while my ear learnt to catch up stray words and phrases, till the general conversation became clear to me in parts, and at last in its entirety. The more ease I acquired in expressing myself, the stronger grew my desire to talk of something better than mere commonplace. I longed to exchange ideas—to be myself in my own proper person. [. . .] Meanwhile, I felt more and more at home. (Andersen 186–87)

Dickens, however, does not seem to have noticed his visitor's increasing fluency in English. In exaggerating Andersen's foibles and linguistic shortcomings, he may have been distracting himself, and perhaps his correspondents, from domestic problems that were about to implode, by turning a distressing situation into comedy. Barry turns it into a tragi-comedy of miscommunication.

For Andersen had blundered into a toxic combination of coinciding crises, which his poor English, his unfamiliarity with English ways, and his inability to read social signals prevented him from understanding. Those crises are the subject of Barry's play. We watch them unfold before the uncomprehending Andersen, who in a brief prologue twelve years after the visit reads in a newspaper that Dickens has died, and remembers Gad's Hill as a paradise of human hearts. I suppose I was dimly aware of mysteries. But I did not suspect troubles so great, no, no. I wrote about my stay among them shortly after, and it seemed natural to describe them as happy [. . .] I sensed not enough. Such it is to have no language. So are the passions of intimates hidden from the stranger [. . .] Andersen's English [. . .] a horror and a hindrance. (Barry, *Andersen's English* 10)

Dickens and his family had moved into Gad's Hill ten days before Andersen arrived, and there were problems about the water supply. Dickens, with his nervous energy no longer engaged by *Little Dorrit* or by the excitement of buying the new house, was facing up to his own conviction that his marriage was a failure and was ready to end it. Meanwhile, he needed distraction, as he had so often in recent years. After the sudden death of Douglas Jerrold on June 8, Dickens threw himself into raising a fund for Jerrold's family, offering two readings of *A Christmas Carol* and arranging to direct and act in several performances of *The Frozen Deep*, the Arctic melodrama he had written with Wilkie Collins. Andersen, who arrived on June 11, "could not help lamenting that our intercourse was so much limited and shortened by [Dickens] being obliged, oftener than would have otherwise been the case, to run up to London and spend the whole day there" (Andersen 185).

In that summer of 1857, Barry's Dickens and his daughter Kate are portrayed as already at odds over his refusal to let her marry Charles Collins. Dickens's son Walter, only sixteen, is unwillingly about to embark for India as a cadet in the East India Company army. Dickens describes Catherine as a cold and incompetent mother to their children, a grievance he had long felt but not yet shared with confidants. "She has never attached one of them to herself, never played with them in their infancy, never attracted their confidence as they have grown older, never presented herself before them in the aspect of a mother," he told Miss Coutts, describing Catherine's sister, Georgina Hogarth, in the next paragraph as "the best, the most unselfish, and the most devoted of human Creatures" (*Letters* 8: 559–60). "She does not—and she never did—care for the children; and the children do not—and they never did—care for her [. . .] she is glad to be rid of them, and they are glad to be rid of her" (632). The editors of Dickens's letters have been skeptical about these comments, and Michael Slater has characterized them as something Dickens "had to get himself to believe so that he could the more freely pity himself in the image of his own children" (*Dickens and Women* 146–47). There was also Dickens's sense, at the age of forty-six, that he was still a vigorous young man, resentful that Catherine's lack of vigor and evident aging after bearing ten children continually reminded him of how old he was. "She is my mirror and I have the urge to smash it in pieces," he tells Georgina. "I peer in there and see my face" (Barry, *Andersen's English* 62). His "Tour of Two Idle Apprentices" in September 1857 with Wilkie Collins, fourteen years younger, was an attempt to shed for a time his responsibilities and problems. "I want to escape from myself," he told Collins; "my blankness is inconceivable—indescribable—my misery, amazing" (*Letters* 8: 423). Barry makes Wilkie Collins Dickens's adviser in arranging the separation from Catherine; Collins "knows these subtle matters," he remarks (*Andersen's English* 63). And Collins has selected Ellen Ternan as the remedy for Dickens's unhappiness: "He said something would happen, and that when it did, I would know what to do," Dickens tells Catherine. "There would be clarity" (47). When Ellen appears to audition for a role in *The Frozen Deep*, Dickens does know what to do. "Wilkie Collins chooses wisely," he comments; "I am sure you will do very well," and a moment later Barry adds two stage directions: "*Dickens holds her by the shoulder quite fiercely.* [. . .] *He pulls her to him a little with a strange energy*" (74–75, emphasis in the original).

Barry uses passages from letters Dickens later wrote to portray tension in the summer of 1857 between Catherine and Georgina, who had long ago taken over the management of household and children. He turns Dickens's claim that Georgina ran the house and supervised the children into Catherine's complaints about Georgina usurping her place as woman of the house. Dickens's descriptions of Catherine's lethargy and inefficiency in his letters use all his rhetorical skill, and Barry draws on them for dramatic dialogue, along with his expressed conviction that, after twenty-one years of marriage, he could no longer stand living with her. The theme is introduced as the play begins, by Kate Dickens singing one of Thomas Moore's then popular *Irish Melodies*:

Believe me, if all those endearing young charms,
   Which I gaze on so fondly today,
Were to change by tomorrow, and fleet in my arms,
   Like fairy gifts fading away,
Thou wouldst still be adored, as this moment thou art,
   Let thy loveliness fade as it will,
And around the dear ruin each wish of my heart
   Would entwine itself verdantly still. (Moore 189)

The Moore melody is our first reminder that this is an Irish play by an Irish playwright, with an Irish view of Dickens, Victorian England, and the British imperial mission. Niamh Cusack, an Irish actress, played Catherine in the 2010 production. Barry's play subtly evokes Irish issues in his portrait of Dickens and his troubled household: colonialism, the loss or suppression of the Irish language, and *Gorta mor*, the Great Hunger, the Famine of 1845–49.

For Dickens, Catherine Dickens's charms had faded. Less than two months after Andersen's visit, he would tell John Forster that "Poor Catherine and I are not made for each other [. . .] nothing on earth could make her understand me, or suit us to each other. Her temperament will not go with mine" (*Letters* 8: 430). Within a year, Dickens had demanded and obtained a formal separation and had published the fact in the *Times* (June 7, 1858) and in *Household Words* (June 12). His "Personal Statement" was intended to quash rumors of an affair with Georgina—he later had her examined by a doctor and found to be virgo intacta. It was also written to refute any potential gossip about Ellen Ternan.

Commenting on his play in the program for *Andersen's English*, Barry saw the crisis in the Dickens marriage as

> strange [. . .] dark, something rather terrible at the heart of [Dickens's] story. We might say he did something that a thousand thousand men have done [. . .] There is a cruelty in the play but it seems to me part of the business of being alive, of being human. And sometimes we mete out such a cruelty, and sometimes we are the recipient of it. In marriage, that may occur in the one conversation [. . .] just in here, in the tiny parenthesis of this play, and a merely imagined play at that, he seems to me like a man possessed of an idea that he cannot put aside, that would have killed him to put aside. Everything with Dickens emotionally is high stakes in that sense. But this is why over the years I came more and more to care for Catherine, well, to be very alarmed on her behalf, let us say. ("Interview" n.p.)

To the crisis in the Dickens marriage, Barry adds crises that did not actually surface during Andersen's visit but that were already implicit by June and July 1857. They would very soon trouble what Andersen called "the land of Dicken" (*Andersen's English* 14). Dickens sets up a bed in his dressing room and nails up a door to deny Catherine access, a change he did not introduce until October (*Letters* 8: 465). He even explains to Catherine what the terms of their separation are to be, accelerating a process that was not settled until June 1858. By anticipating and emphasizing the breakup of the Dickens marriage, Barry increases the tensions in his play and guarantees Andersen's farewell to Catherine its full measure of irony: "I wish you all happiness, in your life, Mrs Dickens, and in your perfect and holy marriage," to which she replies, with equal irony, "Now, truly, your English is perfect" (*Andersen's English* 81–82).

Kate Dickens tells her father that he is "becoming almost brutal" in his evident disdain for Catherine. To his "Be my daughter. [. . .] Do not torment me," she replies, "I do not wish to be *authored* by you" (49–50). Later she tells him she will marry Charlie Collins against his wishes, a step she would not take until the summer of 1860. When he asks, "What causes this change?" she prophetically replies, "All that you are, all that you have done, all that you are going to do" (71), at once a recollection and an anticipation of her later claim that she married Collins to escape from "an unhappy home" and that Dickens knew this (Slater, *Charles Dickens* 484). Barry synchronizes the real disasters, Andersen's visit and the deteriorating Dickens marriage, juxtaposing Andersen's linguistic isolation at Gad's Hill with Catherine's increasing exclusion from her marriage, her children, and her home. As he thought about making a play out of Andersen's visit, Barry suggests that "maybe there was something in Andersen's outsiderness that struck a chord with me. Mutis mutandis, his 'Irishness'; his not-knowing (a very good condition for a writer sometimes, strangely)" ("Interview"). Recalling rumors that Sir John Franklin and his men turned cannibal while stranded in the Arctic, Dickens denies "this calumny" as

> a tale told [. . .] by an Esquimaux. A savage, sir, worse than an Irishman. My friend Carlisle [sic] has written, if the Irish cannot be improved a little, perhaps they ought to be exterminated [. . .] There is something noble and essential in the English character [. . .] that [. . .] forbids dark conduct [...] a man is redeemed by his—Englishness. (Barry, *Andersen's English* 58–59)

Finally, as Dickens creates ordeals for his fictional characters, Barry introduces several crises of his own invention into these five summer weeks at Gad's Hill. "Is fact really reliable?" he asks his interviewer. "Is fiction not a sort of factual picture of an emotional state?" Barry inserts a character not part of the historical record: Aggie, the Irish maid who is part of the household but also, similar to Andersen, is an "other," as a kind of commentary on some of the action. Aggie is pregnant by young Walter Dickens, carrying Dickens's grandchild, a fact Dickens refuses to believe. He dismisses her, recommending only a stay at Urania Cottage. Barry's Andersen is sexually attracted to men and boys, as the original probably was, but here he may have some designs on Dickens: "He has the habit of kissing me on the lips, which is frightful," Dickens complains. "Surely there should be a law against that" (65). When Andersen touches Walter Dickens on the arm, a stage direction suggests that "*There is something of a proposition in the gesture*" (40). Gad's Hill, the kingdom of "Dickens," is as full of domestic and sexual tension as the court at Elsinore, with occasional overtones of Almaviva's estate in *The Marriage of Figaro*. Gad's Hill is a little court, revolving around its ruler and managed by Georgina: "I merely wish to create tranquility and general pleasantness, so Charles can work" (37), she insists to Catherine when Catherine accuses her of taking over her husband, her children, and her position. Dickens increasingly ignores Andersen and Catherine, and dismisses Walter's anxieties about dying in India. When Ellen Ternan enters Dickens's life near the end of Andersen's visit, she arrives several weeks before she actually met Dickens for the first time and tried out for *The Frozen Deep*, in mid-August 1857.

Barry's Dickens is himself a frozen deep: remote, cold, and ruthlessly evasive. Barry underlines his coldness by reminding us how cold an English summer can be; Gad's Hill seems like the castle of the Snow Queen. Andersen complains that his bed is cold (*Andersen's English* 19). "You have taken the cold out of us," Dickens tells Aggie when she brings tea. "If Franklin and his men had had this tea in their icy world at the frozen North [. . .] there would have been no death and dying" (28–29). On a sunny day, Aggie offers to "keep the fire going" for Catherine, who feels that "this cold creeps about my legs [. . .] keep the fire going, Aggie, and do it discreetly. That is how things are done in a good household" (38). Later, when we see Aggie reviving a dying fire, Andersen calls her "the Ash Girl—among the ashes. The Ash Girl becomes princess, little maid, at end of story. Not all stories end so happy" (43). As the play ends, Dickens reports that Andersen is finally gone:

> Catherine: (*with effort*) He was a good, kind, dear man.
> Georgie: He was a terrible old bore, that is the truth.
> Catherine: What will happen to us now?
> Dickens: Only splendid things.
> Aggie: Will I light the fire now, ma'am?
> Dickens: No need, Aggie. (82–83)

"We will have the proper summer soon," he goes on, as if Andersen's departure made all well again while completely ignoring the shattered dreams of domestic happiness around him. "We will be English folk in England—the happiest people on earth in the happiest country" (83). Such a complacent remark is out of character for Dickens, who hardly considered England with its slums and workhouses, Chancery and Circumlocution Office, "the happiest country."

As an Irish writer, Barry interrogates the myth of domestic tranquility that Dickens hoped to preside over at Gad's Hill and that he created so often in his novels, as his characters, their troubles behind them, settle down in a comfortable country house. Here Barry challenges the contrived happy ending of Dickens's fictions and the novelist's inability to contrive one in his own life.

Dickens made himself the hero of *David Copperfield* and with his other novels created "Charles Dickens," a narrating persona, shrewd observer, jovial, kindly, defender of the poor and oppressed, intolerant of hypocrisy, pride, and the inadequacies of most government bodies, from Parliament and the Court of Chancery to parish councils and workhouse committees. But that public Dickens is not the hero of Barry's play about domestic politics at Gad's Hill. Barry's sympathies are with the three outsiders, Andersen, Catherine, and Aggie. Barry stresses Dickens's disdain for his sons, and his assertion of control over those children he blamed Catherine for producing. In *Andersen's English*, actors play Kate and Walter, but the other children are represented by puppets. Dickens was a domestic tyrant, a martinet about order in his house, who "inspected his children's bedrooms like a drill sergeant every morning" (Johnson 2: 905). Walter describes himself as "a son superfluous to requirements." There is a whiff of incest in Dickens's reaction to the idea of Kate marrying: "how could I countenance anyone taking you away from me?" (Barry, *Andersen's English* 33), and Barry suggests that the parts of Kate and Ellen Ternan be doubled.

In introducing Andersen into this troubled house and emphasizing his difficulties with spoken English, Barry is writing a play about language, and so about communication and lack of communication, in the tradition of recent Irish plays such as Brian Friel's *Translations* (1980) and *The Communication Cord* (1982). Ireland and the Irish language are a presence in this play, but only as outsiders. Aggie is a survivor of *Gorta mor*. "I am an Irish girl," she tells Walter. "The land of the dead. My mam and daddy died in a ditch, and four brothers and sisters were thrun in after. I survived all that, only to be tormented by you" (57). "I am not an *amadán* [fool]" (61), she insists. She teaches Andersen the Irish term for applause, *bualadh bos,* which he later teaches to Queen Victoria. "Ah, the Irish, sir. The Irish," the Queen vaguely replies (69–70). Andersen, a gifted and popular writer in his own language, is to Dickens and his household "like listening to the *Iliad* in a Hottentot translation" (31). A black actor, Danny Sapani, played Andersen in the premiere of *Andersen's English*, as a way of underlining Andersen's situation as an outsider at Gad's Hill, his otherness.

Barry draws on Dickens's comic fantasies about Andersen to set up a confrontation between Prospero and Caliban, insider and outsider, a master of the English language and a struggler with its intricacies, and then turns the comedy of misunderstanding into a sad meditation on being misunderstood. No other voice than Charles Dickens's can be allowed to be heard at Gad's Hill or to interrupt the fiction of a happy family he is inventing. He does not listen to Walter's fears about India, and when Walter confesses that he has made Aggie pregnant, he refuses to believe it. "I know something about Fiction" he declares, preferring to believe Aggie's story about a soldier-lover who received the Victoria Cross for heroism at Sebastopol but has now died fighting in Madagascar. Aggie declines to enter Urania Cottage. Expelled from Gad's Hill, she returns to Ireland with money Andersen has given her: "I am not blind in the eyes. I cannot say English, but I see, I see [. . .] you will need it" (81). She supports little Walter as a prostitute in the Monto, Dublin's red-light district, where Stephen Dedalus would later wander. Walter Jr. eventually joins the Dublin Fusiliers, as would Barry's Eneas McNulty. Her story is one of enduring to die "an old old woman in Calgary, Alberta" (83). Kate Dickens also rebels. Her "I will not be *authored* by you" announces her awareness that she is rebelling against the fiction her father is creating and his manipulation of reality in his life as well as in his novels.

The play consists of scenes that represent Andersen's vivid but often uncomprehending memories of his visit to Gad's Hill. As the play ends,

Dickens is dead. Dickens's women, now free to speak for themselves, remain enthralled by the fantasies he has invented for them. Catherine mourns the separation from most of her children that Dickens had imposed and wants "the whole nation [to] know that he loved me once" (84). Georgina defends her decision to remain at Gad's Hill after the separation, speaks of the scandals that decision provoked, and adds that she "did what I could to understand Miss Ternan" (85). She imagines herself as his acolyte, a keeper of the flame, publishing Dickens's papers and comparing herself to the saucer-eyed dog that guards the treasure in Andersen's "The Tinderbox." Ellen Ternan, "if I may be allowed to speak," declares, "I loved him," tells an implausible story of transporting the dying Dickens to Gad's Hill, and briefly summarizes her uneventful later life (84–86). Barry supplies a brief epilogue, as the Andersen of 1870 recalls his last view of Dickens, "waving his hat in farewell, faithfully, faithfully waving [. . .] Dickens himself. Great friendship, like a conflagration, cooling to silence." There is a final stage direction: "*More light on Dickens. He sings 'The Last Rose of Summer', the company join in, then a last flourish of his hat, raised high, banishing everything*" (86).

For Barry, Dickens and his household become a metaphor for England's oppression of Ireland, an oppression that combines suppression, indifference, and hostility. Dickens dismisses Aggie and her claims, and he disdains Andersen's imperfect English, metaphors for England's sins and omissions toward the neighboring island. That Dickens could arouse such hostility is an indication of his continued importance at the bicentenary of his birth. While the current near obsession with Ellen Ternan makes it seem as if Dickens the lover/unfaithful husband is now more interesting than Dickens the novelist, the very fact that his personality and its paradoxes, and their role in shaping his novels, still absorb us indicate that he will continue to be a major figure in the consciousness of the twenty-first century and will send us back to closer examination of his work, at once so elusive and so accessible. Dickens still matters. As an agent of change, he tried in his novels to awaken his contemporaries to England's dangerous refusals to change, and the play dramatizes his determination to provoke a change in his personal life, just after he had imagined Arthur Clennam at forty, discontented with his lonely life, and married him to the much younger Little Dorrit. The Dickens who began his concealed liaison with Ellen Ternan was a novelist who concealed many things in his novels, and as English literature's Artful Dodger, he still has much to teach us, or rather, much for us to discover. Barry's play invites us to ponder one of Dickens's personae, an artifact capable of great kindness and great cruelty, on the verge of rejecting that dream of respectable domesticity that in his life and art he had so frequently endorsed, of changing as so many of his fictional characters change. Barry asks us to question the Dickens we think we know.

BIBLIOGRAPHY

Andersen, Hans Christian. "A Visit with Charles Dickens." *Eclectic Magazine* 13.2 (1871): 183–96.
Barry, Sebastian. *Andersen's English*. London, 2010.
———. "An Interview with Sebastian Barry." Hampstead Theatre program for *Andersen's English*. London, 2010.
Bredsdorff, Elias. *Hans Christian Andersen: The Story of His Life and Work, 1805–75*. New York, 1975.
Dickens, Charles. *The Letters of Charles Dickens*. Ed. Madeline House, Graham Storey et al. 12 vols. Oxford, 1965–2002.
Johnson, Edgar. *Charles Dickens: His Tragedy and Triumph*. 2 vols. New York, 1952.
Moore, Thomas. *Poetical Works*. Ed. A. D. Godley. Oxford, 1924.
Slater, Michael. *Charles Dickens*. New Haven, 2009.
———. *Dickens and Women*. London, 1983.

How to Read Dickens in English: A Last Retrospect

Edgar Rosenberg
Cornell University

Seventy years ago, I lay burning in the sun, one day, reading *A Tale of Two Cities*. (The editor's name I forget.)

Toward the end of *A Tale*, Sydney Carton asks the seventy-eight-year-old London banker Jarvis Lorry—the two are chatting in Lorry's Paris quarters the night before Dr. Manette's explosive disclosure—whether his childhood seems far off to him. "Do the days when you sat at your mother's knee, seem days of very long ago?" No, Lorry tells him, or rather "Twenty years back, yes; at this time of my life, no. For, as I draw closer and closer to the end, I travel in the circle, nearer and nearer to the beginning." With Lorry and Carton as my gentle pilots, what I want to do here is to retrieve my earliest links to these two good people, to retrieve my first love affair with Dickens the novelist, and to recapture some of my first feeble attempts to come to terms with the language in which he wrote. Although I have taught English to the natives for nearly fifty years, I spoke barely a word of English before I turned fourteen, apart from homegrown idioms such as "pshaw," "uff uff," "yonder wigwam," "behold, a papoose" (which I naturally pluralized into "papeese" the moment I picked up my first crumbs of more digestible stuff)—or again imbecilities such as "yon hellish Apache," "behold, a tomahawk," or interlingual beauties such as "'Egad,' *bruellte der dicke Sam*, 's'death,' *kreischte er*, '*ein* redskin! *Wo hast Du jetzt wieder Dein Pony gelassen*, by Jove!'" I am indebted for these pre-Dickensian lessons in literature to a depraved German imitator of Fenimore Cooper's, an enormously popular writer named

Karl May, a native of Dresden, and May's English conformed at least partly to Sam Veller's topographical know-how: mighty peculiar, but none too extensive. May had a remarkable ear for American usages such as invectives and social niceties, so that you were forever tripping over landmines like "fie fie, Sir Brown"; "lackaday, Sir Smith"; "faugh, Sir Kelly"; and "zounds, Sir Webster" ("Spell it with a V")—Sir Webster and the rest of the Dakota swells were all of them sleazy, potbellied charcoal burners, who, unlike the lean and lenten Apaches, outdid each other in swilling gallons of "stinking firewater, by the good Lord Harry." Besides, May assailed my eardrums with a steady barrage of palefaces, blackfaces, rednecks, greenhorns, goldbricks, and yellowbellies, as if he had written his Wild West stories with a color chart next to him, like his French double, Flaubert. It goes without saying that May had never set foot on American soil: as far as I know, he wrote reams of his stuff in debtors' prison, a sort of Dresden-based Marshalsea, without English aids for reflection. Even so, as the Widow May recalls in a somewhat tearful self-serving memoir, some ten years after May's death, President Harding received her at the White House in recognition of her late husband's lasting contributions to German–American ties. Whether they exchanged civilities in English or presidential German (*"Ich bin ein Dresdener*, M'lady," and "Pshaw, *ich bin eine waschechte Chippewa*, Sir Harding!"), she does not say. And it is good to know that May gave not only Mr. Harding and me our first notions of America, but also, if their words can be trusted, to susceptible souls such as Albert Schweitzer, Einstein, Hitler, and Kafka. So my taste could not have been all bad. May himself, by the way, anticipated his wife in writing his own confessions. Instead of taxing the reader's attention span with some such title as *The Personal History, Surprising Adventures, Considered Opinions, and Hellish Misfortunes of Karl May the Younger of Dresden, As Told By Himself to His Twenty-One Grandchildren and Their Wives and In-Laws: With Sixteen Woodcuts*, he just called the book "*Ich.*" "*Ich!*" "*I!*" "*Moi!*" He could have taught Dickens (as well as Frau M.) a lesson in economy.

It is convenient to mention that of the four of us (father, mother, smart eleven-year-old kid brother Hans, and myself *aet*. 14) who came to the States in February 1940, after cooling our heels on the hot sands of Port-au-Prince, only my father, who had attended Master Brownrigg's public school in Haslemere or Godalming, Conan Doyle popping over every so often to play cricket with the boys, and who later served out a term at Edinburgh and one at Oxford, talking into his cups about Maudlin College—only my Dad spoke English at all, a mildly archaic English, though he knew better than to browbeat me with a "s'death, Edgar" when I collected a 55 in algebra. And even he still called the neighbor's brand-new Plymouth a "Ply-Mouth," as if the car, not the neighbor, required dental adjustments; referred to elderly elevator operators as liftboys; and read Austen Chamberlain, Lord Vansittart, *Three Men in a Boat*, and Pollard's history of the Tudors in German. Or (unsurprisingly, given his newly hatched interest in U.S. motor cars) the Two Doors, as if bluff King Hal, instead of hauling the royal barge out of dry dock, hired an inexpensive Chevy sedan to escort his lady friends from Richmond to Tower Hill.

* * *

I came on Dickens long after I came on Karl May. Stanley Kubrick might have captured my progress in some such title as *Witch Doctor Dickens, or How I Learned to Jilt My Last Mohican Squaw and to Love Lucie Manette*. I'm fairly sure that I was fifteen when I first read *A Tale of Two Cities*. I remember reading it on a Saturday. Saturdays (speaking of Kubrick) were undeviatingly consecrated to movies, and this was the first Sabbath in creation on which a book—any book— kept me from trotting up to the Uptown Theater one block from our homestead or to the nearest Loew's, the one next to the funeral parlor on 175th Street. The idea was that movies were the best way to teach me English—correct idiomatic English, the way educated people expressed themselves. I must have seen easily two hundred movies in my first three or four years in the States, and naturally I do not recall the order in which I saw them—whether I saw *Abe Lincoln in Illinois* before I saw *Dumbo* or I saw *Dumbo* before I saw *The Return of the Cat People* or I saw *The Return of the Cat People* before I saw *Citizen Kane* or I saw *Citizen Kane* before I saw *Pardon My Sarong* or I saw *Pardon My Sarong* before I saw Winston Churchill's pet flick, *That Hamilton Woman* (Hitler's favorites were rumored to be that antediluvian-bore *King Kong* and *Krach im Hinterhaus*, and the pope, though he left no record of this, must have cast a fatherly eye on *The Song of Bernadette*, *All This and Heaven Too*, *The Bells of St. Mary's*, and *The Saint in Palm Springs*). And I do not recall whether I saw *That Hamilton Woman* before I saw *Gilda*, *Laura*, *Gigi*, *Bambi*, or *Kitty Foyle*. In the middle of *Bambi*, I burst out laughing at Bambi's mother, and the usherette at the "Uptown," a mannish creature who carried her pencil flashlight as if it were Rommel's marshal's baton, said, "Would you please leave the theater, young man," but somehow I talked myself into staying put by blaming it all on my Latvian Exent. I was not born yesterday. "Well, don't let it happen again," said the lady, who did not know Latvia from the Suez Canal, and went after some other child martyr, the next available Oliver Twist or Smike de nos jours.

I have recently revisited some of these films on Turner Classics, and I do not suppose that as teaching aids to spoken English, they were any more useful to me than May's *Collected Works*. I cannot imagine myself walking up Broadway or Amsterdam Avenue, shouting at Mrs. Mahoney upstairs, "Get away from that window, smartpants! Somebody might blow you a kisser!" or putting it to that redhead flirt and teacher's pet, Honey Augenlicht, who scored 500 on every I.Q. test and knew the names of all the vice presidents from Adams to Nance Garner by heart, "Why don't you slip out of that wet coat into a dry martini?" or "Have you ever noticed, dearest, that the Danube is blue only to people in love?" Instead of "Pshaw" and "Uff uff," the actors commenced every other sentence with some such fog bomb as "Shiver my timbers!" "Holy Toledo!" or "Holy mackerel!" or again they addressed each other as "baby," "lady," and "kid"—the three could be used interchangeably, to the greater confusion of refugee teens: "I got no time to mess around, lady." "Fix your face, baby; we're going to Buckingham Palace." "Listen, kid, we're going to get you to Piccadilly if I have to carry you piggyback!" Many people apparently went to England in those days, probably to track down that Hamilton woman. Nor was I likely to tell Nancy Nussbaum, the slightly sullen bubble-gumming eighteen-year-old dropout who sold candy in the scarlet-upholstered lobby of the RKO on 181st Street, "We love each other beyond time and place," or "Good Heavens, a woman!" or "We don't need the moon when we have the stars." Not that Nancy was any more likely to shrug me off with a snooty "Pardon my French, Mister, but you ain't my idea of a valentine!" And although America was about to enter the war, I obviously had nothing to learn from your enlisted men: "*Achtung! Achtung!* Red River Five to Red River Six! Come in as directed, Red River Six!" and again "Knock off the baloney, Sarge, or should I say Dr. Freud! I got a mission to fly!" And totally less than nothing from your preacherly types: "You're helping mankind, Knute Rockne, and anybody who helps mankind helps the Almighty Himself." "Four hundred years ago a man said it better than I could: No man is an island," or, for all I know, "Four hundred years ago a man said it better than I could, 'There is some corner of a foreign field that is forever England.'"

* * *

By the time Dickens cheated the Uptown of its most hyperkinetic client, I had seen a fraction of the movies I soaked up during my first years in the States. Nor did Dickens "replace" the movies. Very likely nobody really knows why anyone should prefer one book to another. Why Dickens? Why *A Tale of Two Cities*? The novelist Isaac Bashevis Singer once said that falling in love with a writer is like falling in love with a woman. But perhaps a library ought not to be confused with a harem. In view of my linguistic handicaps, it's perhaps all the more astonishing that the spell Dickens cast on me originated not primarily in his plots but in his language, a language I grasped very imperfectly. I don't believe that I was drawn into *A Tale of Two Cities* by the quick fiery turn of events—I never managed to get the hang of John Barsad's slippery maneuvers nor the virtuous servant Roger Cly's, though this in no way diminished my pleasure in their shifts and dodges. No, what captivated me even then were the spectacular verbal fireworks. (I may just note here that the failure of so many Dickens adaptations for film and TV seems to me to lie precisely in their tone-deafness to Dickens's music, and I might as well air my flinty conviction—which not only insults all PC orthodoxies but flies in the face of the steadily mounting trend—that as far as I'm concerned the studios ought to keep their hands, their pickers and stealers, off Dickens's novels; please.)

So I began by simply *listening* to Dickens's Carton, to Darnay, to Miss Pross, to The Vengeance, to Jacques One through Five, and their many friends. Those gorgeous sounds, those dazzling phrases—what movie could begin to do justice to them? I remember standing in front of the hallway mirror in our new U.S. quarters in Washington Heights, mouthing these syllables for minutes on end: "Sadly, sadly the sun rose; it rose upon no sadder sight than the man of goodly abilities and goodly emotions [. . .] sensible of the blight on him and resigning to let it eat him away." (Frankly, Dickens assigns Sydney merely "good abilities and emotions," but the two "goodlies," I thought, greatly enhanced the poor devil's despondency, and Dickens himself would have used them, if he hadn't been pressed for time.) Or finely honed questions such as "'Pray, Dr. Manette,' said Mr. Darnay, / as they sat under the plane-tree [. . .] / 'have you seen much of the Tower?'"—things I thought deserved to be scanned, such as the poet Schiller. And Madame Defarge's withering Anglo-French Old Testamentary hocus-pocus sent chills down my spine. "I tell thee that the lightning is on the road and coming. Consider thou but the rage which our Jacquerie feels with more and more of a certainty every hour. Bah! I mock thee." But this, too, I may have doctored a little. Of Dickens himself I knew nothing: I couldn't know, for example, that he anticipated my mummeries in front of his own mirror—though very likely he mimicked gestures, not words. How would he have acted out Sydney's haunting swansongs? "'The time will come, the time will not be long in coming, Miss Manette, when new ties will be formed about you—the dearest ties that will ever grace and gladden you. O Miss Manette [. . .]' He said, 'Farewell!,' said a last 'God bless you!' and left her." "O Miss Manette," mind you, not "Oh, Miss Manette": the absence of the *h* deepened my pleasure in the pathos of his address, for even then I could sound the distance between the passionate *O* and the merely chatty *Oh*. If I came across a phrase I could not follow, instead of breaking the rhythm by looking it up in a dictionary, I went on to the next gem. Now what could old Lorry mean by telling Lucie that he passes his life in "turning an immense pecuniary Mangle"? And once or twice Dickens strays perilously close to Karl May's turf: "'Silence,' croaked the man with the red cap, raising his hatchet, 'hold thy peace, Aristocrat!'" "'My blood,' ejaculated the vexed coachman, 'not atop of Shooter's hill yet! Tst! Yah!'" But no more often than once or twice.

It may be objected here that I was no more likely to woo Honey Augenlicht, in or out of her dry martinis, with benedictions such as Sydney's "God bless you for your sweet compassion" or "You have been the last dream of my soul" than with Jack Warner's "We love each other beyond time and place." But I suspect that what drew me to Dickens was precisely the artifice of expression, not the proximity and availability of the medium to common usage. In other words, it never occurred to me that in surrendering to these ravishing phrases and sentences I was really learning a new language or was being brought closer to the requirements of social intercourse. In looking back at the novel now, I am in fact startled by the number of hurdles Dickens had placed in my way. To be sure, every so often he met me halfway. Thus, he might lead off with a perfectly simple passage, a lyric sequence made to order for an audition before the hallway mirror, only to lose me completely after the half. Take the narrator's reveries on the Dover Road in I, iii: "My friend is dead, my neighbour is dead, my love, the darling of my soul is dead" (so far, perfect; then, separated by a semicolon): "it is the inexorable consolidation and perpetuation of the secret that was always in that individuality, and which I shall carry in mine to my life's end." And the echo murmurs, was ever reader in this humour woo'd?

Besides, I can hardly be the only reader to whom the famous first chapter of the novel is all but totally unintelligible. Very likely, I simply yielded to the mildly soporific rhythm of the opening sentence—all 120 words of it: almost certainly to the first of Dickens's pairings, "It was the best of times, it was the worst of times," which is all that most people remember. But then—never mind the vocabulary—what is young Edgar to do with the "information" that "Mrs. Southcott had recently attained her five-and-twentieth blessed birthday, of whom a prophetic private in the Life Guards had heralded the sublime appearance by announcing that arrangements were made for the swallowing up of London and Westminster"? This halfway down on page 1! Mrs. Southcott? Surely she sounded older than twenty-five. In light of her eerie powers and accomplishments, she might have sat for a portrait of Reka, the Hun Atilla's wife, or of one of your poisonous Borgia women or the scandalous Lupescu person who seduced King Carol away from his regal responsibilities, or for a preliminary sketch for Therese Defarge herself. A private in the Life Guards? And a prophetic one at that? Astonishing! If it had not been for the prophetic-ness, the young man might have passed for Johnny Weissmuller, or the teenage Ron Reagan. And no sooner have Mrs. S. and her soothsaying gigolo waltzed onstage than something or somebody called the Cock-lane Ghost materializes two lines down. Of *it* we are told that it "has been laid only a round dozen of years, after rapping out its messages as the spirits of this very year last past (supernaturally deficient in originality) rapped out theirs." Only! There are also the Fantastic Convulsionists. But Dickens keeps *them* up his sleeve. Very strange.

It has to be remembered here that until about fifty years ago our texts lacked any and all editorial and critical apparatus, apart, occasionally, from a lazy eight-page introduction or "appreciation," a genre perfected and patented in the twenties by Professor Phelps of Yale. Today we simply reach for the novel in the Oxford World's Classic edition with Andrew Sanders's impeccable notes, and on page 370, we find out all we need to know about the sublime lady, Ron Reagan, the ghost, and the epileptics, as well as the ingurgitation of London and Westminster. Failing annotated paperbacks, there is always that instant resort of the curious—Wikipedia. But in those days, we were left without any such godsends and had to fend for ourselves. And perhaps it was just as well that we did. Very likely, all those academic braces with which we support our pedagogy and which we in our turn fabricate ("This edition includes Author's Prefaces. General Introduction. Textual Note. A Dickens Chronology. Dating the Narrative. Explanatory Notes. Illustrations. Contemporary Reviews. Bibliography. Critical Essays") would have acted, all perversely, as a bar to enjoyment, a blot on the purity of the story. In the event, Ms. Southcott and her Mark Spitzes did quite well without being explained to me—for "explained" read "explained away." And if any historical Mme. Defarge ever trod the pavements of Saint Antoine's, I would have been just as lief be kept in the dark about her. One of Dickens's own great mistakes, by the way (for I was by no means a wholly uncritical reader), seemed to me to lie in the fuss he made about Madame D's toothpick and its everlasting application. Dickens no doubt intends this to act as what is nowadays called a "diminishing trait," but it's just as well that this foolish instrument is dropped long before the knitting needles vanish from sight. La Defarge has no business sharpening her incisors as if they were removable toy guillotines.

* * *

What else did I bring away from my first encounter with Dickens?

Dickens the wordsmith—then also I fell almost instantly under the spell of Dickens the iconographer and image maker. Very few readers, I imagine, remember the conceit Dickens deploys (he rather works it to death) in the first Darnay trial scene in II, 3, in which he likens the blood-thirsty spectators at the Old Bailey to "a cloud of great blue-flies swarming about." Although (again) I had no clear idea about the shape and condition of blue flies, any more than I made sense of Lorry's tiresome Mangle or the Cock-lane Ghost's supernatural deficiencies,

I thought them the last word in poetic inventiveness, too good not to be filched. I have an especially soft spot in my heart for the blue flies because they got me a 95 (or A+) on my first oral book report, when I did in fact pilfer these lyric termites and transferred the whole buzzing crowd from the Old Bailey to a supermarket on Broadway and 171st Street. Miss McInness, the English teacher, a chubby, dimpled, elderly lady, the sort you call a "fading beauty," who, had she been twenty years younger, might have given Dolly Varden a run for her money (but this obviously is hindsight: Dolly I had yet to meet)—Miss McInness, apparently no more sensitive than I to the toxic effects of the blue flies on all that fresh meat, those lumps of Gorgonzola and Liederkranz cheese, and the double Gloucesters, thought the theme sufficiently massive and concrete to have it ventilated in class, and she asked for volunteers. There was no point in *my* auditioning it. Unlike my improvements in "reading skills" and even, within a year, of "writing skills" (by the end of the school year I collected the medal for having written the best essay in my class) my spoken English was still so awful that I could not get through a sentence without having the class in stitches, and even McInness could not suppress a smile—or, in Dickens's words, refrain from agitating her countenance from one auricular organ to the other—whenever I opened my mouth. *Vehicle* came out "vee-hi-cul," *purpose* kept striking a "poor pose"; I bandied about my beehapses and percauses, and for weeks, innocent adverbs such as *always*, *almost*, and *already*, gave me the fantods. "Edgar, haven't you finished that paragraph yet?" "Always." "How long have you lived with your grandmother?" "Almost." And so on, world without end. I asked my refugee-classmate Ilse Breslauer, the Fürth rabbi's daughter, a shy, flaxen-haired slip of a thing, why everybody, especially the guys in class, and most especially bullies such as George Blekas and Milton Petrides, began every sentence with "Cheese." "It means," Ilse whispered, a deep flush veiling her freckles, as if she were about to blaspheme, "it means Yaysus." "What do you know," I said. "Back in Fürth they start every sentence with Jesus too. Even the brownshirts."

Although it got me my 95 all right, the blue-fly publicity was thoroughly dampened by my stand-in, a perfect lowbrow—literally, like Jerry Cruncher, of whom Dickens writes that "he had just enough forehead to knuckle," or more precisely his look-alike offspring. And his written English was nothing to write home about: whenever McInness called him to the blackboard, the Hinfant Cruncher compounded his limitations by turning into a perfect juvenile Bunsby (whose acquaintance, too, I was to make years later) "abstaining, with characteristic modesty, from the use of capital letters." This grisly urchin (I think that his name was Virgil Slopes—something, anyhow, that spelled a brief but complete sentence) prowled through my essay with nerve-wracking melancholy, the tristesse endemic to professional body snatchers and their children, and after class Miss McInness called me up to the rostrum. In the novel, the chapter that inspired my sketch is titled "A Disappointment" (disappointment, that is, at Darnay's acquittal) and the chapter following "Congratulatory" (congratulatory at his acquittal); thus, McInness's homage, coming after Cruncher's blunted bite, followed the script to a "T." I remember our brief exchange of civilities. You have to recall here that in addressing refugees, your grown-ups, and some of the kids, one must assume the tone (offensively courteous "Chin-up," "Well done!") that people habitually assume in the presence of dwarfs and halfwits and that they speak three times more slowly than they would in addressing a normal subject. Thus Honey Augenlicht, who walked to school with me every morning, batting her unmade bedroom eyes at me, ostensibly to explain what happens in *Treasure Island*, the first book assigned in English, dawdled so insufferably in a (futile) effort to reconstruct the teenage hero's itinerary in his bumboats, jolly boats, schooners, and more of the same and to demystify the war games of that gibbering amputee with his parrot and his Pieces of Eight, that Honey and I were stopped by a red light at every intersection between 170th and 177th Street and arrived just in time to find our wordy unidexter perform such tricks before high heaven with his prosthesis or crutch that you wished him deported from Treasure Island to Barnum and Bailey or Sleary's Horse-Riding. I did not think a classic could be so confusing and boring at the same time. But then it was the first English book I had to read—light-years, as they now seem—before I pitched into the Vengeance, the luckless Gabelle, and Monsieur Heretofore the Marquis eight or nine months later. The name of Old Wooden Leg was Mr. Silver, and I remember asking Honey whether she thought he might be Jewish. But Honey did not think that piracy was really a Jewish profession, such as banking, owning delicatessen stores, and selling Fifth Avenue fur coats with hair-raising price tags on them. And, as my smart brother reminded me, our most famous radio star, the Lone Ranger, a cowboy who could have taught Karl May a few tricks, rode a horse named Silver every Monday on the radio, and who ever asked a horse whether he or she was Aryan or non-Aryan. Honey herself gave an excellent book report on a novel titled *Ethan Frome*, enlivening her performance with highly effective theatrical gestures whenever one of the Fromes got into an accident—all this without benefit of hallway mirrors.

* * *

The blue flies. Given my fragile hold on even the crudest barebones of English, it seems astonishing to me now that I could dredge up two or three paragraphs coherent enough to yield even the slightest sense. Moreover, I do not in the least recollect what this composition of mine was all about. I do not, for example, recollect why my blue flies behaved the way they behaved, what I gave them to do (and why) once I'd relocated them from Newgate. It was easy enough to let them loose as spectator substitutes and busybodies at an exciting trial in Mrs. Southcott's backyard, but what was there for them to do in the drab atmosphere of an A & P in upper Manhattan, squeezed in between "Evelyn's Lingerie" and a gas station? I suppose that I could have gotten them to enact a fight between the curator of the dairy section and an obnoxious patron, or between any two or more customers, or I might have introduced a spirited incident involving a burglary that called for the intervention of the police. But who in this day and age would want to steal a jar of peanut butter or mayonnaise? That sort of thing might have gone down very well 150 years ago when Jean Valjean's petty theft activated Inspector Javert of the Paris prefecture, but in the Year of Our Lord one thousand nine hundred and forty-one? Not likely.

This, however, is wishful hindsight, speculation by negative reference. Sadly, I do not recall my first sustained piece of writing in English. On the other hand, as I said, I recall all the more vividly the nice conversation with Miss Dimples that followed the urchin's audition. I remember, too, that one of the first things I learned on my treks with Honey—one of the first things any foreigner learns the minute he passes Ellis Island—is the time-consuming nationwide habit of starting every other sentence with a provisional "Well"—whenever he does not launch into it with George Blekas's godless Cheese.

Thus, Miss M. said, "Well, Edgar, that was a wonderful composition. Why, *whatever* gave you that idea about those horrid . . . those horrid . . . *things*?" As even Cruncher had checked out with her the book he and

I were reporting on and she had explicitly okay'd the assignment, the question struck me as too obtuse for words. Apparently she hadn't been listening. "Well, Dickens," I said, to minimize the suspense between the preliminaries and the subject. "*Charles* Dickens?" McInness asked with a broad smile, specially laid on for handicapped Germans, speaking as if she thought Charles the most nearly obvious Dickens worth mentioning but hardly the only one when half a dozen minor talents in the Dickens family—Elmo Dickens, Chaim Dickens, Spike Dickens, Calamity Dickens, Trixibelle Dickens, and Hamilton Fish Dickens—were even now flooding the high school market.—"Yes, Ma'am," says I. "The late Charles Dickens." Says she, "*Well*. May I venture to hazard a guess which one of Mr. Dickens's novels you chose to write your report on?" But that she had to repeat. "Please?" said I, meaning, say that again. "May I guess the book?" she asked. "Well," I said, "it's a free country." "How about *Oliver Twist*, then?" she said. "Well," says I, "I don't know"—it occurred to me that I couldn't be sure Dickens hadn't let loose some blue flies in *Oliver Twist* as well, having already used them so powerfully in *A Tale of Two Cities*. "What do you *mean*, you don't know!" she burst out. "*Is* it *Oliver Twist*, or isn't it?" "Well, *A Tale of Two Cities*," I said and improved her instruction, adding spitefully, "Well, it's better than your *Treasure Island*." *Your* Treasure Island. I should have said, "Well, it is a far, far better book than I have ever read, especially *Treasure Island*." It then dawned on her to ask, "Oh, by the way, Edgar, why do you begin every sentence with 'Well?'" "Well, you do it," I said. "Well no, I don't," said she.

Well, she meant well. During the first few weeks, whenever she called me up after class, it was to ask, "Well, how are you coming along, Edgar?" or "How are we getting on, young man?"—questions that always propelled me to look at my feet, the phrase "coming along" suggesting to me that I gave the appearance of being lame or crippled and that if things went on in this way, I would end up by being carried piggyback, like Tiny Tim, or hobbling around like Stevenson's Squire One Leg. Moreover, McInness had just been asked to substitute for our music teacher, dainty Miss Kaplan, who had taken a three months' leave to nurse a vexatious woman's grievance, and whenever I couldn't keep up with an assignment, McInness gave me permission to pick an easier one of my own choice. Thus, I might ask her whether I could be excused please from writing from memory the words to the song "Joshua Fought the Battle of Jericho, Jericho, Jericho, and the Walls

Came Tumbling Down" and substitute "Oh Come, All Ye Faithful" (which now strikes me as a *great* deal more difficult than Joshua's wordy battle hymn), or "God Save Our Gracious King," or "The Good Ship Lollipop," or "My Country, 'Tis of Thee," without quite knowing what "'Tis of Thee" meant. "Edgar," says McInness, "you may." "Well," she added on second thought, "perhaps you'll hold off a bit with the English National Anthem . . ." But she did not finish the sentence. One of your early women's rights advocates, she may have meant me to wait "until that unfortunate King George expires and we may all join hands in asking His blessings on Our Gracious Queen, the unfortunate king's nice looking older girl." Or perhaps, like many Americans, she did not particularly fancy the Brits. I mean, living Brits. Dickens, I think, she liked well enough, along with Ethel Vance, Hendrik Willem Van Loon, and a book entitled *Of Lena Geyer*, in which she buried herself while we sat and tried to make sense of the latest I.Q test. Ach, wouldn't you know it. "George Washington and Abraham Lincoln were both born in (a) February (b) June (c) August (d) November." I circled (d). "Edgar," said Miss M. with unaccustomed severity after glancing at my answer, "and you expect to become an American citizen! November indeed!" "Povably Egger thinks Danksgiving is in November too," that horrible Morley Geimke, our resident spastic, said. "Ha ha ha."

* * *

After doing *A Tale of Two Cities*, I took a breather, and a few years later, I read *David Copperfield*. I still have the copy—a 95-cent Modern Library hardcover—that bears at the end the impulsive oddly childish scrawl, "This is a great book." Oddly childish at a time when I was already ankle-deep into Donne and Malcolm Lowry as a Cornell freshman. If impassioned, the comment also betrays a certain detachment, for it ends not in an exclamation mark but a restrained full stop. In reading the book, the impression was very strong on me that these pages, in their twilight mood of retrospection and nostalgia, must have been written by a man in his late fifties or his sixties, a man writing toward the end of his life—someone who resembled the patriarchal Anatole France or Alphonse Daudet (I still had no clear picture of Dickens to guide me, or else too many portraits of him to push the regulative one into the center of my mind): a serene old man who wrote books with titles such as *Le petit Pierre*, *Le Livre de mon ami*, *Le petit Chose*, *Lettres de mon moulin*. To this day I think the first third of *Copperfield* the most magical thing Dickens ever wrote. By and by, I took ten years to edit *Bleak House* for a small vanity press. Naturally, after ten years the first fine raptures have died out forever. Let other pens than mine dwell on Esther Summerson's guilt and misery while I retire for an improving chat or sit down to a game of Hearts with the Orfling, Barkis, and Mr. Dick.

It must have been in my first year in college, too, that I suffered my one brief lapse of faith. These backslidings, like conversions, can, of course, be brought about by the most trifling circumstance, in this case by my perusal of half a sentence. We were assigned to read Butler's *The Way of All Flesh* in the standard course on "The Novel from Austen to Conrad"—strictly speaking from Austen to Butler, presumably the instructor privileged Conrad as a sales pitch. I greatly admired Butler's novel, largely, I think, for its unembarrassed cerebral and dissective "no nonsense" qualities. The central character is a student of theology, Ernest Pontifex, and towards the end of the book, the narrator Overton, Ernest's mentor and Butler's—well, overt—alter ego, in summing up his protégé's studies, notes with dismissive brevity that he had devoured Charles Kingston's *Alton Locke* "as he had devoured [Dean] Stanley's *Life of [Thomas] Arnold*, Dickens's novels, and whatever other literary garbage of the day was most likely to do him harm." There, the harm was done. Instead of my passing it over with mild misgivings, the comment verily shook my belief. Could I be wrong? Could I have been wrong all these years? The very assertiveness of Butler's language compelled assent. As I knew nothing of literary climates, it didn't occur to me that his put-down might itself be the—slightly bromidic—product of an age in which these slurs were becoming the fashionable article. Of course, I got over the lapse in a matter of weeks. Even so, when fifteen years later I took my turn in presiding over "The Novel from Austen to Conrad" I naturally dropped Butler from the syllabus.

* * *

So much for my initiation. And at that I should perhaps leave it. But "art and religion love the somber chord," and it's on rather a somber note I should like to wind down this little retrospect. A few years ago, Michael Slater convened a conference on "The Popularity of

Dickens" at the Senate House. The popularity of Dickens has long been a given; suppose I conclude by citing two testimonials to its limitless reaches. First, a column that appeared in *The Dickensian* for 1 September 1946.

> A curious piece of news appeared in the British press in July, to the effect that Dickens is the most popular author among the twenty-one German war leaders on trial at Nuremberg since last November. Schacht [the head of the Reichsbank and economic wizard, a sort of Alan Greenspan *de ses jours*] is reading *Pickwick Papers*, Rosenberg [no relation: the Party ideologue and Minister for the Occupied Eastern Territories] is deep in *Oliver Twist*, and Seyss-Inquart [the leading Austrian Nazi, later, Commissioner for the Occupied Netherlands] is finishing *A Tale of Two Cities*.

End quote. Because the writer, one of the finest editors of *The Dickensian*, seems to betray a certain queasiness in dishing out this information ("a curious item"—the gentlemanly kid glove "war leaders") one may wonder why he printed the item at all. For the very best of reasons: because (to update—and pin down—Terence) nothing that touches Dickens can be immaterial to the Dickensian, in roman letters, nor obviously in italics.

And then I wonder: could Seyss-Inquart and I really have read the same book?

As the last testimonial, I cite a writer who came on Dickens—read him over the paternal shoulders—at about the time I did and at roughly the same age, give or take a year, at a time when a year was a terribly precious commodity. The book (it eventually outsold any five or ten novels of Dickens) is cast in the form of a journal kept by an adolescent anyhow obsessed with dates, anniversaries, genealogies—not least a headcount of the composer Liszt's mistresses. Thus, under date of August 5, 1943, the notation: "Above one can hear the noise of Mrs. Van Daan's vacuum cleaner [. . .] [Father] goes into a corner with his inseparable Dickens to try and find peace somewhere." Two and a half weeks later:

> Daddy is sitting (with Dickens and the dictionary, of course) on the edge of the sagging, squeaky bed [. . .] Once he is reading, he doesn't look up, or about him, laughs every now and then, takes awful trouble to get Mummy interested [. . . W]hen he comes to something extra amusing, he tries it again. Daddy raises his eyebrows into a funny curve, his reading wrinkle deepens again, and he is lost in his book once more.

The writer (of course) is Anne Frank; the scene, the Secret Annex on the Prinsengracht. The first of these entries is dated almost a year to the day before Anne and the seven other Annex-dwellers were hauled from their shelter—we now know that Anne's father was in the middle of giving Peter Van Daan *his* elementary English lesson, "But Peter, you know that in English 'double' is spelled with a single 'b,'" when the Reich Commissioner's myrmidons terminated the lesson. I shouldn't care to forget that the spirit of Dickens penetrated even that dungeon and brightened a few of the inmates' hours before they were handed their tickets to the stall of night.

A century earlier, of course, you have the testimony of people whose hosannas have found their way into the standard biographies as part and parcel of Dickens lore and perhaps remain of vestigial interest only to students of Adorno, Horkheimer, Loewenthal, and Marcuse: Walter Savage Landor, laying down his leonine and shaggy head, overcome with grief at Little Nell's death, an event that surpassed in tragic depth the death of King Lear; Macaulay bawling at the news of What the Waves Were Saying about Dombey the Son (and Dombey the Father); Tolstoy, a more anal compiler of lists than Anne, ranking the death of Steerforth as the third greatest passage of prose in world lit., preceded only by the Sermon on the Mount and Rousseau's *Confessions*; Tolstoy's smallest boy, the seven-year-old Vanitchka, at death's door of scarlet fever, spilling a child's honest tears at Pip's loss of Biddy; Tolstoy's idolator, the ten-year-old Leo Bronstein (he had yet to turn himself into Leon Trotsky) spilling tears at Oliver Twist's exemplary progress through crime and poverty.

Orwell began his essay with the famous sentence that "Dickens is one of those authors who is worth stealing." What he meant, I suppose, is that Dickens could be appropriated by any ideologue who chose to appropriate him, from Trotsky to the Count de Suzannet. But I like to think that these parties had no more of an axe to grind when they stole him than, say, Otto Frank did, who took up Dickens without bias, as a gratuitous gift. Dickens worth stealing? But so was Karl May, whose books provided Einstein and Kafka with their Baedekers to America. The best I can say for him now is that it's a pity they didn't scalp him before he fathered his first papoose. But I feel an octogenarian's debt to the bright-eyed gent, the wizard and family friend, who seventy years ago taught me to love literature and turned a jittery refugee from another language into one of his most loquacious disciples.

Index

Adorno, Theodor W., 139
aesthetics, xvi, 37, 44, 129, 131, 145, 161–62, 166, 167n12
aetiology, mythological, 90
agency, 77, 80. *See also* power
Aggie (Irish maid), 213–14, 216
allegory, 64, 130, 165–66
alliteration, 115, 117, 119
All the Year Round, 21
Altick, Richard D., 191
America, 75, 180–81
"Amusements of the People, The" (Dickens), 161–62
anacrusis, 116
anagnorisis, 131
analyses, character: Arthur Clennam, 146–50; Eugene Wrayburn, 150–54
anaphora, 115, 119
Andersen, Hans Christian, xvii, 205–9, 213–18; "Visit to Charles Dickens in the Summer of 1857, A," 209
Andersen's English (Barry), xvii, 205–18
Andrews, Malcolm, xvi, 99–110
anti-Semitism, 151
argument, from design, 78. *See also* patterns
Arnold, Matthew, 44, 137, 160; "Hebraism and Hellenism," 44
arrangement, physiognomic, 85–90, 93–94
artists: and social change, 34–45, 49–50; and understanding patterns of life, 38–42
Attridge, Derek, 124n8
audiences, theater, 193–94
Australia, 137–38

Bagehot, Walter, 103
Baker, Ernest, *The History of the English Novel*, 149
Bardell, Martha, 3–4, 6–8
Barnaby Rudge (Dickens), 111, 118, 135
Barry, Sebastian, xvii, 205, 209–10, 212, 215–18; *Andersen's English*, xvii, 205–18
bastard, 132–33
Battle of Life, The (Dickens), 195
Bauer, Matthias, xvi, 111–25
beats, 114–19, 122, 124n8. *See also* offbeats; rhythm
Beattie, James, *The Minstrel; or, The Progress of Genius and Other Poems*, 113
bells, 113–14, 117–22
benevolence, 4, 7, 9, 11, 47–49. *See also* doing good
Benjamin, Walter, 87
Berard, Jane H., 82
Bergson, Henri, 99
Bhownagary, Jehangir, 177
bildungsroman, 130, 136, 140
Blake, William, 131, 134; "London," 134
Bleak House (Dickens), xv, xvii, 12, 19–30, 34, 51–54, 56, 66–67, 192–203
"*Bleak House* and the Playhouse" (Bolton), 200
Bohème, La (Puccini), 91
Bolton, H. Philip, 194–95; "*Bleak House* and the Playhouse," 200; *Dickens Dramatized*, 194
Boots. *See* Weller, Samuel
Bosch, Hieronymous, *The Conjurer*, 176–77
Bounderby, Josiah, 88, 165

236   Dickens as an Agent of Change

Bowen, John, 182
Boythorn, Lawrence, 23–24
Brass, Sampson, 181–82
Brattin, Joel J., xv, 19–30, 45
Broadstone of Honour (Digby), 67
Brontë, Charlotte, 133; *Jane Eyre,* 133, 140
Browne, Hablot Knight, 89, 176–77, 183, 197
Brownlow, Mr., 48–49, 51, 132
Buckley, Jerome H., 140
Bunyan, John, 130–31; *The Pilgrim's Progress,* 130
Buzard, James, 174, 177
Byron, Lord, *Childe Harold's Pilgrimage,* 137

capitalism, xvi, 85–86, 89–90, 93, 95, 160, 166
"Captains of Industry," 19–20
caricatures, 102–3, 112, 121
Carker, James, xii, 87–90, 92–93
Carlyle, Thomas, 19, 62, 64, 107–9, 133, 185; *Chartism,* 64; *Sartor Resartus,* 133
Carper, Thomas, 124n8
Carton, Sydney, 54–55
catastrophism, xvi, 4, 10, 12, 75, 77
Cervantes, Miguel de, 107–8
Chancery, Court of, 23–24, 51–52, 198, 202
change: acoustic, xvi, 112–25; literary, xvi; personal, effecting social change, 27; in popular culture, xvi; of power, xv–xvi; social, xv, 19–30, 34–45, 49–52, 166; desire by Dickens to cause, 50, 76–77, 82–83, 217; work to bring about, 53, 55
characterization: as comedic method, 103; of East End theater audiences, 193–94
characters: analysis, xvi; Arthur Clennam, 146–50; Eugene Wrayburn, 150–54; comic, 147; as literary concept, 145; modern, 146–54; picaresque, 11, 139, 147; Victorian, 154
charity. *See* benevolence; doing good

Chartism (Carlyle), 64
Chesterton, Gilbert Keith, 129, 145, 150
Chick, Louisa, xiv–xv, 92
Childe Harold's Pilgrimage (Byron), 137
children, sympathy towards, 66, 108, 131, 200
Child's History of England, A (Dickens), 24–26, 77–78
chimes, 113–14, 117–22
Chimes, The (Dickens), xvi, 67, 112–25
"Chimes" (Rossetti), 114
Christmas Carol, A (Dickens), 50, 56, 83, 120
Church of England, 65
Chuzzlewit, Martin, 10, 51, 77–78, 81
circus, 163–65
City of London Theatre, 193–94, 199–201
classes, social. *See* divisions, cultural
Clennam, Arthur, 146–50, 154
Cockton, Henry, *The Life and Adventures of Valentine Vox, the Ventriloquist,* 184
Collins, Wilkie, 211; "Tour of Two Idle Apprentices," 211
comedy, xvi, 93, 152, 198–99, 209, 216; physical, 103–5. *See also* humor; wit
commentary, political, by Dickens, 64–65
"commodity text," 161
Communication Card, The (Friel), 216
Conjurer, The (Bosch), 176–77
conjuring, xvi, 173–80, 184–88
Coppa, Francesca, 179
Copperfield, David, 34, 42, 51–53, 56, 136–37
copyright, xvii, 174, 180–81, 184, 186–87. *See also* patent; property, intellectual
Copyright Act: of 1814, 180–81; of 1842, 180
Cordery, Gareth, 36, 42
Corn Laws, 67
Court Magazine, 101–2
Coutts, Angela Burdett, 71, 138
Cowley, Malcolm, 50
criticism: of Dickens (historical), 129,

Index

161; political, 147; radical, 138; social, 48–49, 52, 201
cronyism, 202
culture: changing definition of, 160; divisions of, 130, 134, 160–61, 163, 191, 202; folk, 163; functions of, 164–65; money, xvi, 86–95; popular, xvi–xvii, 161–62, 164, 167n12, 174, 192–93, 197
Cunningham, Hugh, 37
Cuttle, Captain, 94–95

Daily News, 70–71, 76
dandyism, 66, 107, 202
Datchery, Dick, 55–56
David Copperfield (Dickens), xvi, 33–34, 36–37, 42, 51–54, 56, 131, 136–40
Davis, Jim, *Reflecting the Audience: London Theatregoing, 1840-1880*, 193–94
Dedlock, Sir Leicester, 20–22, 24–25
deluge, imagery, 140
design, argument from, 78. See also patterns
devices, comedic. See methods, comedic
Dick, Mr., 51–52
Dickens, Charles: and America, 75, 180–81; awareness by, of influence, 37–38, 44, 52; desire of, to cause social change, 50, 76–77, 82–83, 217; and methods of political influence, 63–64; personal life of, xvii, 206, 209–18; political commentary by, 64–65; political ideology of, 61–68, 71, 192; public reception of, x, xvii, 100–101, 191–92, 202, 233–34; and public service, 68–69, 71; on religious establishments, 65–67, 79; theatrical reception of, 194–97
Dickens, Charles, works of: "The Amusements of the People," 161–62; *Barnaby Rudge*, 111, 118, 135; *The Battle of Life*, 195; *Bleak House*, xv, xvii, 12, 19–30, 34, 51–54, 56, 66–67, 192–203; *A Child's History of England*, 24–26, 77–78; *The Chimes*, xvi, 67, 112–25; *A Christmas Carol*, 50, 56, 83, 120; *David Copperfield*,

xvi, 33–34, 36–37, 42, 51–54, 56, 131, 136–40; *Dombey and Son*, xi–xv, xiv–xv, xvi, 85–95; "The Fine Old English Gentleman," 63; *Great Expectations*, xv, 10, 34, 38–42, 55, 57; *Hard Times*, xvi, 21, 25, 28, 35, 52–53, 88, 159–69; *Little Dorrit*, xvi, 21, 25, 28, 35, 52–54, 56–57, 146–50, 185–86; *Martin Chuzzlewit*, xv–xvi, 50, 75–84; *Master Humphrey's Clock*, 109, 177–78; *The Mystery of Edwin Drood*, ix–x, 55–57; *Nicholas Nickleby*, 54, 119–20; *The Old Curiosity Shop*, xvi, 33–34, 111, 139, 173–88; *Oliver Twist*, xvi, 48–49, 130–35, 138–39; *Our Mutual Friend*, xvi, 42–45, 52, 55, 57, 145, 150–54; *Pickwick Papers*, xv, xvi, 3–15, 47–48, 50–51, 99–104, 107–9; *The Seven Poor Travellers*, 195; *Sketches by Boz*, xiii, 102; "'The Story without a Beginning' (Translated from the German by Boz)," 64; *Sunday under Three Heads*, 65; *A Tale of Two Cities*, 12, 26, 28, 34, 36, 39, 54–55, 219, 223–25
Dickens, Kate, 210, 213, 215–16
Dickens, Novel Reading, and the Victorian Popular Theatre (Vlock), 196
Dickens, Walter, 210, 215–16
Dickens and the Popular Radical Imagination (Ledger), 199
Dickens Dramatized (Bolton), 194
Digby, Kenlam, 66–67; *Broadstone of Honour*, 67
disappearance, as reversal, 12
discontinuities, ideological, 166
Disraeli, Benjamin, 63, 66–69; *The Letters of Runnymede*, 67; *Vindication of the English Constitution in a Letter to a Noble and Learned Lord*, 67
divisions, cultural, 130, 134, 160–61, 163, 191, 202
doing good, 27, 37, 49, 52, 80. See also benevolence
Dombey, Paul, xii, 85–95
Dombey, Paul Jr., 85–86

Dombey and Son (Dickens), xi–xv, xiv–xv, xvi, 85–95
Donne, John, 121
Douglas-Fairhurst, Robert, 118
Doyce, Daniel, 147–48
During, Simon, 174

East End, 192–203
economy, political, 159
education, 90
egalitarianism, 134, 137
Eliot, George, *Felix Holt the Radical*, 135
"Elizabeth and Victoria" (Jerrold), 62–63
Elphinstone, James, *London Labour and the London Poor*, 197
Emeljanow, Victor, *Reflecting the Audience: London Theatregoing, 1840-1880*, 193–94
Emily *(David Copperfield)*, 138
Endell, Martha, 138
Engels, Friedrich, 184
England's Trust (Manners), 118
entertainment, popular, 161–62, 164, 174, 193
Era, 194–95
escapism, 164
establishments, religious, Dickens on, 65–67, 79
Etymologiarum sive originum libri XX (Isidore), 120
Examiner, 63, 65–66, 71

fact, 159, 162–63
Fagin *(Oliver Twist)*, 132
faith, loss of, 78–79
families, depiction of, 132–33, 140
fancy (imagination), 159, 162, 165–66
Fawkes, Guy, 23–24, 26
Feather, John, 184
Feldmann, Doris, xvi, 159–69
Felix Holt the Radical (Eliot), 135
Fern, Will, 112–13, 121
figures, 145
Figur und Person (Jannides), 145
"Fine Old English Gentleman, The" (Dickens), 63
Flanders, Moll, 139
flies, blue, 226–27, 229

Foltinek, Herbert, xvi, 145–55
Ford, George, 103–4
Forster, John, x, 69, 131, 173
Fox, Caroline, 108
Frank, Anne, 233–34
freedom, 135
Frenk, Joachim, ix–xvii
Freud, Sigmund, 177
Friel, Brian: *The Communication Card*, 216; *Translations*, 216
functions, of culture, 164–65

Gad's Hill, x, 207, 209–10, 214
Game Chicken, The, 93
generosity. *See* benevolence; doing good
Gertsman, Elina, 176–77
Gilbert, John, 109
Gill, Stephen, 34
goblins, 113, 118–19
good. *See* benevolence; doing good
Gordon Riots (1780), 135
Gradgrind, Thomas, 165
Granger, Edith, 90–92
Great Expectations (Dickens), xv, 10, 34, 38–42, 55, 57
Gridley *(Bleak House)*, 22–23
Gunpowder Plot (1605), 23–24, 26

Hafenreffer, Samuel, 120
Hall, William, 100
Hard Times (Dickens), xvi, 21, 25, 28, 35, 52–53, 88, 159–69
Harlot's Progress, The (W. Hogarth), 130
Harmon, John, 43
Havisham, Miss, 40–41
Haywood, Ian, 192
Hazlitt, William, 65, 106, 131, 135, 140
Headstone, Bradley, 152–53
Heaman, Bob, xv, 33–45
Hebraism, 44, 137
"Hebraism and Hellenism" (Arnold), 44
Heine, Heinrich, xvii
Hellenism, 44, 137
Hennelly, Mark M., 177
Herophilos of Chalcedon, 120
heterotopia, 137–39
Hexam, Lizzie, 43–44, 151–53
history, revisionist, 78

History of the English Novel, The
(Baker), 149
Hogarth, Catherine, 68, 210–14, 217
Hogarth, Georgina, 210, 214, 217
Hogarth, William: *The Harlot's
Progress*, 130; *The Rake's Progress*,
130
Holder, Hiedi J., 197, 202
Holland, Lady, 69–70
Hollington, Michael, xvi, 85–95
"homoerotic fixation," 136
Hook, Theodore, 102
Hornback, Bert, xv, 33, 42, 47–57, 150
Horne, R. H., 105–7; *New Spirit of the
Age, A*, 105–6
"Hospital Dinner," 62
humor: affirmative, 129; as comedic
method, 105–8; popular, changes in,
99–110. *See also* comedy; wit

iconicity, 122
ideology, 167n12; political, of Dickens,
61–68, 71, 192
Illuminated Magazine, 62
illustrations, 89, 109, 176–77, 183, 197
imagery: animal, 62–63; deluge, 75, 140;
linguistic, 226
individualism, 77
industrialism, 67
Industrial Revolution, xv, 19–21, 28–29
influence: awareness by Dickens of,
37–38, 44, 52; political, of Dickens,
63–64
interruption, of rhythm, 116–19
Ireland, influence of, 205, 212, 216–17
Irish Melodies (Moore), 211–12
Ironmaster, 19–22
irony, xiii, xv, 6–7, 55, 89–90, 92–93,
95, 121, 183, 198
Irving, Washington, 108
Isidore of Seville, *Etymologiarum sive
originum libri XX*, 120

Jackson, T. A., 139
James, Henry, 145, 150
Jane Eyre (Brontë), 133, 140
Jannides, Fotis, *Figur und Person*, 145
Jerdan, William, 100

Jerrold, Douglas, 61–63; "Elizabeth and
Victoria," 62–63
Jingle, Alfred, 3–8
Jo *(Bleak House)*, 200–201
John, Juliet, 167n12
Jones, Graham M., 185

kalokagathia, 133
Kant, Immanuel, 135
Krook *(Bleak House)*, 12, 24

language: figurative, 159, 166; as
manipulative tool, 165
Leavis, F. R., 35
Ledger, Sally, 130, 132, 192;
*Dickens and the Popular Radical
Imagination*, 199
Lee, Austin, 200–201
Leech, John, 104–5
Leeford, Edward, 133
Lennartz, Norbert, xvi, 129–41
Letters of Runnymede, The (Disraeli), 67
Levine, George, 78–79
Lewes, George Henry, 191
life, money style of, 86–95
*Life and Adventures of Valentine Vox,
the Ventriloquist, The* (Cockton), 184
Lightwood, Mortimer, 150–51
limitations: spatial, 40–41; temporal,
40–41
Lister, T. H., 107–8
Literary Gazette, 100
Little Dorrit (Dickens), xvi, 21, 25, 28,
35, 52–54, 56–57, 146–50, 185–86
"London" (Blake), 134
London Labour and the London Poor
(Elphinstone), 197
London Medical Gazette, 82
Louttit, Chris, xvii, 191–203
love, revolutions of, xv, 26–29, 45
Lucas, John, 135

Macready, William, 197
magic, xvi, 173–80, 184–88
Malthus, Thomas Robert, 131
Manners, Lord John, 118; *England's
Trust*, 118
Marcus, Steven, 3–4

Marston, John, *The Patrician's Daughter*, 82–83
Martin Chuzzlewit (Dickens), xv–xvi, 50, 75–84
Marx, Karl, xi, 184
Master Humphrey's Clock (Dickens), 109, 177–78
Mattacks, Kate, 193
May, Karl, 220, 234
Maylie, Harry, 134–35
McCalman, Iain, 135
Meckier, Jerome, xv, 3–15, 47
Meditation 18 (Donne), 121
melodrama, 12, 161, 166, 193, 195, 197–99
Memoirs of Robert-Houdin: Ambassador, Author and Conjurer (Robert-Houdin), 184–86
memory, cultural, 163
metaphors, 6, 10, 165–66, 217
methods, comedic, 99–110
metonymy, 121, 160
Metropolitan Magazine, 108
Metz, Nancy Aycock, xv, 75–84
Middle Temple, 68
Miller, D. A., 178, 187
mimesis, 177
Minstrel, The; or, The Progress of Genius and Other Poems (Beattie), 113
money, style of life, xvi, 86–95
Monks *(Oliver Twist)*, 133
Monod, Sylvère, 149
monologues, 149, 153
Moore, Thomas, *Irish Melodies*, 211–12
Morley, Henry: "Need Railway Travellers Be Smashed?," 21; "Patent Wrongs," 186
Morning Chronicle, 63, 76
Morris, Pam, 43
Mystery of Edwin Drood, The (Dickens), ix–x, 55–57

Neale, Frederick, 195
"Need Railway Travellers Be Smashed?" (Morley), 21
Newey, Vincent, 137
Newgate novels, 161
New Poor Law (1834), 131
New Spirit of the Age, A (Horne), 105–6

Nicholas Nickleby (Dickens), 54, 119–20
novels: allegorical, 130; condition-of-England, 34, 42, 77; Newgate, 130, 161; political, 159; romantic, 140; of social criticism, 48–49; Victorian, 36, 140

offbeats, 114–19, 122, 124n8. *See also* beats; rhythm
Old Curiosity Shop, The (Dickens), xvi, 33–34, 111, 139, 173–88
Oliver Twist (Dickens), xvi, 48–49, 130–35, 138–39
onomatopoeia, 122
originality, 181–82, 184–85
Orwell, George, 3, 9, 13, 103, 234
Our Mutual Friend (Dickens), xvi, 42–45, 52, 55, 57, 145, 150–54
outsiders, portrayal of, 133, 213, 215–16
Oxford Movement, 65–66

Paine, Thomas, 65
pantisocracy, 137
Panza, Sancho, 108
Paroissien, David, xv, 33, 35, 61–73
patent, 185–87. *See also* copyright; property, intellectual
"Patent Wrongs" (Morley), 186
Patrician's Daughter, The (Marston), 82–83
patter (linguistic routine), 176, 186
patterns: allegorical, 130; physiognomic, 85–90, 93–94; picaresque, 5, 8, 47, 184; of social change, 3–13; structural, 3–4; temporal, 111–25
Peasant's Revolt (1381), 24–26
Pecksniff, Mercy, 80–81
Pecksniff, Seth, 78–79
Peel, Sir Robert, 64
Penny Dreadful, 161
personal life, of Dickens, xvii, 206, 209–18
perspective: historical, 38–42; literary, 149
Pettitt, Claire, 184–85, 187
Philosophie des Als Ob, Die (The Philosophy of As If) (Vaihinger), 85
Philosophie des Geldes (The Philosophy of Money) (Simmel), xvi, 85, 87

philosophy, social, 49–50
Philpotts, Trey, 186
Phiz. *See* Browne, Hablot Knight
physiognomy, 85–90, 93–94
Pickwick, Samuel, 3–15, 47–48, 51, 108
Pickwick Papers (Dickens), xv, xvi, 3–15, 47–48, 50–51, 99–104, 107–9
Pictures of Life and Character (Leech), 104–5
Pilgrim's Progress, The (Bunyan), 130
Pinch, Tom, 78–79, 83
Pip (Phillip Pirrip), 10, 38–42
Pitt, George Dibdin, 195, 198–99
Pittard, Chris, xvi, 173–88
Plummer, Patricia, 138
politics: cultural, 160, 166; domestic, 215
poor, plight of the, 33, 47, 76, 197–202
"potency of the small," 80, 82
power: from money, 93–95; from spatial arrangement, 86–88
"power of doing good," xv
principles, Malthusian, 131
Pritchett, V. S., 103
property, intellectual, xvii, 174, 178–82, 184–87. *See also* copyright; patent
psycho-narration, 149–50
Puccini, Giacomo, *La Bohème*, 91
pulse, human, 120–21

Quantz, Johann Joachim, 120
Quarterly Review, 100–101
Quilp, Daniel, 175–76, 182–83, 188
Quixote, Don, 108

Radcliffe, Caroline, 193
radicalism, xvi–xvii, 50–51, 130–31, 133–40, 159, 192–93, 198–99, 201–2
railways, xi–xiii, 21
Rake's Progress, The (W. Hogarth), 130
realism, 3, 12, 102–3, 145, 197
reappearance, 10–11
rebellion, 24–26
reception, of Dickens: critical, 129, 161; popular, 233–34; public, 191–92, 202; theatrical, 194–97
Reflecting the Audience: London Theatregoing, 1840-1880 (Davis and Emeljanow), 193–94

Reform Bill (1832), 63
relationships, spatial, 86–88
religion. *See* establishments, religious
"Remonstrance with Dickens," 101
repetitions, 4–11, 27, 183; acoustic, 114–17, 122–23
retribution, 10–11
revenge, 4, 6
reversals, xv, 3, 7–13, 41, 43, 47–48, 133
revolutions, xv, 3, 12, 19–29, 45, 48, 135. *See also* Industrial Revolution
rhetoric, 115
rhymes, nursery, 163
rhythm, xii, xvi, xvii, 111–25, 176
Riah, 151
Richard II (Shakespeare), 116
Richter, Jean Paul, 107
riding, horse, 163–65
Robert-Houdin, Jean Eugène, *Memoirs of Robert-Houdin: Ambassador, Author and Conjurer*, 184–86
Romanticism, 130, 136, 166
Rose, Jonathan, 191–92
Rose, Mark, 181
Rosenberg, Edgar, xvii, 219–34
Rossetti, Dante Gabriel, "Chimes," 114
Rouncewell, Mr., 19–22
Rouncewell, Watt, 20, 28–29
Royal Pavilion Theatre, 193–95, 198–202
Rudge, Barnaby, 51

Sanders, Andrew, 36–39
Sartor Resartus (Carlyle), 133
satire, xiv, xvi, 10, 63–64, 112, 118, 121, 164, 183, 197–98, 202, 207
Schivelbusch, Wolfgang, xiii
Schlicke, Paul, 173–74
Screw (ship), 81–82
Scrooge, Ebenezer, 10
secrecy, 178–79, 184
self-reflexivity, 174, 180, 187
service, public, and Dickens, 68–69, 71
Seven Poor Travellers, The (Dickens), 195
Shakespeare, William, 116, 122; *Richard II*, 116; Sonnet 18, 122
Shaw, George Bernard, xi, 35
Simmel, Georg, xvi, 85–93, 95; *Philosophie des Geldes (The*

Philosophy of Money), xvi, 85, 87
Single Gentleman, The, 186, 188
Sketches by Boz (Dickens), xiii, 102
Slater, Michael, x, 33–35, 118, 210, 232
Sleary, Mr., 162–65
Smelfunguses, 131
Smiles, Samuel, 186
society, money, xvi, 86–95
Sonnet 18 (Shakespeare), 122
Steerforth, James, 136
Steinmeyer, Jim, 179
Steveker, Lena, ix–xvii
Stewart, Garrett, 176, 183
Stiggins, Reverend, 3, 10–12
"'Story without a Beginning, The' (Translated from the German by Boz)" (Dickens), 64
structuralists, 145
structure, literary, 3–4, 9, 11, 152
Summerson, Esther, xv, 26–29, 53
Sunday under Three Heads (Dickens), 65
Sweet William, 174–75, 179–80, 187–88
Swiveller, Dick, 175–76, 183, 188

Tale of Two Cities, A (Dickens), 12, 26, 28, 34, 36, 39, 54–55, 219, 223–25
tales, fairy, 163
Talfourd, Thomas Noon, 180–81
Tapley, Mark, 77–78, 81
Ternan, Ellen, 211–12, 214, 217
Thackeray, W. M., 104–6
theaters, East End, xvii, 192–203
theory, cognitive, 165
time: denial of, 119–20; as literary component, 83; relationship to money, 92
Tom Tiddler's ground, 88, 91–92
Tories, 63, 66
Tormes, Lazarillo de, 9, 11
"Tour of Two Idle Apprentices" (Dickens and W. Collins), 211
Tracy, Robert, xvii, 34, 205–18
Traddles, Tommy, 136
Translations (Friel), 216
Trollope, Anthony, 50
Trotter, Job, 3–5, 7–8
Trotty, 113–19
Tyler, Wat, 24–26, 28–29

uniformitarianism, 75
Unitarians, 79–80
University of Oxford, 66
usefulness, 54, 68. *See also* benevolence; doing good
utilitarianism, 131, 159, 165–66

Vaihinger, Hans, *Die Philosophie des Als Ob (The Philosophy of As If)*, 85
Veck, Toby, 113–19
Victorianism, xiii, xvi, 33, 35, 42, 44, 107–8, 129–30, 132–34, 136–40, 145, 161
Vindication of the English Constitution in a Letter to a Noble and Learned Lord (Disraeli), 67
"Visit to Charles Dickens in the Summer of 1857, A" (Andersen), 209
Vlock, Deborah, 196–97; *Dickens, Novel Reading, and the Victorian Popular Theatre*, 196

Watt, James, 20–21
Waugh, Arthur, 99
Weller, Samuel, 3, 10–12, 100, 107–8
Weller, Tony, 3, 10–12, 104
Welsh, Alexander, 113, 121
Westminster Review, 102
Whigs, 61, 63–64, 66–67, 70–71
Whipple, Edmund, 191
Whittington, Sir Richard, 111
William, Sweet, 174–75, 179–80, 187–88
Williams, Raymond, 87, 160
Wiltshire, 82
wit, 105–8. *See also* comedy; humor
women, fallen, 71, 138
Woodcourt, Alan, 27
Wordsworth, William, 99, 135, 180
work, to effect change, 53, 55
Wrayburn, Eugene, 43–44, 150–54
Wu, Duncan, 131

Young England Movement, 66–67, 118

Zimmerman, Virginia, 80
Zweig, Stefan, 129

CPSIA information can be obtained
at www.ICGtesting.com
Printed in the USA
LVHW041716010319
609210LV00003B/282